The Atlas of Billy Dean

Billy Thomas

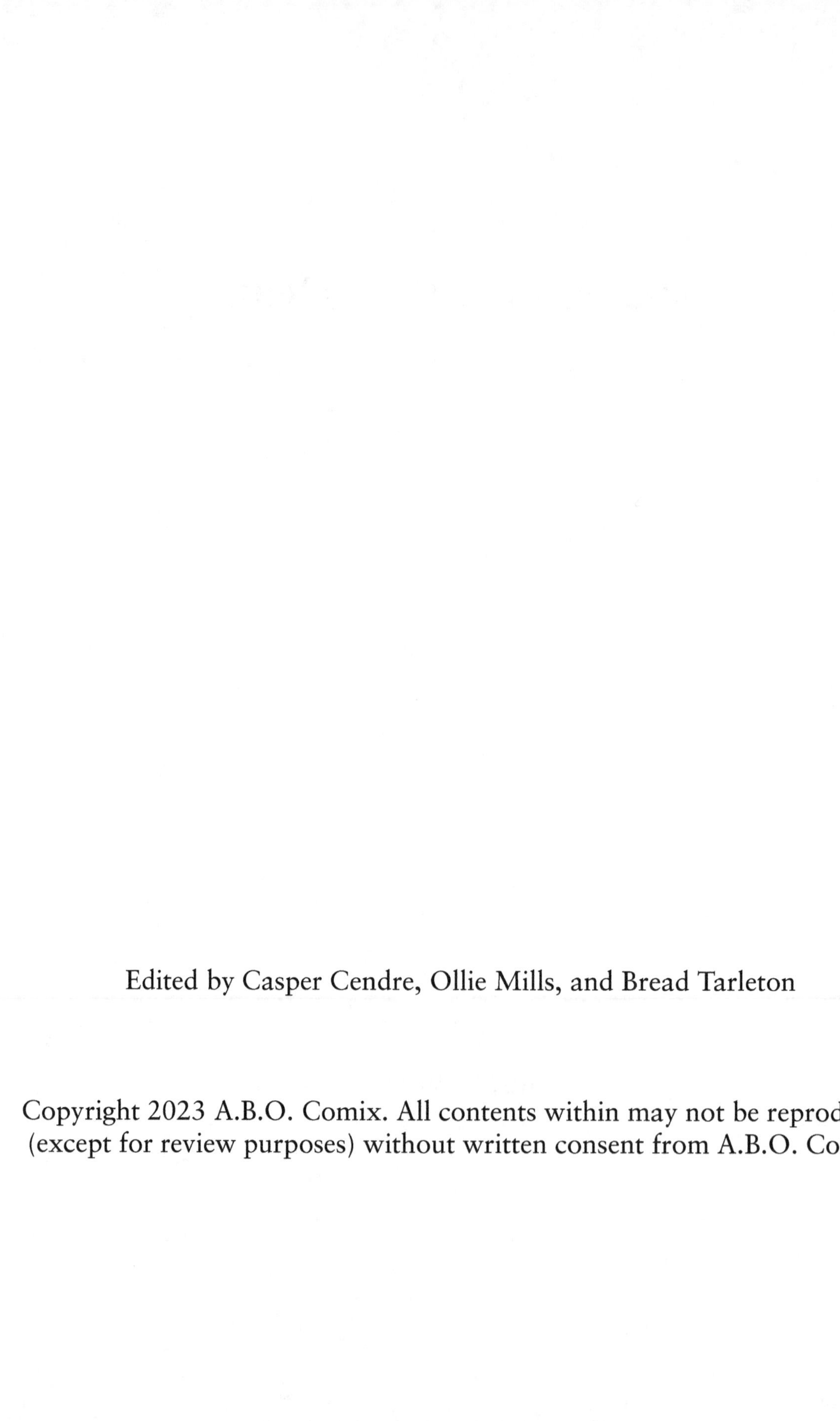

Edited by Casper Cendre, Ollie Mills, and Bread Tarleton

Foreword

Sometimes tears are the only thing I can accomplish when I open Billy's mail. Often the tears flow with incredible sadness at the things he is going through; even more common is the feeling of overwhelming gratitude for the prolific package of artwork he has sent; yet always my heart grows with affection for the extraordinary person who has blessed me with his friendship. It is not always easy for people inside prison to trust and be vulnerable with their stories. Trust is not easily achieved within prison walls. But somehow, Billy has trusted me with both the darkest trenches and the brightest light that has permeated his life.

Since 2017, I have gotten to know Billy through letter writing, art sharing, and phone calls. These pages could not begin to adequately sum up his experiences, but I feel his story should accompany these pages of art so that you too can know this beautiful soul that the world, shamefully, has locked away.

Billy's experiences and his art are one and the same, and his history permeates the art he makes. These pages are filled with his hope and pain, his desires and reality. Billy's art helps you see the world through his eyes, and opens you to a new way of perceiving. His art is filled with vibrant colors, expressionist imagery, and real stories. These works are incomplete without Billy's stories, and his story is incomplete without his art.

Billy was taken from his family by Child Protective Services at age 5. He grew up in Texas state hospitals and homes where he experienced ongoing sexual abuse. At the mental state hospitals and without his consent, he was put on a mind-altering medication that kept him from speaking out about the rape he endured under the care of CPS. He remained unschooled throughout his youth.

In 1992, Billy was diagnosed with an organic mental disorder with Psychosis and illiteracy. Vernon State Hospital deemed Billy "mentally retarded" and advised that if Billy did not receive mental health care/treatment, his illness would worsen.

During his trial in 1997, the Johnson County Judge overlooked the 1992 request of a mental health professional asking that Billy be returned to Vernon State Hospital for treatment. Had he received the treatment requested by this doctor, the circumstances that led to his conviction would never have been possible.

Billy underwent a complete psychiatric evaluation by E. Clay Griffith, M.D. to determine Billy's competency to stand trial. At the trial, Billy's rights were read to him, but he did not understand the words. He was cooperative to the best of his ability, but had a limited understanding of what was happening, was experiencing auditory and visual hallucinations, and was reported to seem confused.

The doctor's medical opinion was that Billy did not have sufficient present ability to consult with his lawyer, did not have a factual or rational understanding of the proceedings against him, and was not competent to stand trial. He was deemed seriously mentally ill and likely to cause harm to himself or others, and would continue to suffer significant distress without treatment. He was sentenced to prison time regardless.

In 1997, as a person with mental illness and an IQ of 70, he was forced into a cell with gang members where he was beaten and raped. Then, upon being moved to a new unit, he was tossed from a third-row tier, breaking his right wrist, hand, and bones in his face in the fall.

In 1998, Billy was released from prison with no mental health treatment, schooling, or job skills. He met a woman and had four children together. After many years together, Billy found out the unfortunate information that his wife was also his half-sister, and CPS took custody of their children in Waco, TX. Losing his three sons and daughter to the same system that had taken him from his own home as a child worsened his mental health state. He began having blackouts and in one episode, Billy killed a man.

In 2002, the court in Fort Worth, Texas, withheld his past and present mental history from the jury. Billy was sentenced to capital life in prison where he has been sexually assaulted and raped, and forced to work in prison without pay under the duress of disciplinary cases, harsher living conditions, and the loss of visitation.

In 2017, Billy's best friend hanged himself. In August 2020, Billy's mother passed away from lung cancer. He wrote, "I'll miss her...I just pray I get this case overturned before my dad passes away. This is not the place to be when some loved one dies."

During the 2020 outbreak of COVID-19 within the prison system, Billy endured staff putting queer prisoners in two-man cells despite social distancing protocol, being kept from accessing medical care because co-pays could not be charged during the outbreak, and guards spreading COVID-19 within the prison and gassing prisoners that requested help. He was kept from mental health treatment, forced to work still without pay, and received spoiled meat and vegetables in brown bags as meals, all while gang extortion became the norm. During this time, he caught COVID-19 twice.

In 2021, Billy went on a hunger strike to protest the ongoing mental, physical, and sexual misconduct from Allred Unit staff and the large outbreak of gang hits put on GBTQ (gay, bisexual, transgender, queer), elderly, and mentally ill prisoners that went unstopped by guards.

Billy sees a psychiatrist 2-3 times a year, and his past mental and physical health history is always overlooked. He has asked to be moved back to a DDP mental health unit where he is not forced into cells with gang members, but his requests have been ignored. He has frequent nightmares of the sexual trauma he has endured.

Billy likes swimming, hiking, biking, weight lifting, watching movies, cooking & eating, penpalling, sex, and Dungeons & Dragons. Billy has found hope in prison through God and his Jewish faith. Billy writes, "I have capitol life yet my love for God tells me Ill overturn it or recev erly perole any day now. For God opens the hears of peppol to stand for us that cant stand 4 are selfs."

[I have capital life yet my love for God tells me I'll overturn or receive early parole any day now. For God opens the hearts of people to stand for us that can't stand for ourselves.]

Art has become his life's joy.

We are hoping the Texas Governor will look at the details of Billy's circumstances, pardon him, grant him early parole, or move him back to Vernon State Mental Hospital for treatment, not ongoing punishment. He is seeking legal support and a new trial.

To get in touch with Billy or offer assistance, send us an email at abocomix@gmail.com.

With love and everlasting hope,
Casper Cendre,
Director of A.B.O. Comix

Table of Contents

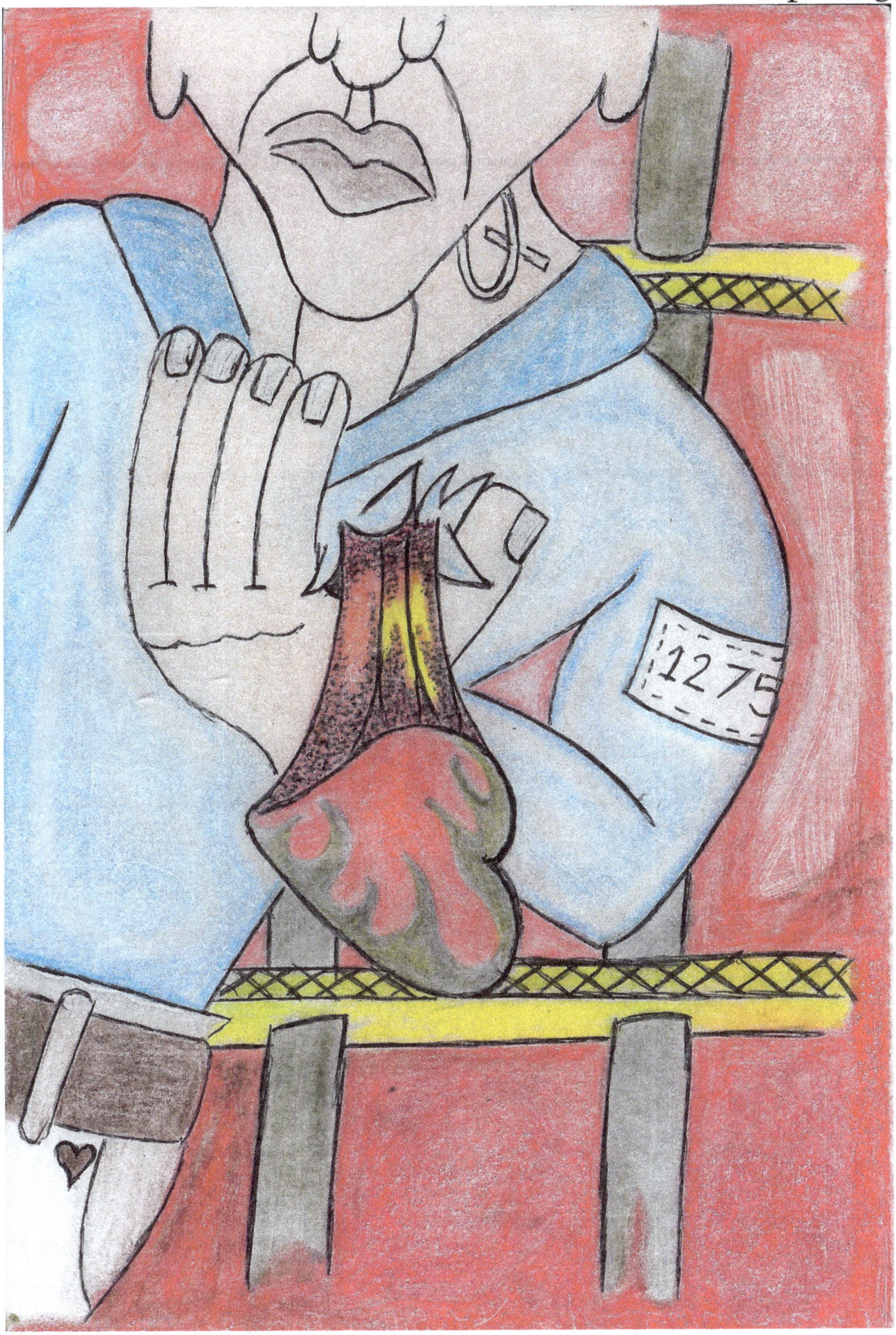

12 75

I am a Texas prisoner and a serviver of mental Fisical & Sexual abuse. while in The cear of Texas c.p.s. & TDCJ, I Have over came The mind altering meds But I still live with The sidefects of The meds & sexual abuse Dun To me while in state kussid & cear

I am 47 man Thats life Becous History was From The Fort Worth Tx The DA & The Attorneys That a Fear Tril: a BI Queer Doing capitol my mentol with Heald Jurry in in 2002 By court apponted Denied me

I am Billy Artist At and mentor is Family is and Thank You Wish get With Comic Hope In Your

#1275621
#683892

a Friend and To A B O Comic my Casper my Frend & Casper all my Hope is To Casper If To Help Fund me Casper At ABO- You Can Shin into my life support.

Sincerly With
♡ Billy. D. Thomas

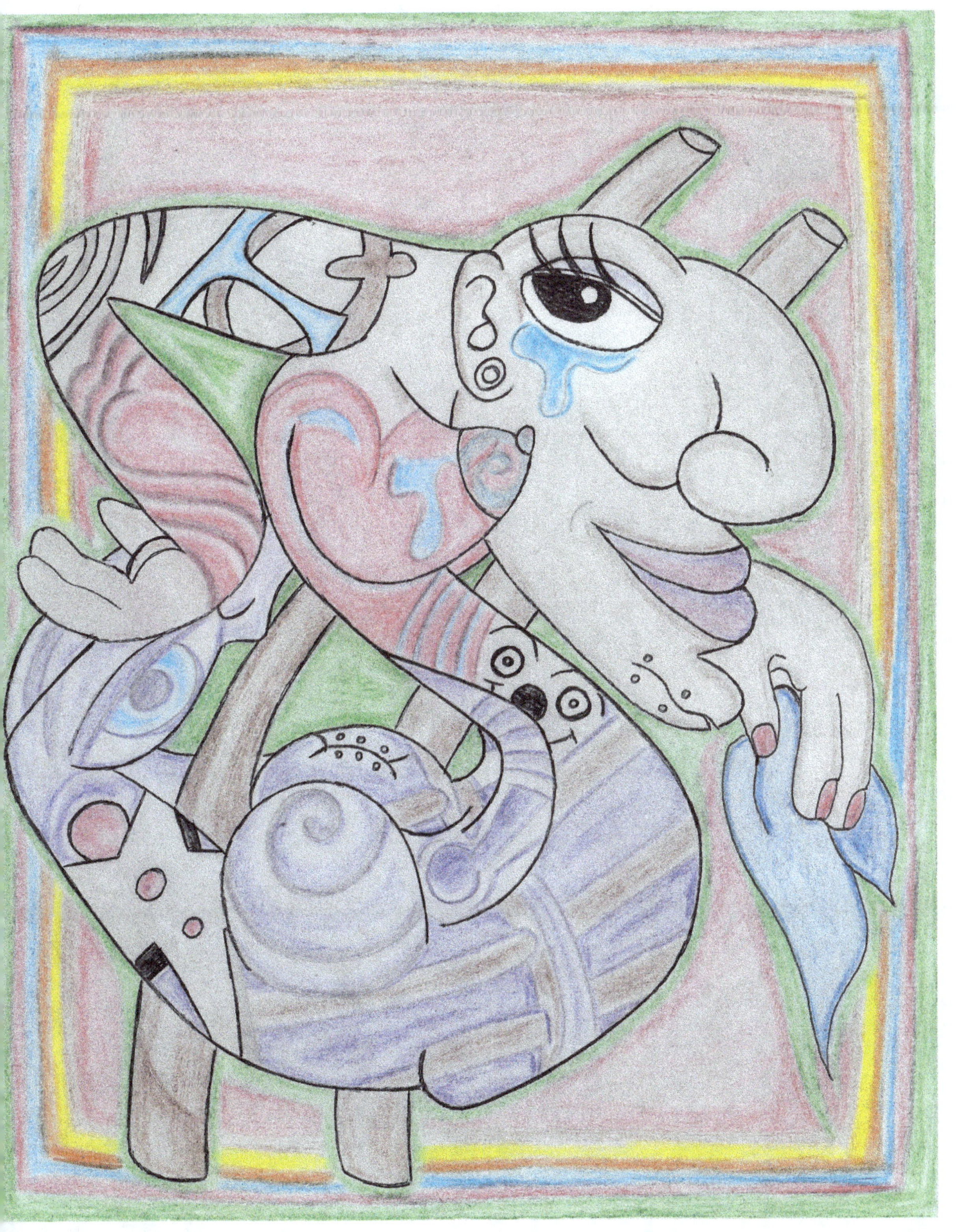

Opening

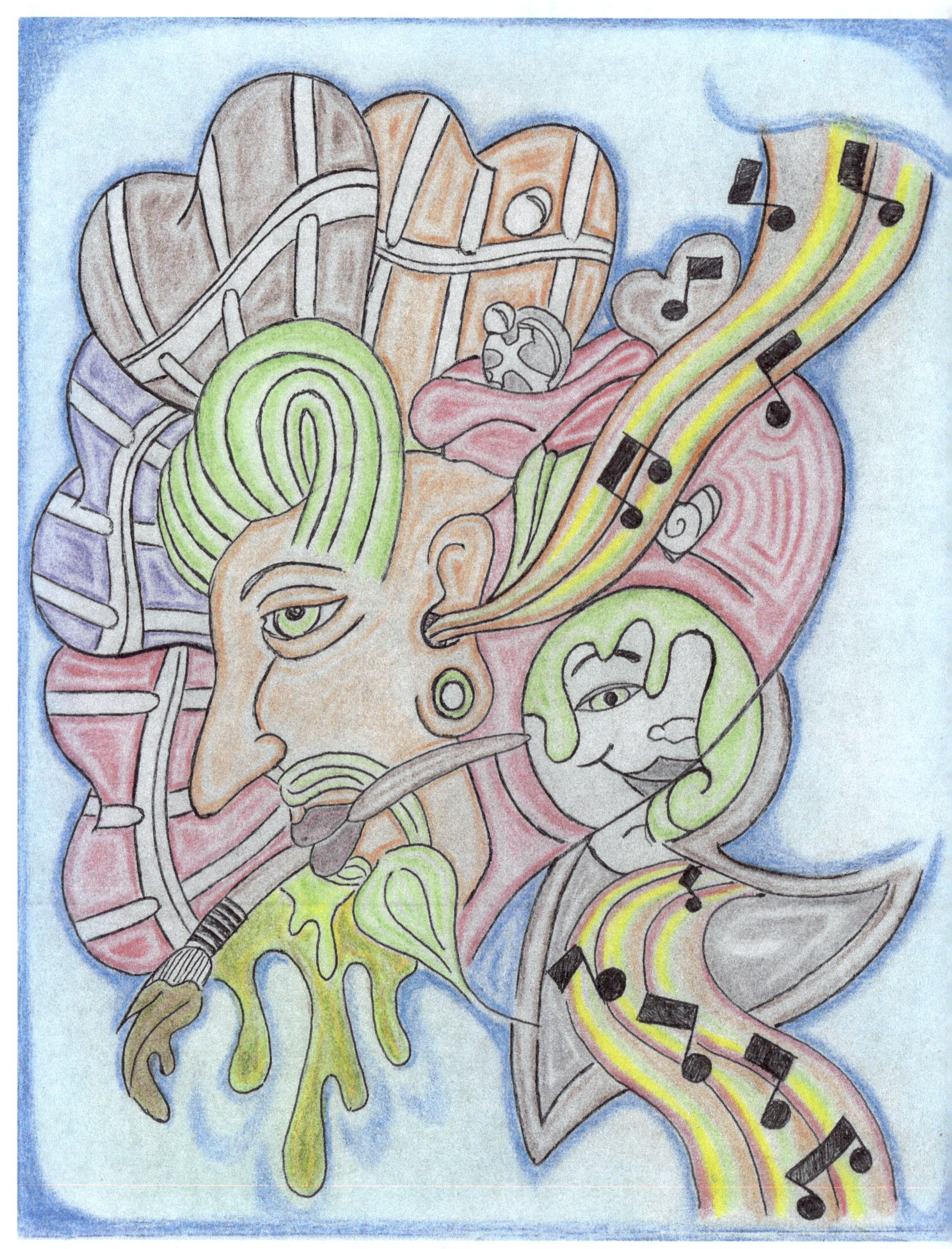

Billy
omeing To
now A
riend

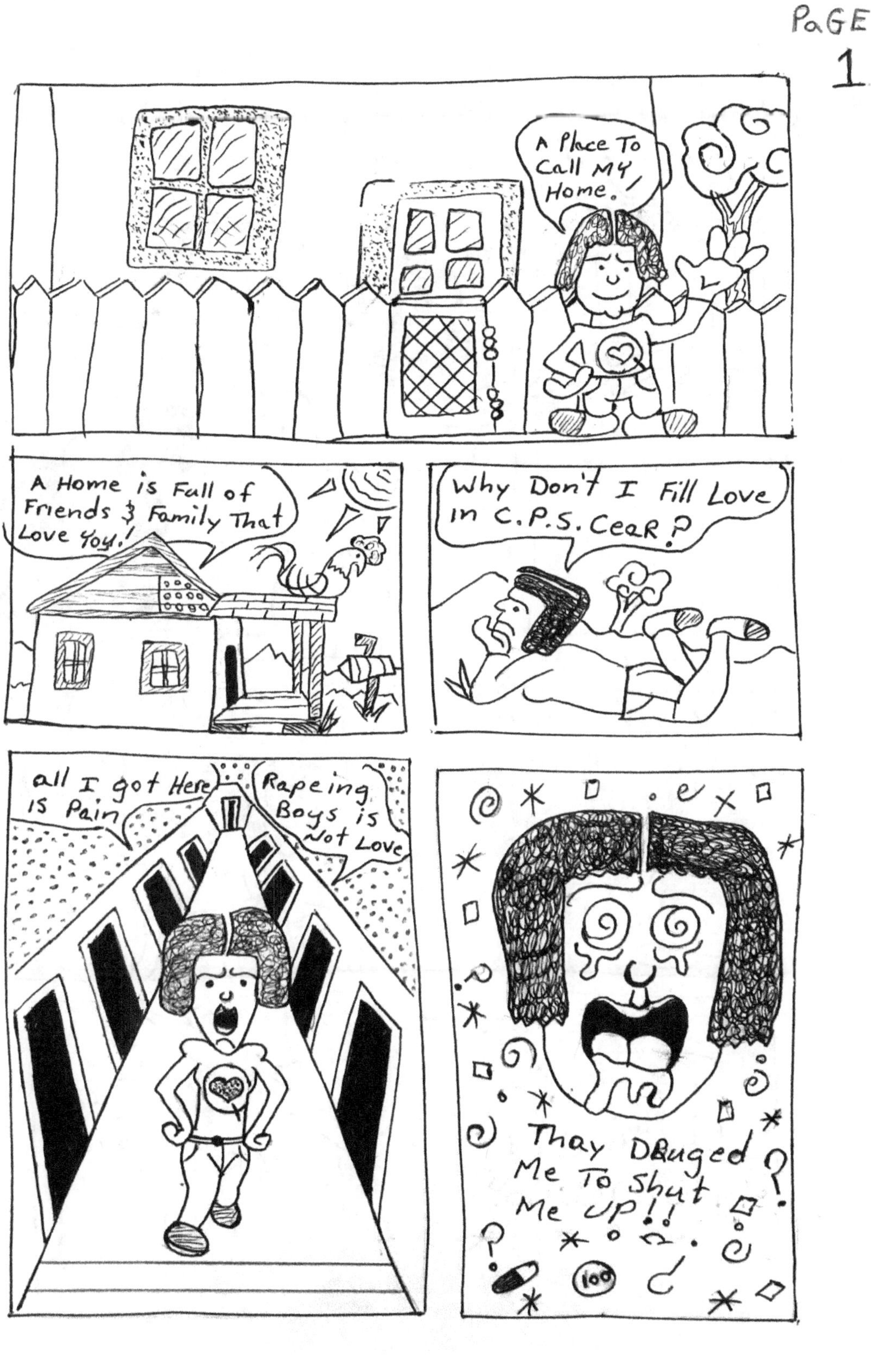

Billy

knowing
Where To
Look For
Help!

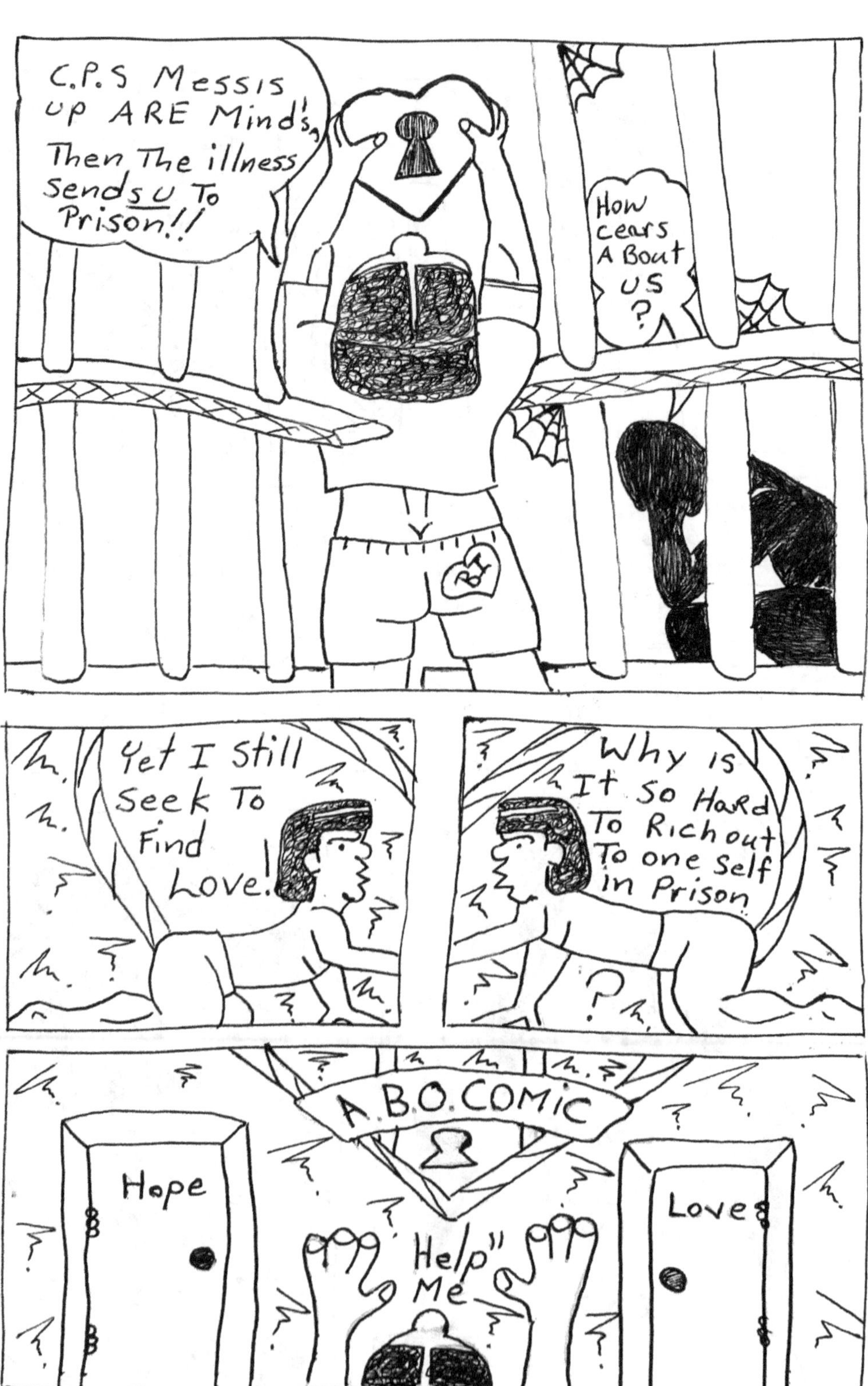

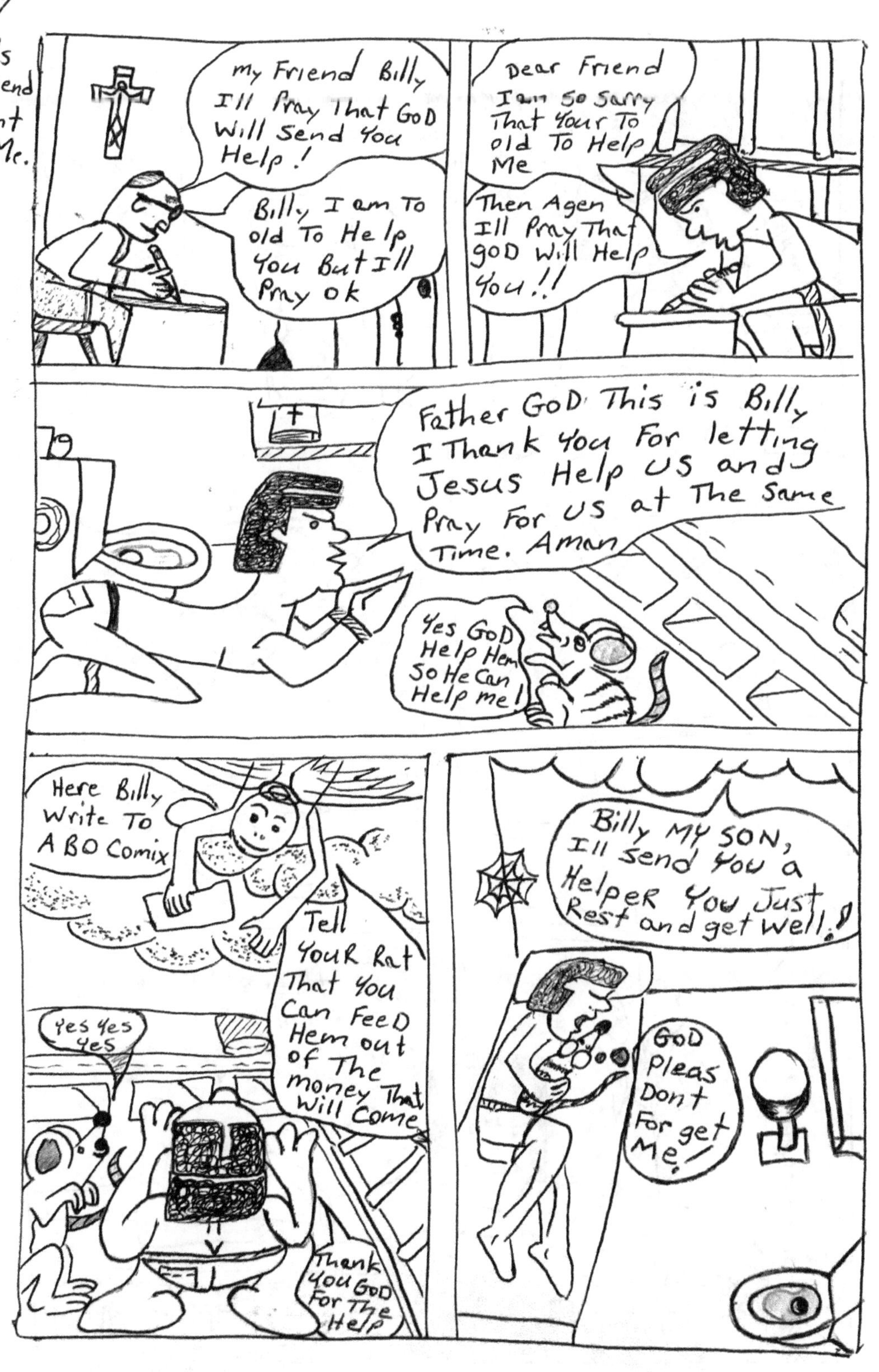
Billy
Calls
Friend
Dont
Help Me.
my Friend Billy I'll Pray That GoD Will Send You Help!
Billy, I am To old To Help You But I'll Pray ok
Dear Friend I am So Sorry That Your To old To Help Me
Then Agen I'll Pray That goD Will Help You!!
Father GoD This is Billy I Thank You For letting Jesus Help US and Pray For US at The Same Time. Aman
Yes GoD Help Hem So He Can Help me!
Here Billy Write To A BO Comix
Tell Your Rat That You Can FeeD Hem out of The money That Will Come
Yes Yes Yes
Thank You GoD For The Help
Billy MY SON, I'll send You a Helper You Just Rest and get well.
GoD Pleas Dont For get Me!

Early Life

Helping
others
out of are
Blessings.

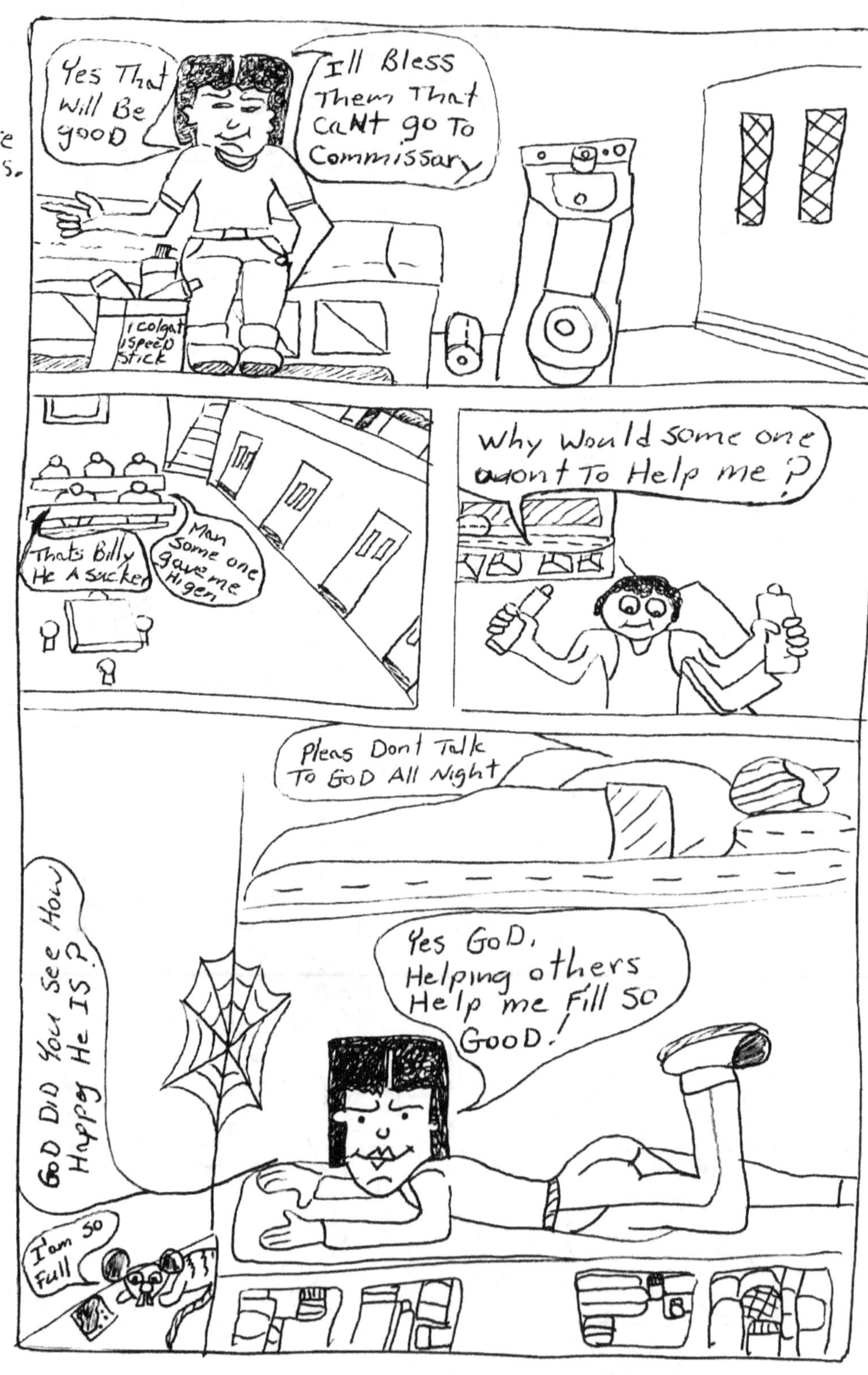

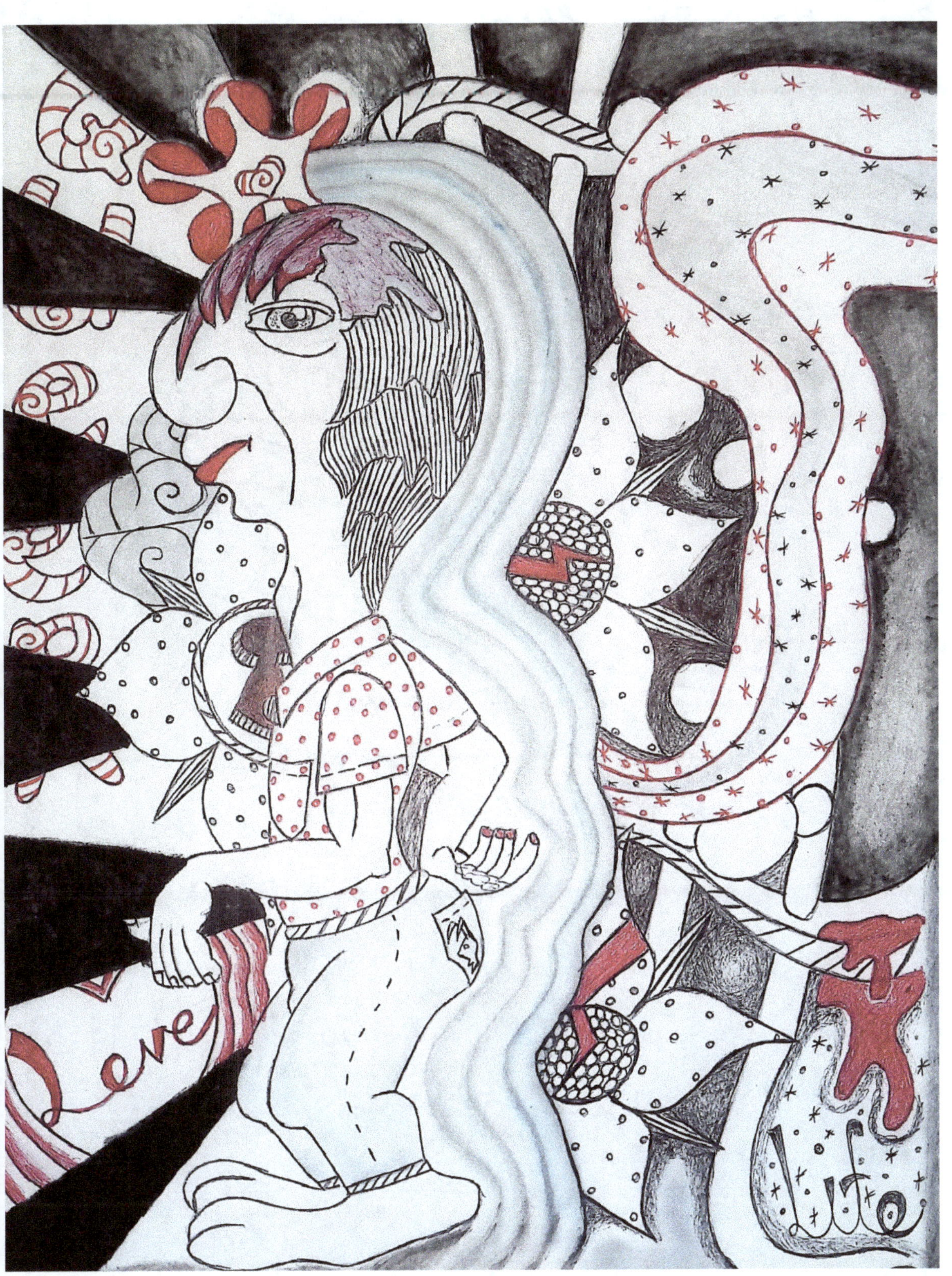
Love
Early Life

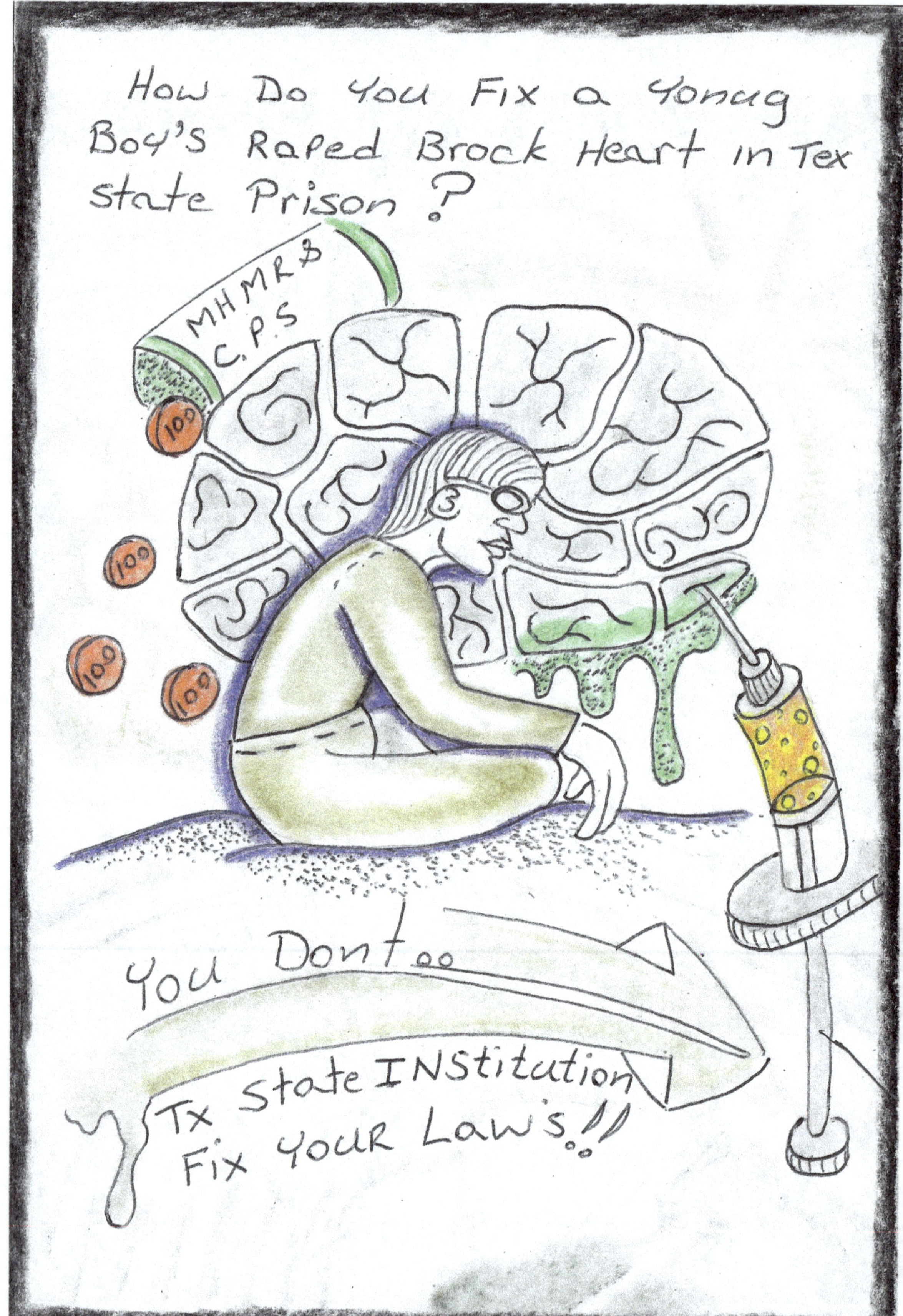
How Do You Fix a Yonug Boy's Raped Brock Heart in Tex state Prison ?
MHMR &
C.P.S
100
100
100
100
You Dont..
Tx State INSTitution
Fix YOUR Law's..

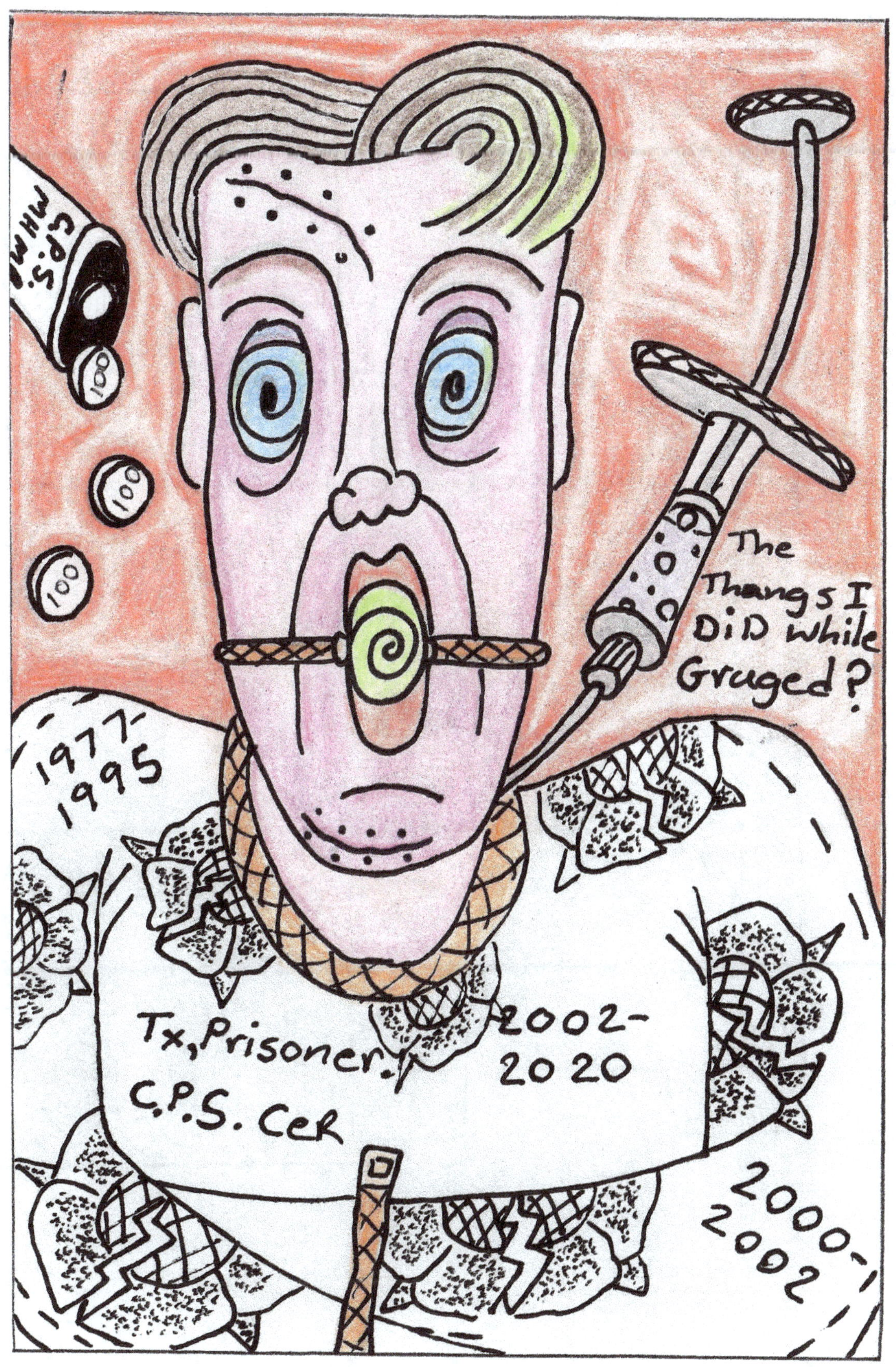
CPS MHMR
100
100
100
1977-
1995
The
Thangs I
DiD while
Gruged?
Tx, Prisoner.
C.P.S. CeR
2002-
2020
2000-
2002

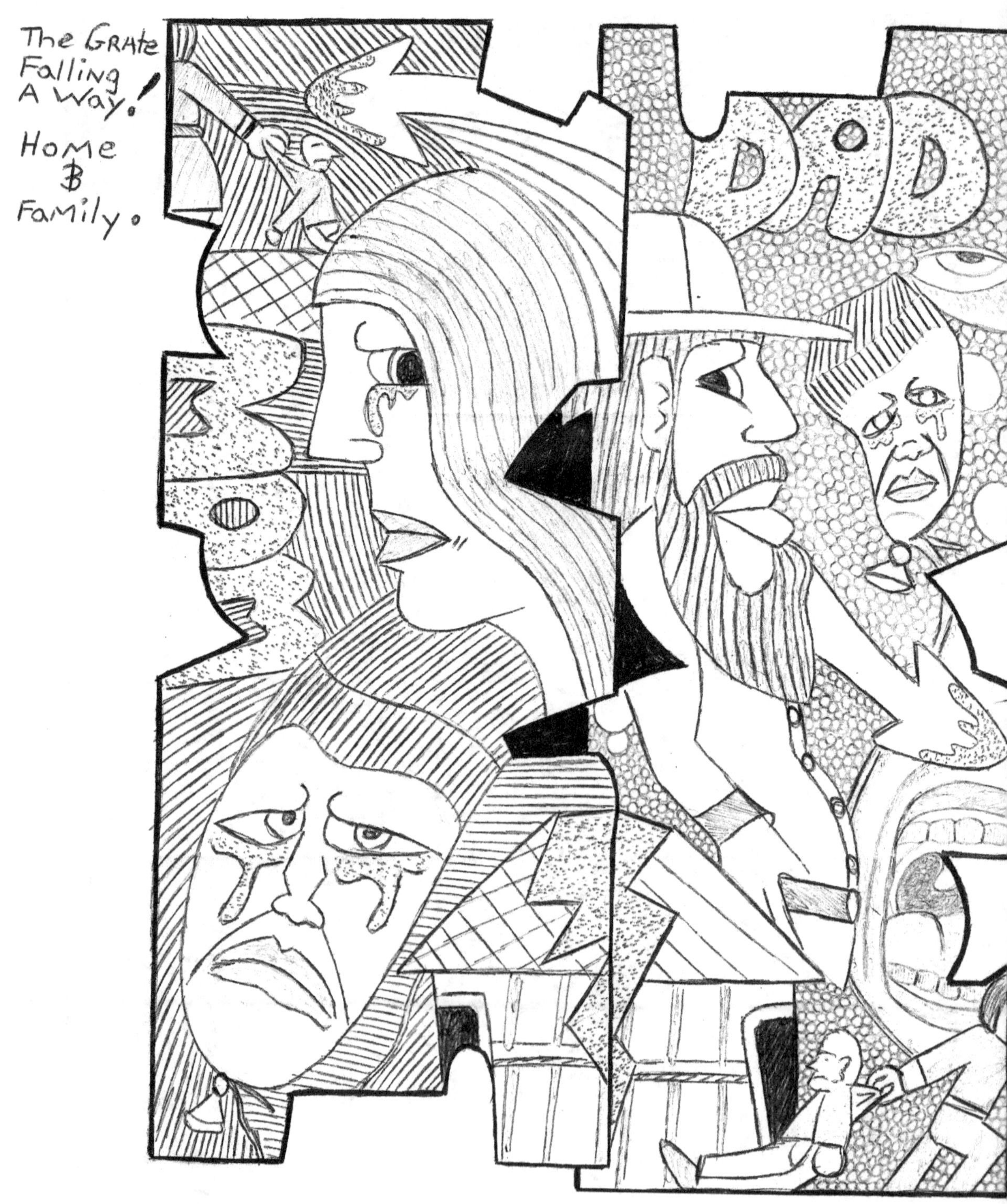
The Grate
Falling
A way!
Home
&
Family.
DAD

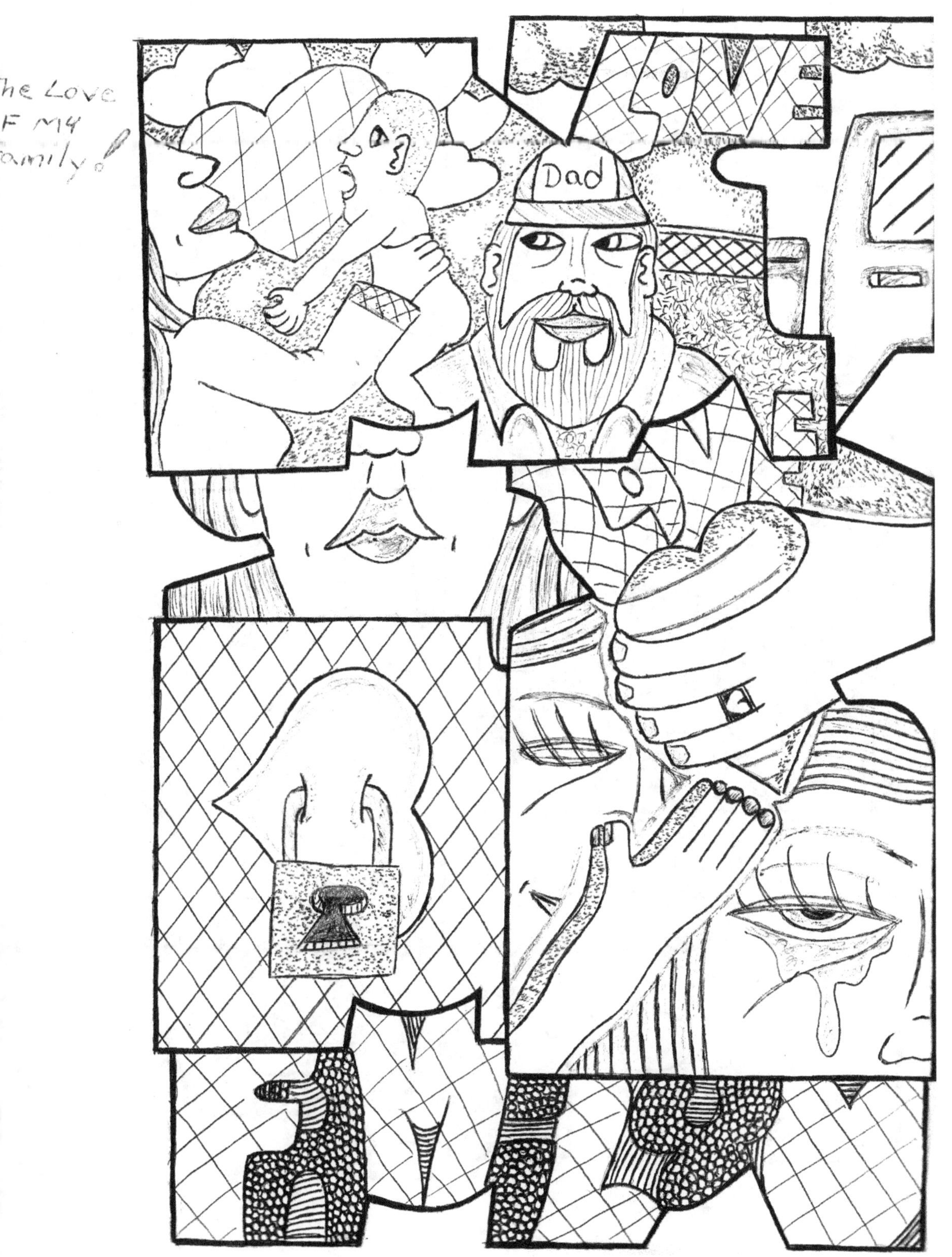
the Love
F MY
Family!
Dad
LOVE
FAMILY

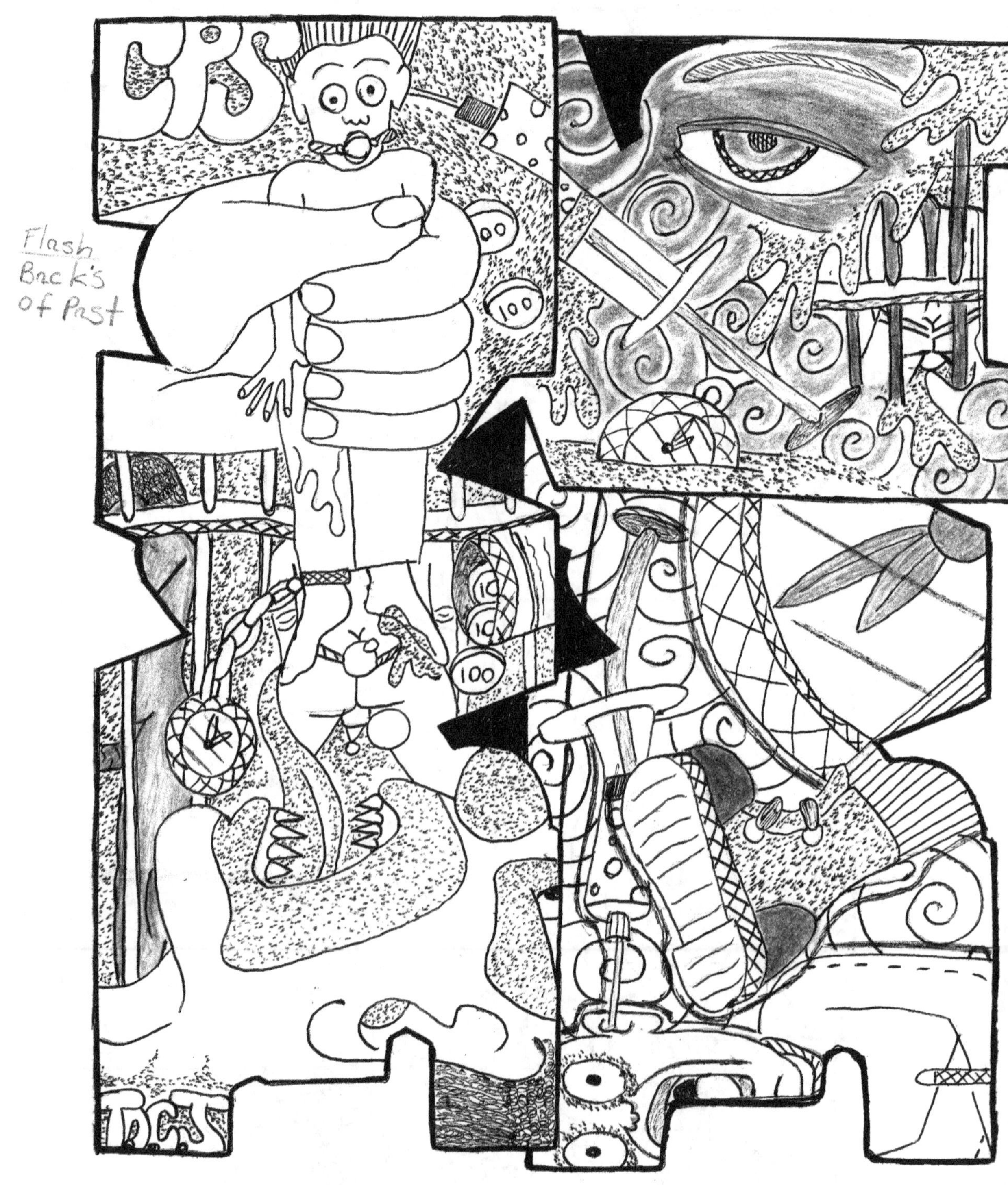
Flash
Back's
of Past
100
100
100

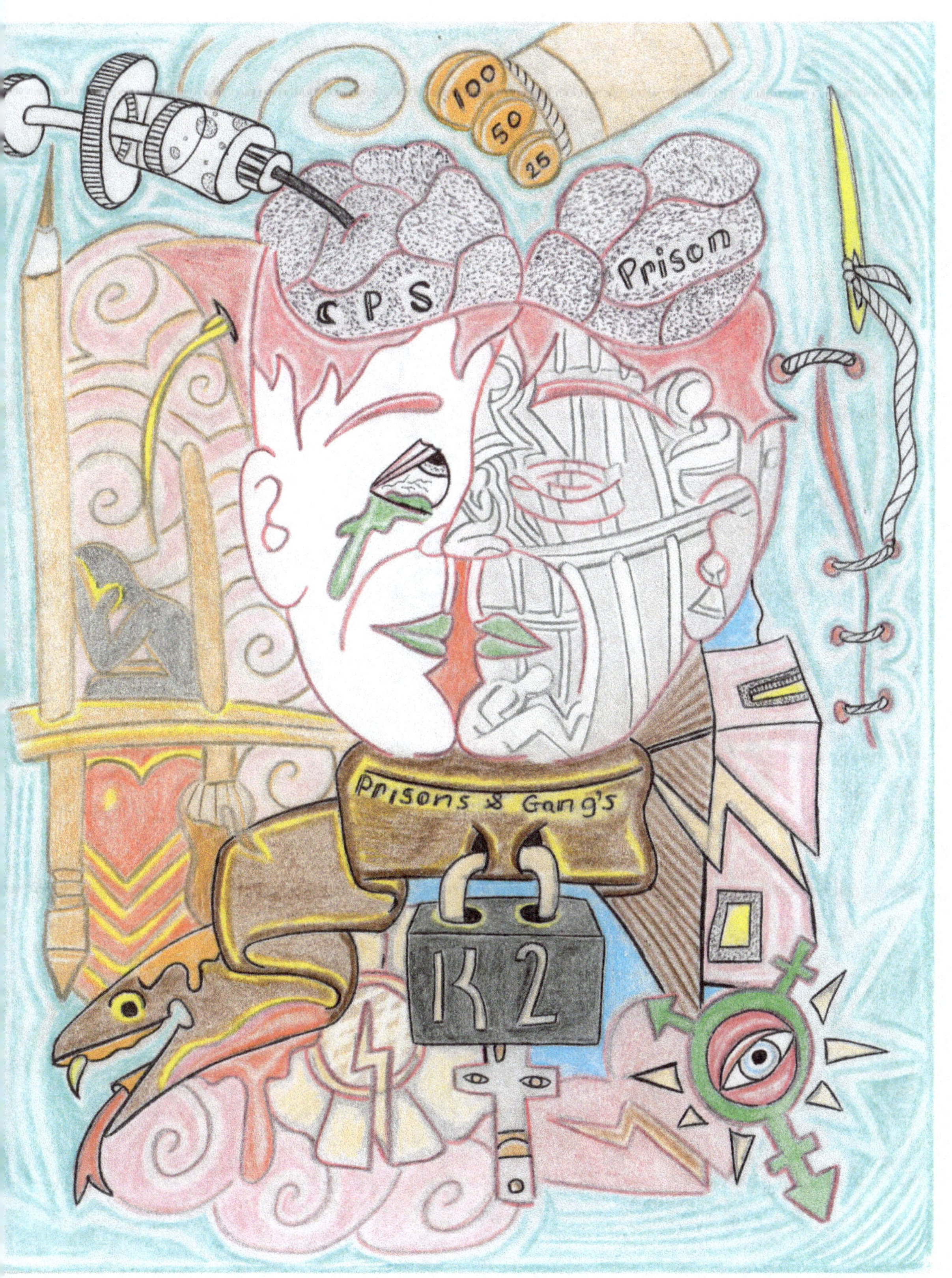
100
50
25
C P S
Prison
Prisons & Gang's
K2

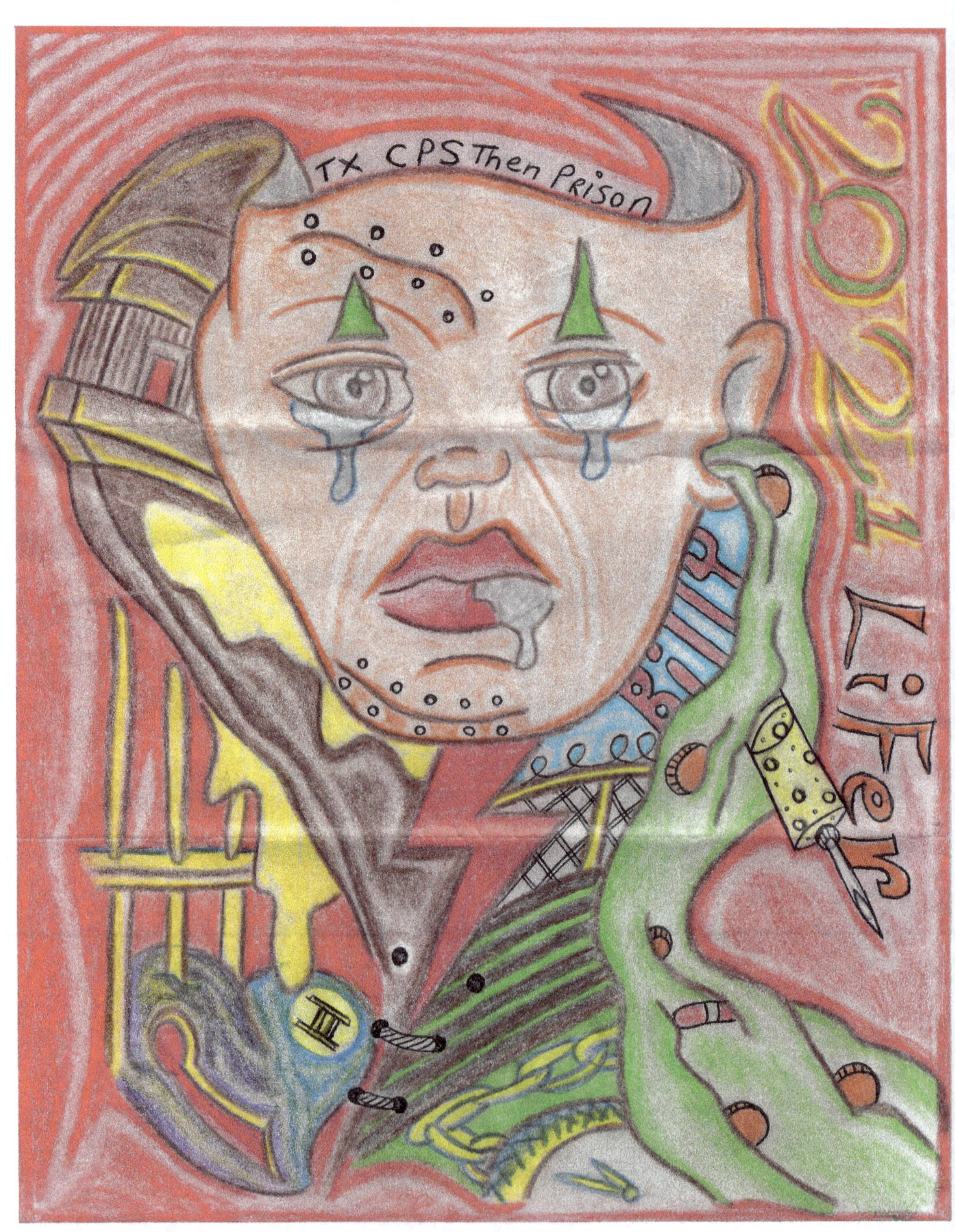
TX CPS Then Prison
2021 Lifer
Billy

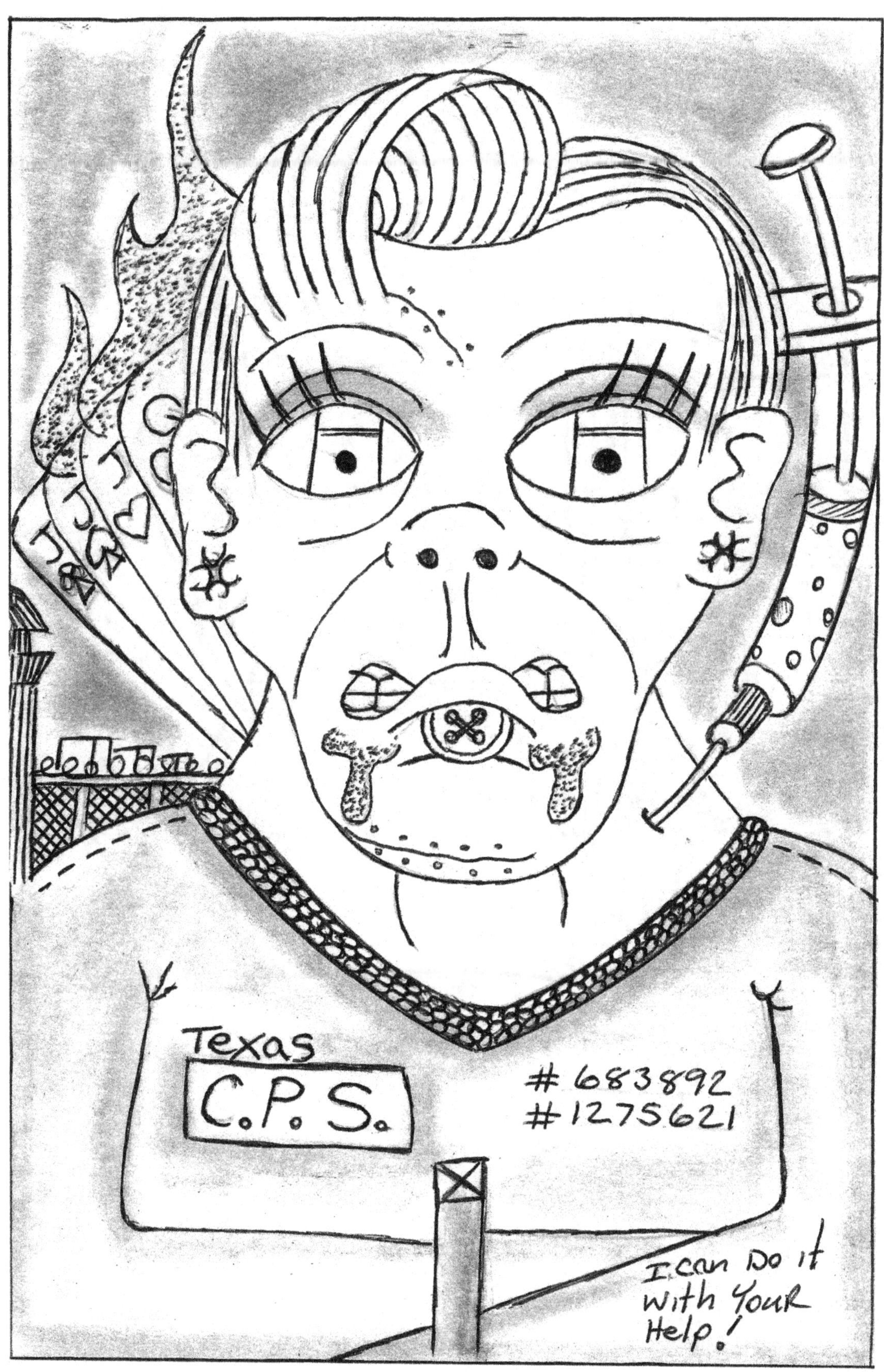
Texas
C.P.S.
#683892
#1275621
I can Do it with Your Help!

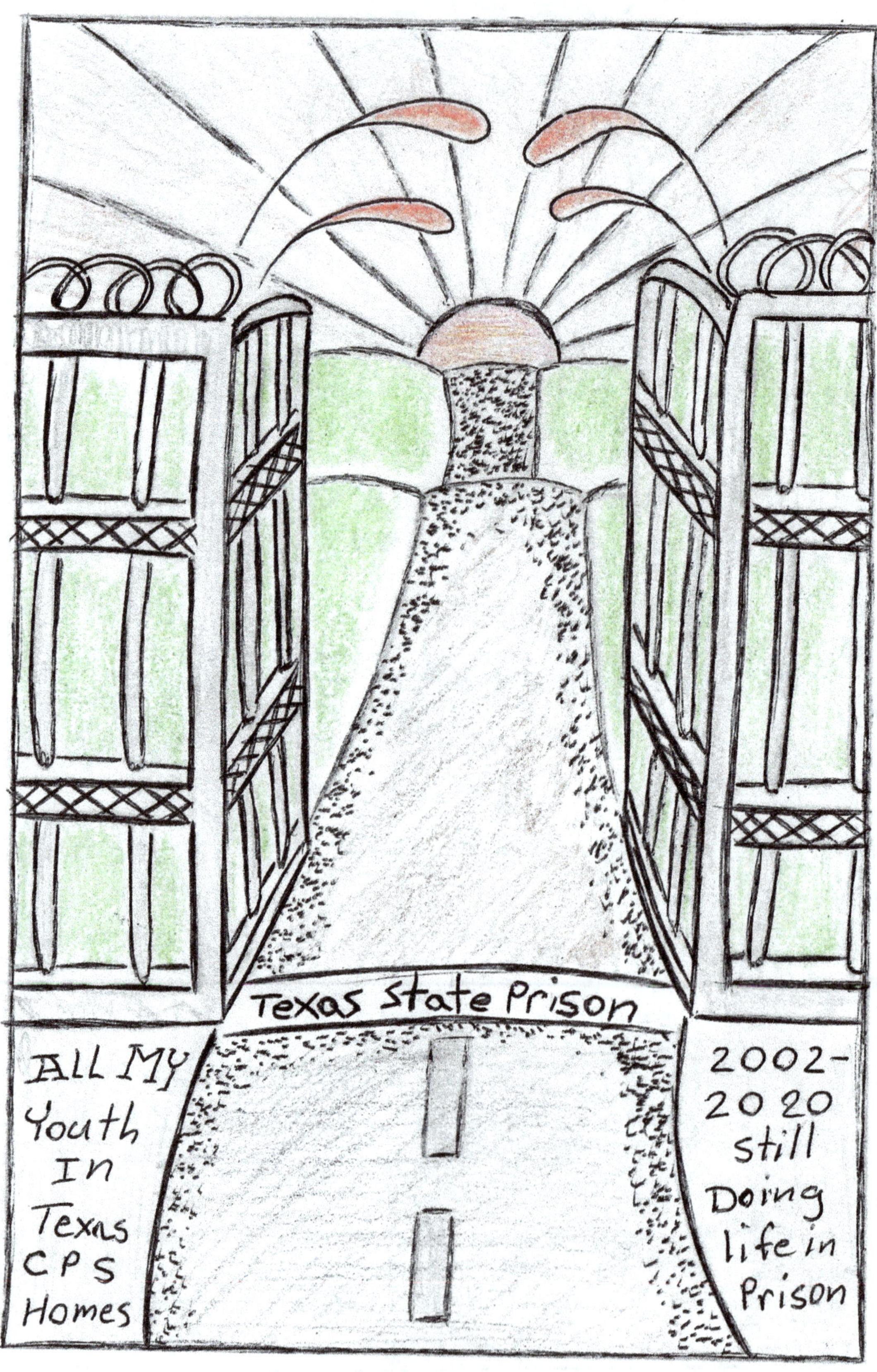

Texas State Prison
All My Youth In Texas CPS Homes
2002-2020 still Doing life in Prison

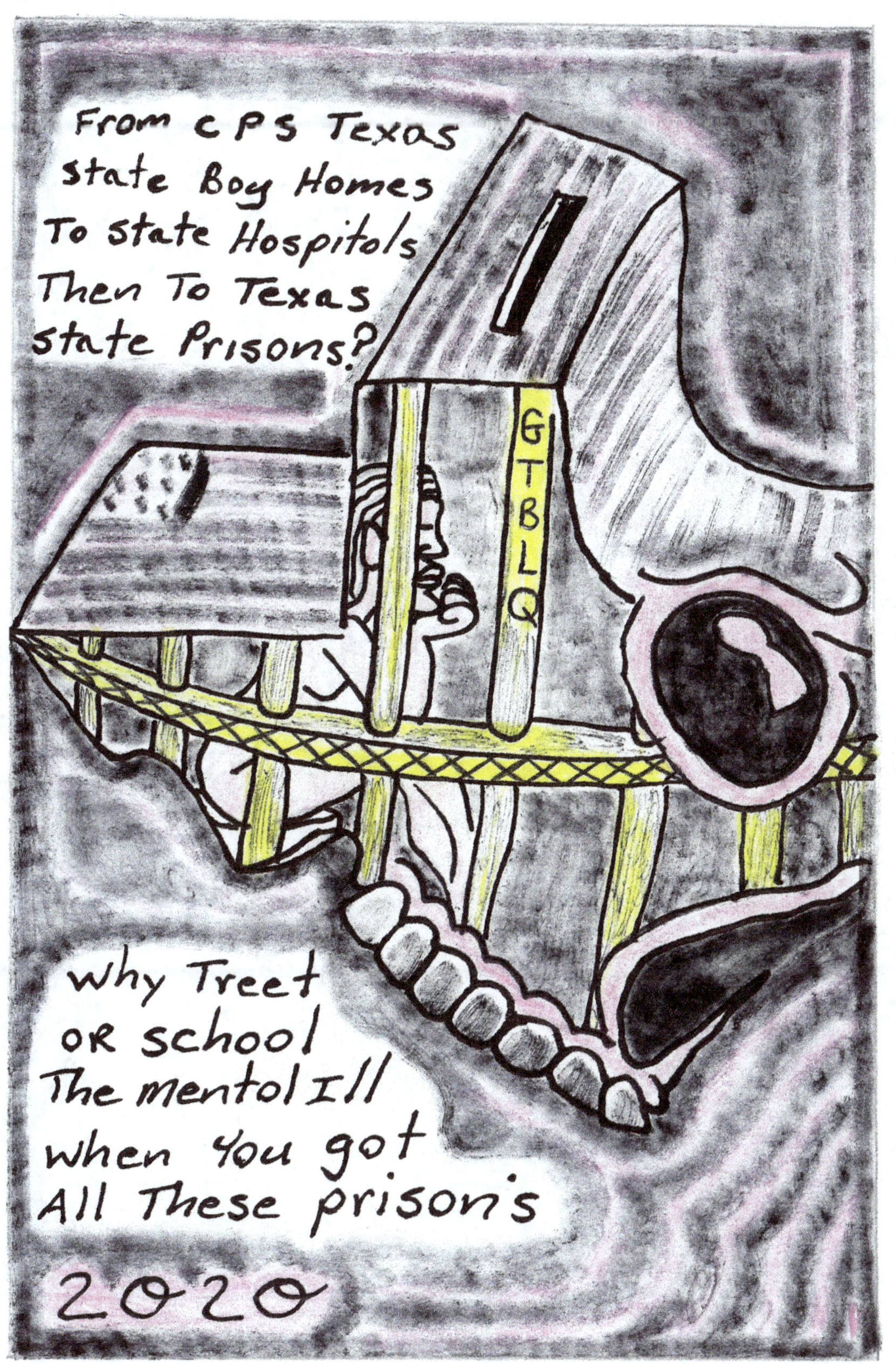
From C P S Texas
state Boy Homes
To state Hospitols
Then To Texas
state Prisons?
GTBLQ
Why Treet
oR school
The mentol Ill
when You got
All These prison's
2020

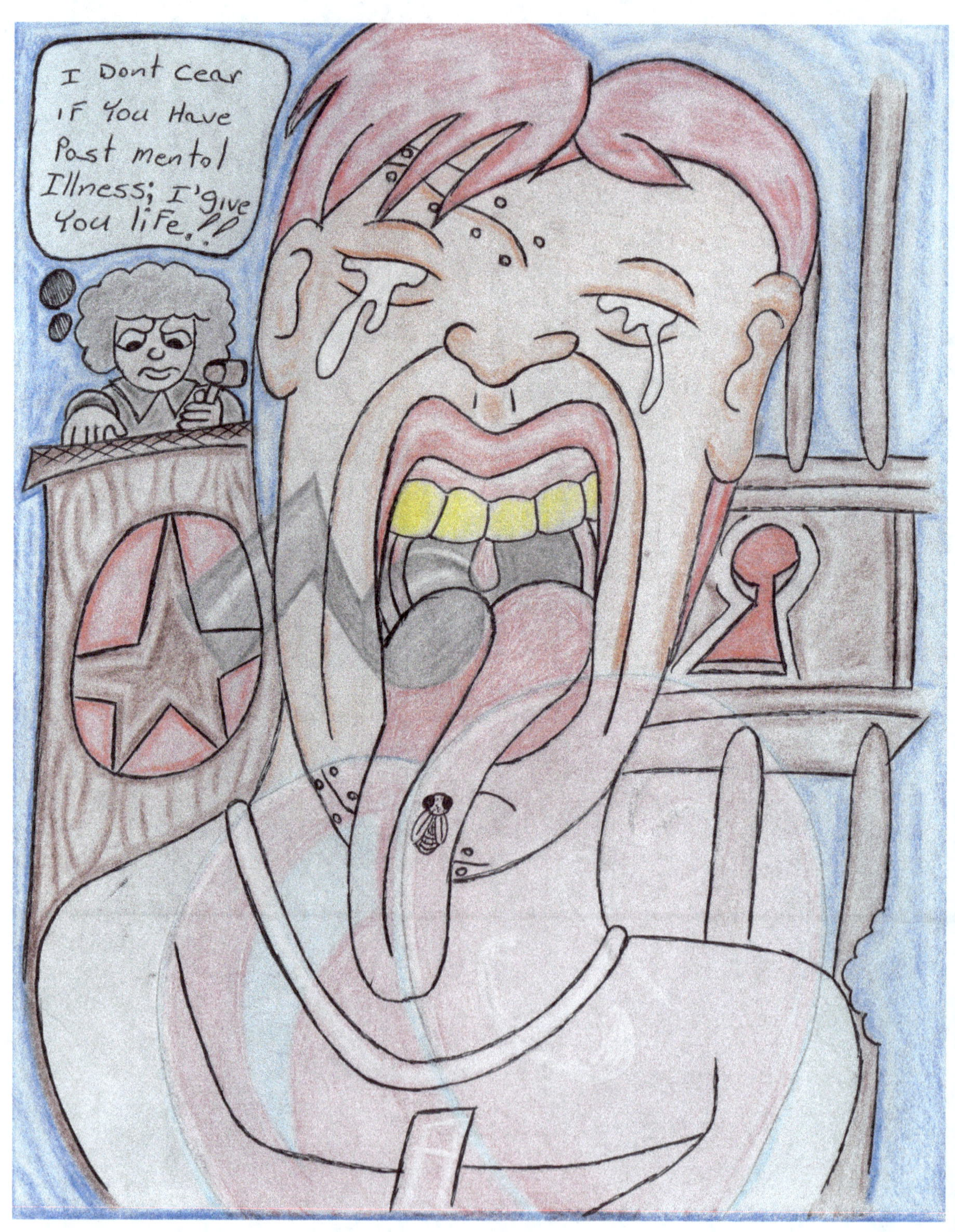
I Dont cear
iF You Have
Past mentol
Illness; I'give
You life.!!

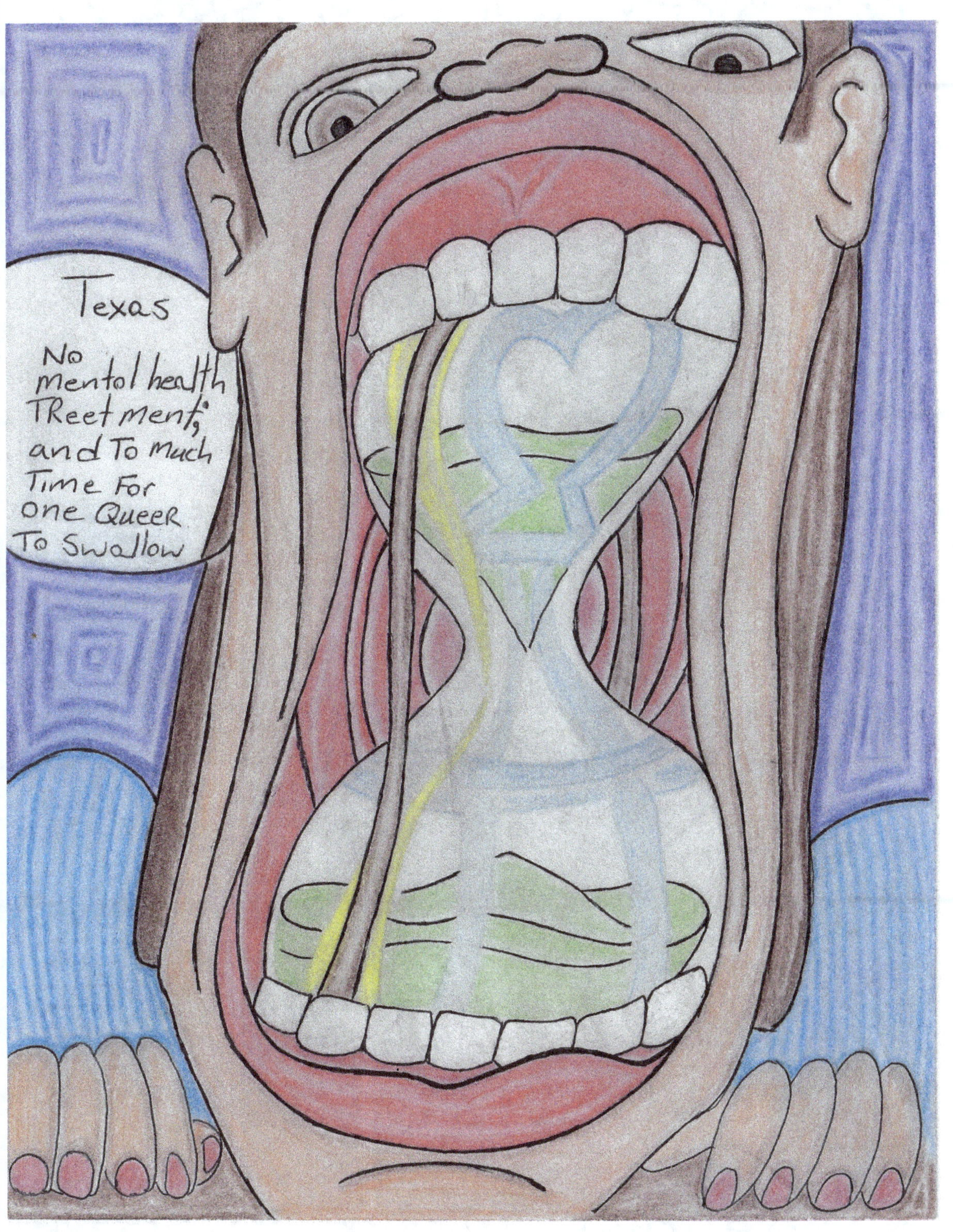

Texas
No mentol health TReetment, and To much Time For one Queer To Swallow

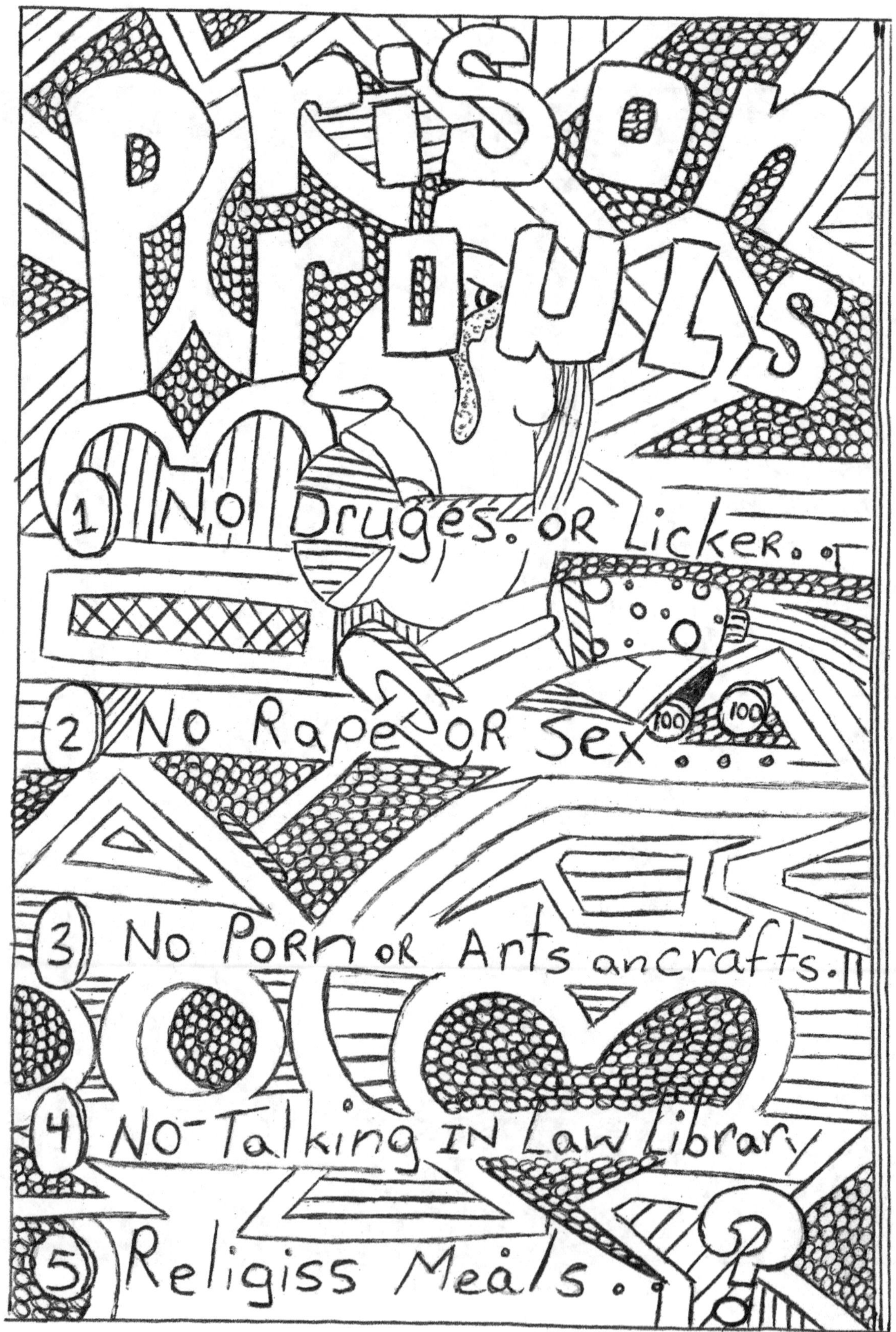
PRISON PROWLS
1 No Druges. or Licker..
2 No Rape OR Sex....
3 No Porn or Arts ancrafts.
4 No Talking IN Law Library
5 Religiss Meals..

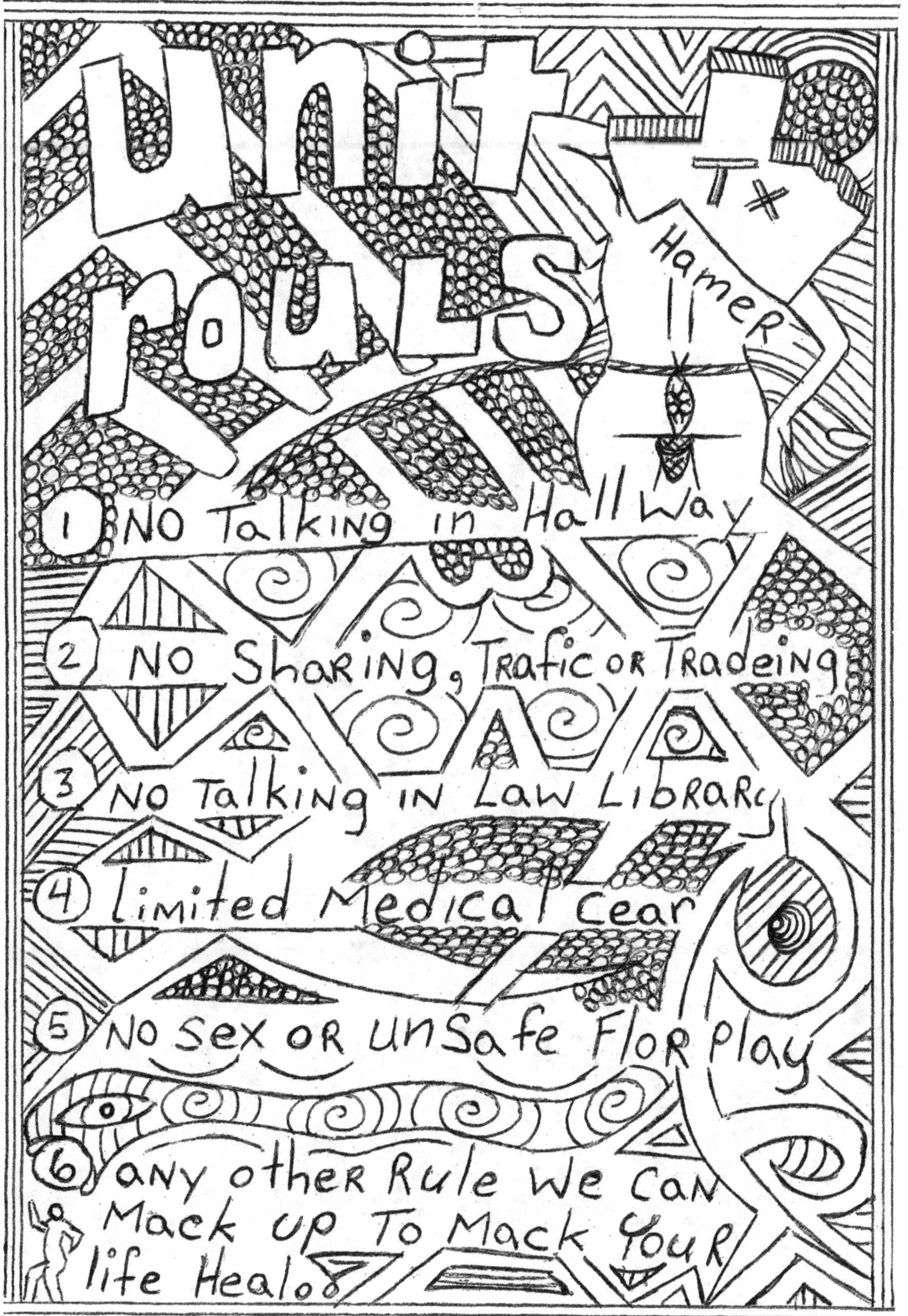
unit 4 rouLS
Tx
HameR
1 NO Talking in Hall way
2 NO Sharing, Trafic or Tradeing
3 No Talking in Law LibraRc
4 limited MediCal cear
5 No sex or unSafe Flor play
6 any other Rule We Can Mack up To Mack YouR life Heal..

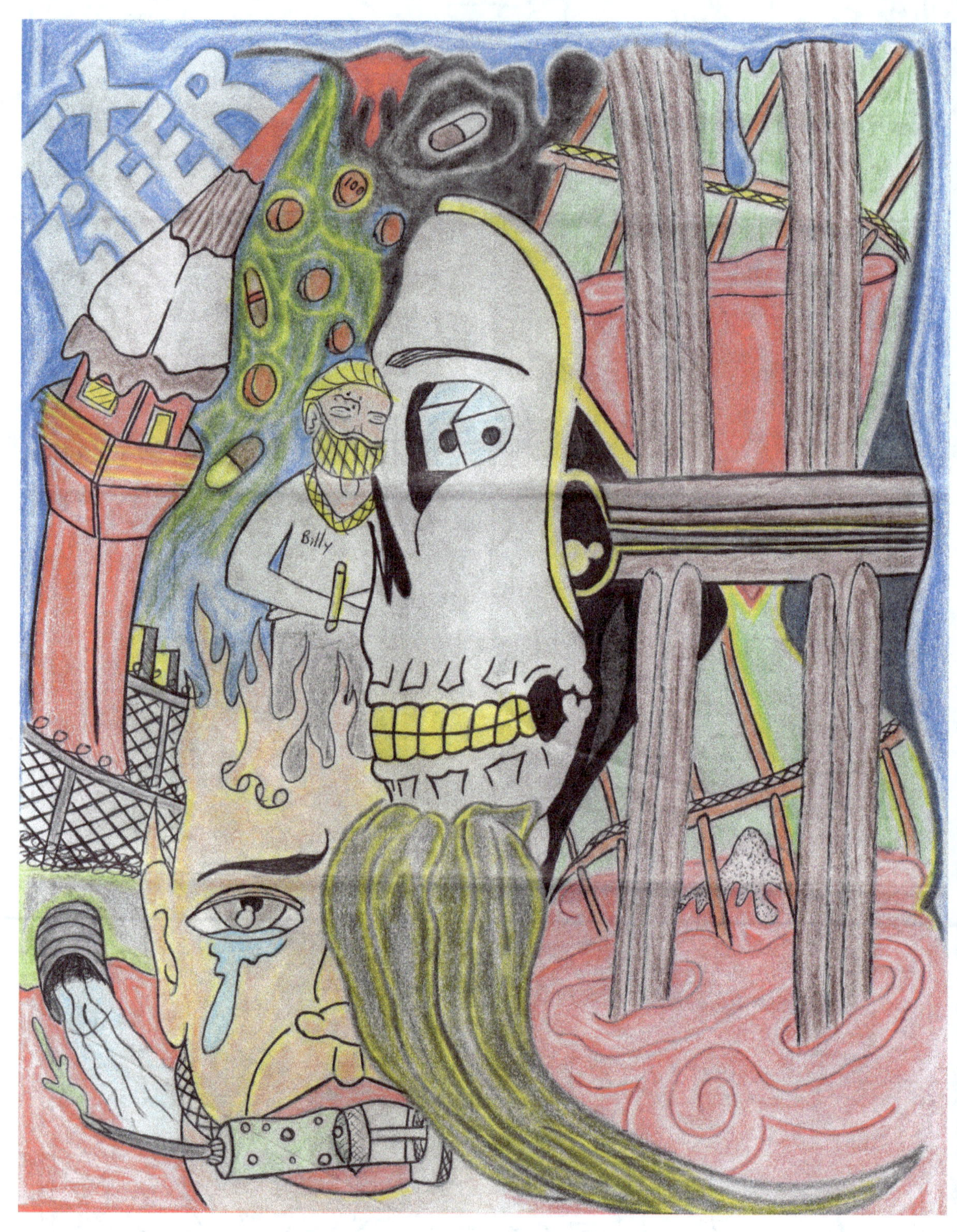
Billy

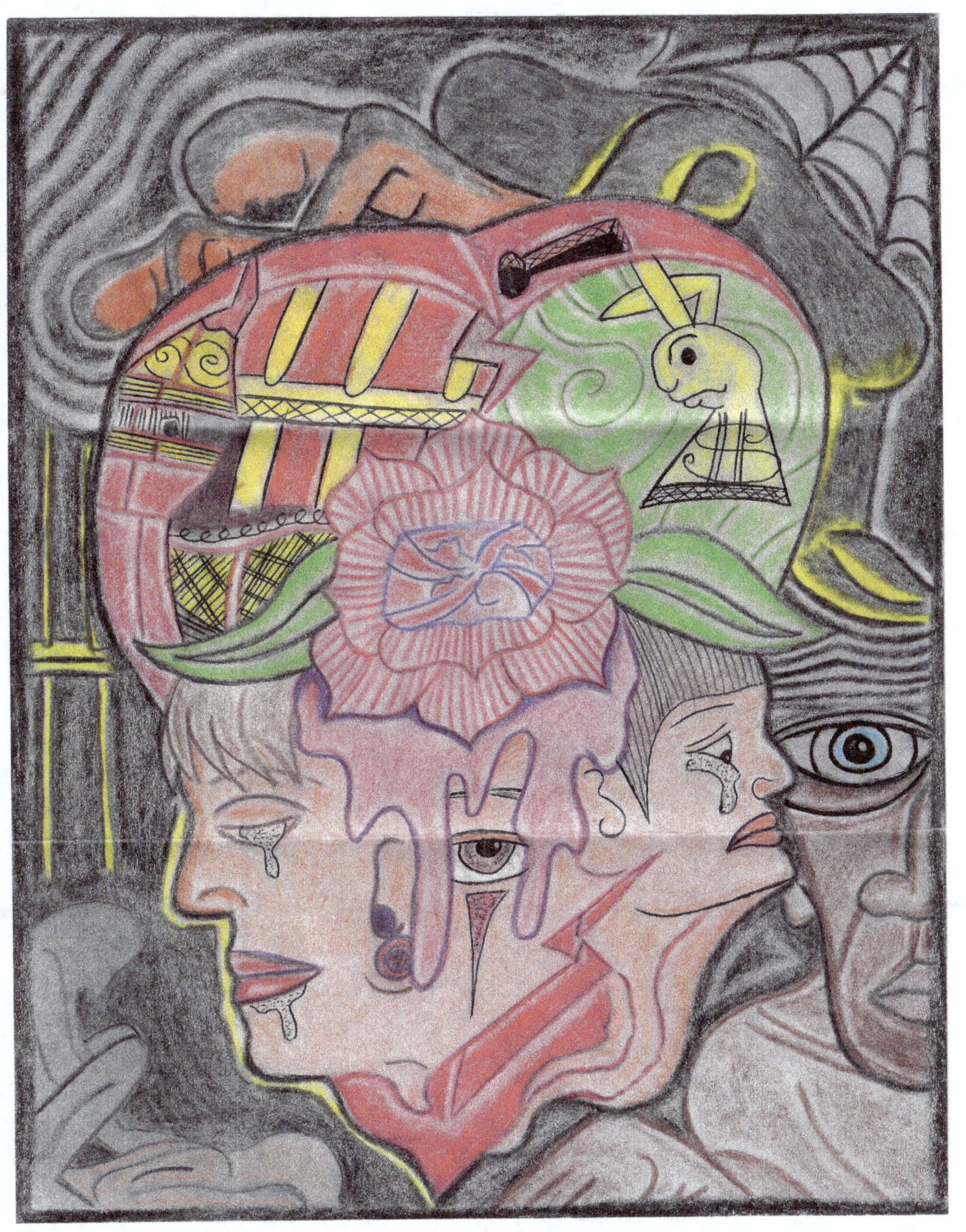

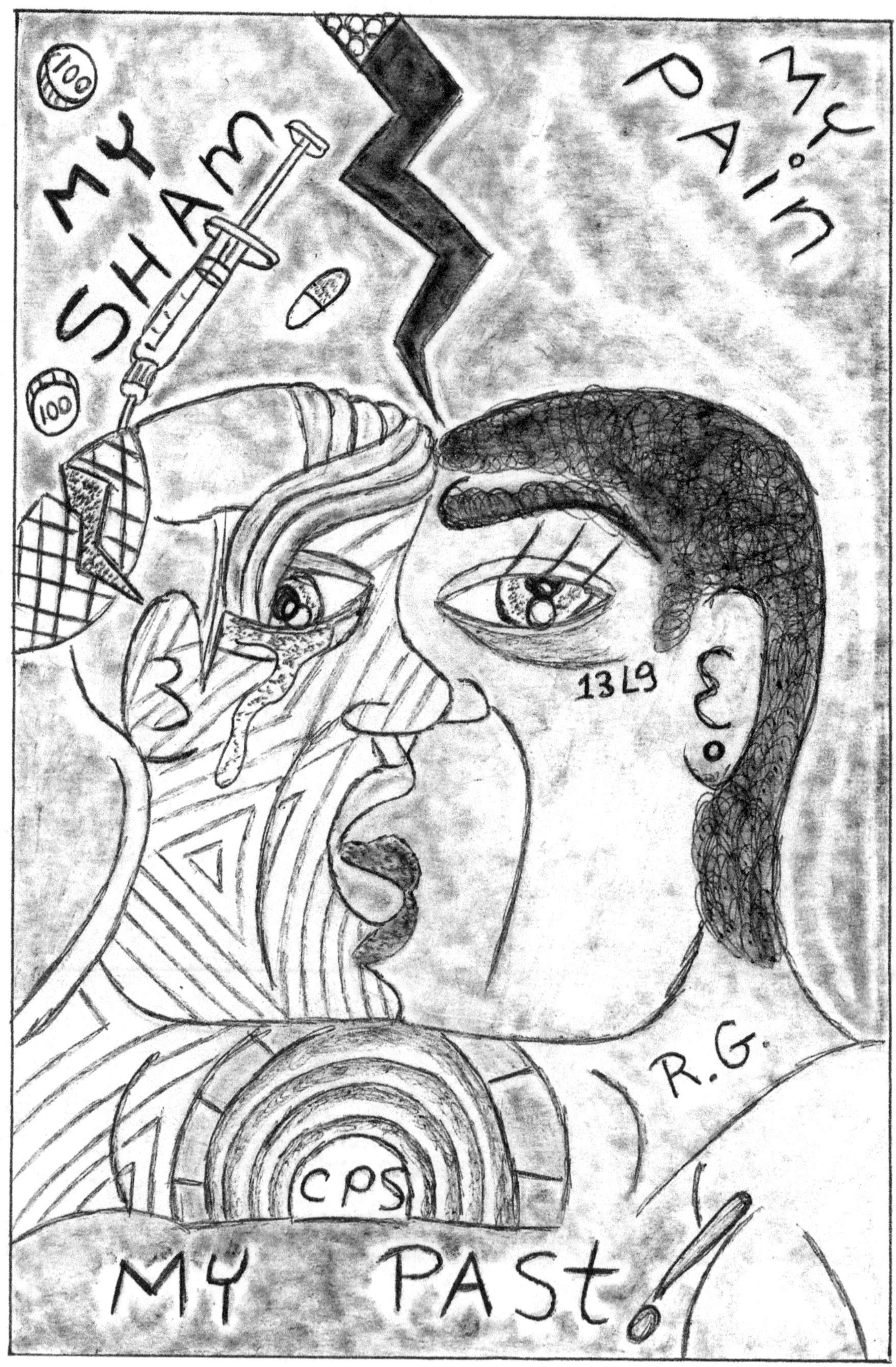
MY PAIN
MY SHAM
MY PAST
100
100
CPS
R.G.

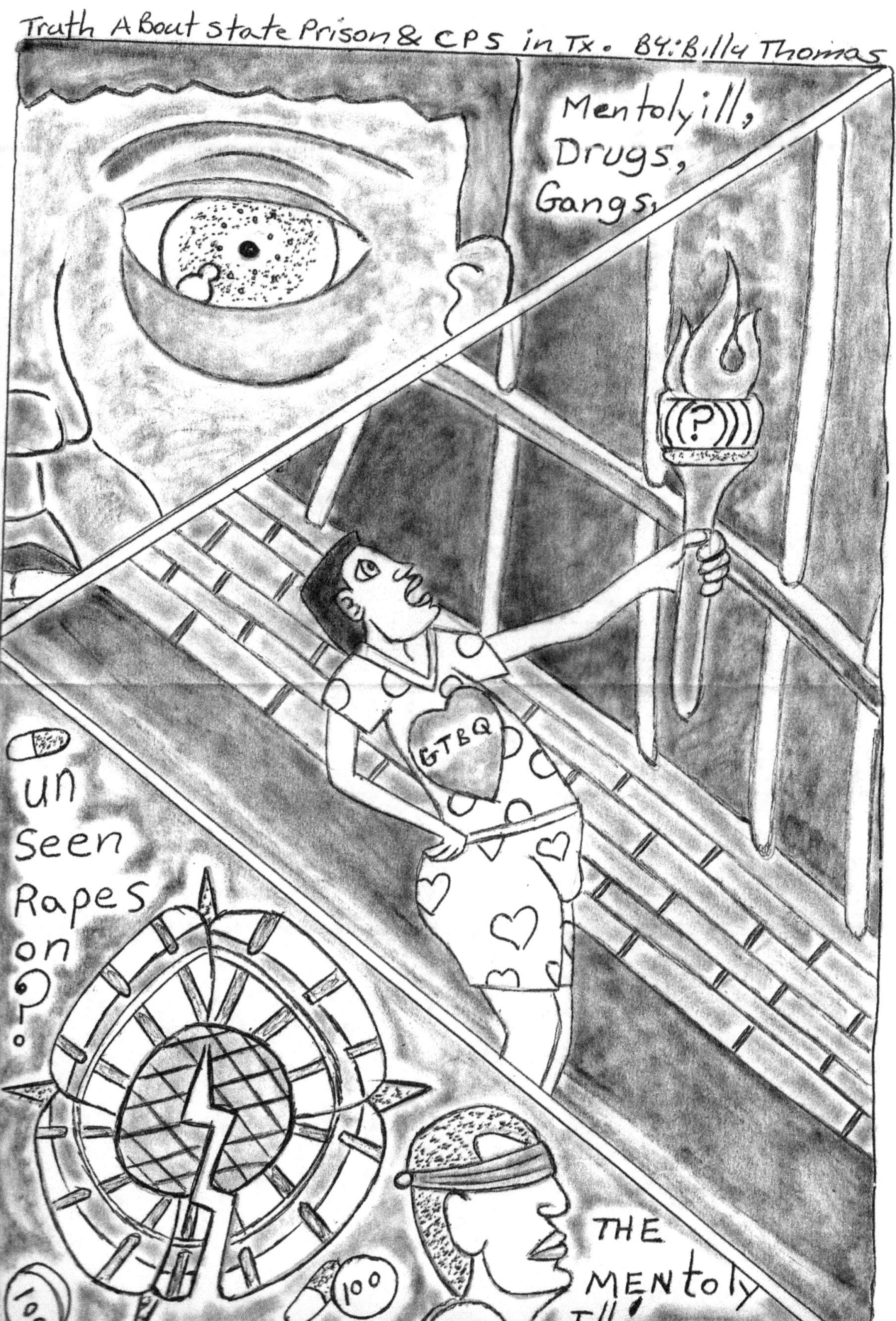
Truth About state Prison & CPS in Tx. BY: Billy Thomas
Mentoly ill, Drugs, Gangs,
?
GTBQ
un Seen Rapes on ?
100
THE Mentoly ill

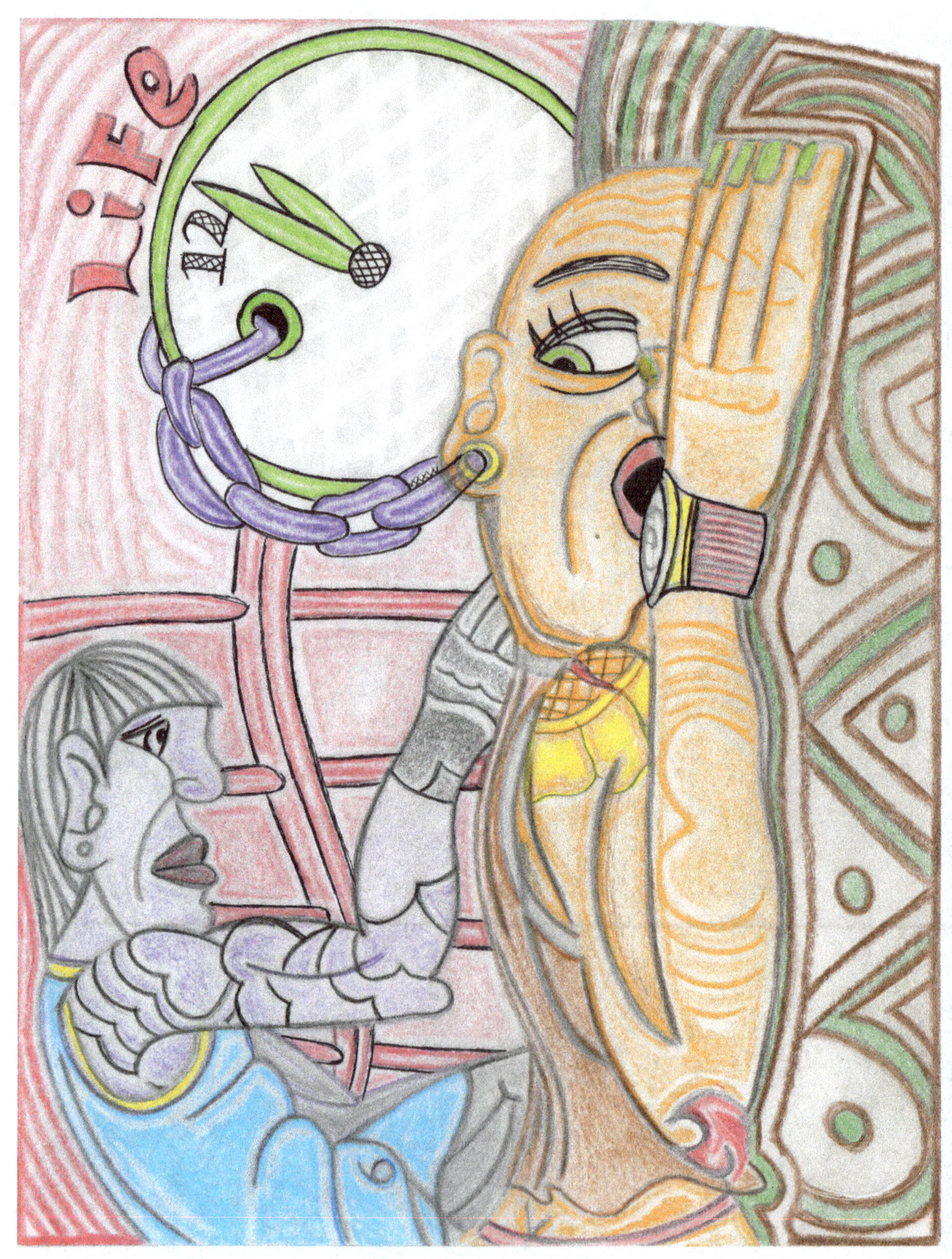
LiFe
12
6

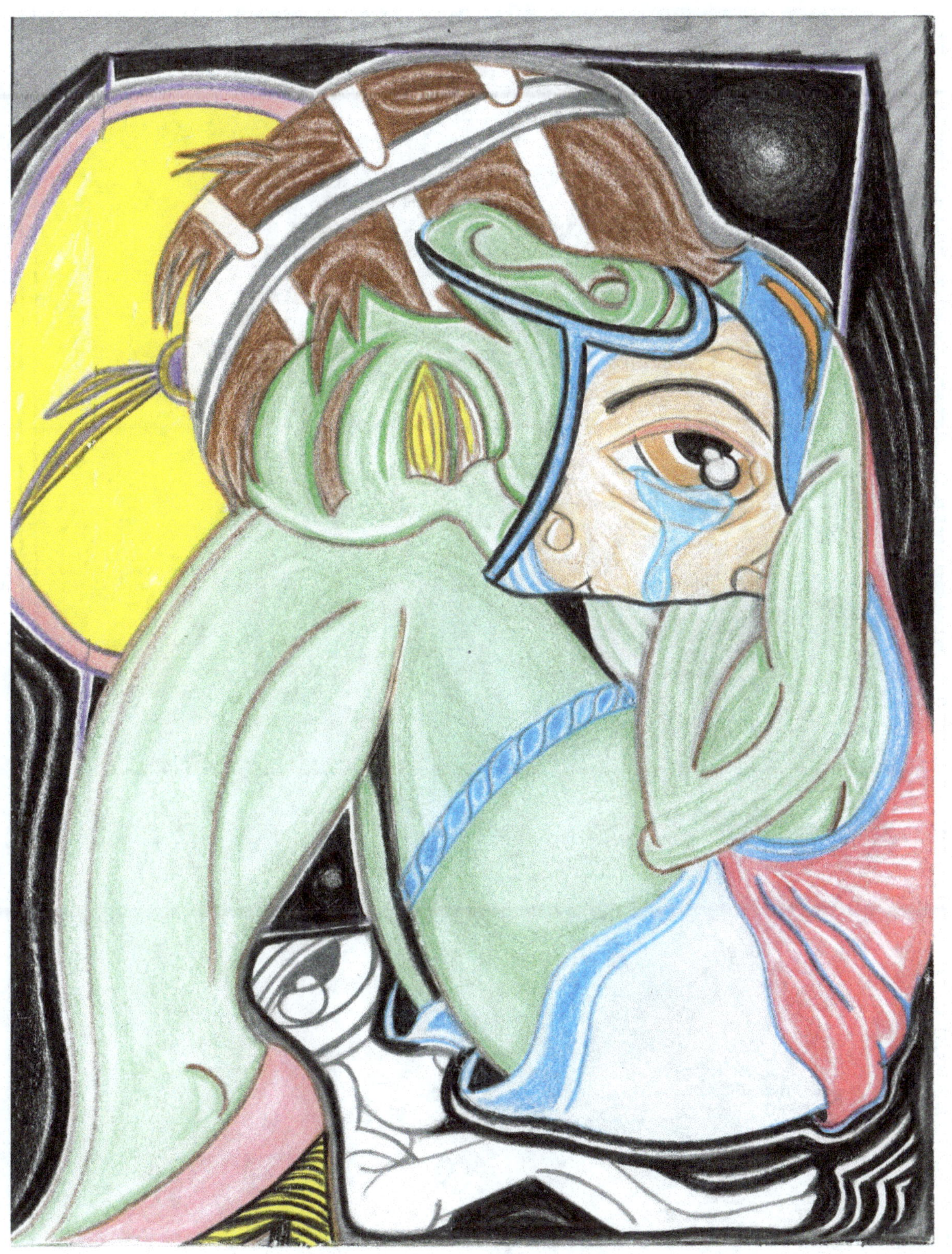

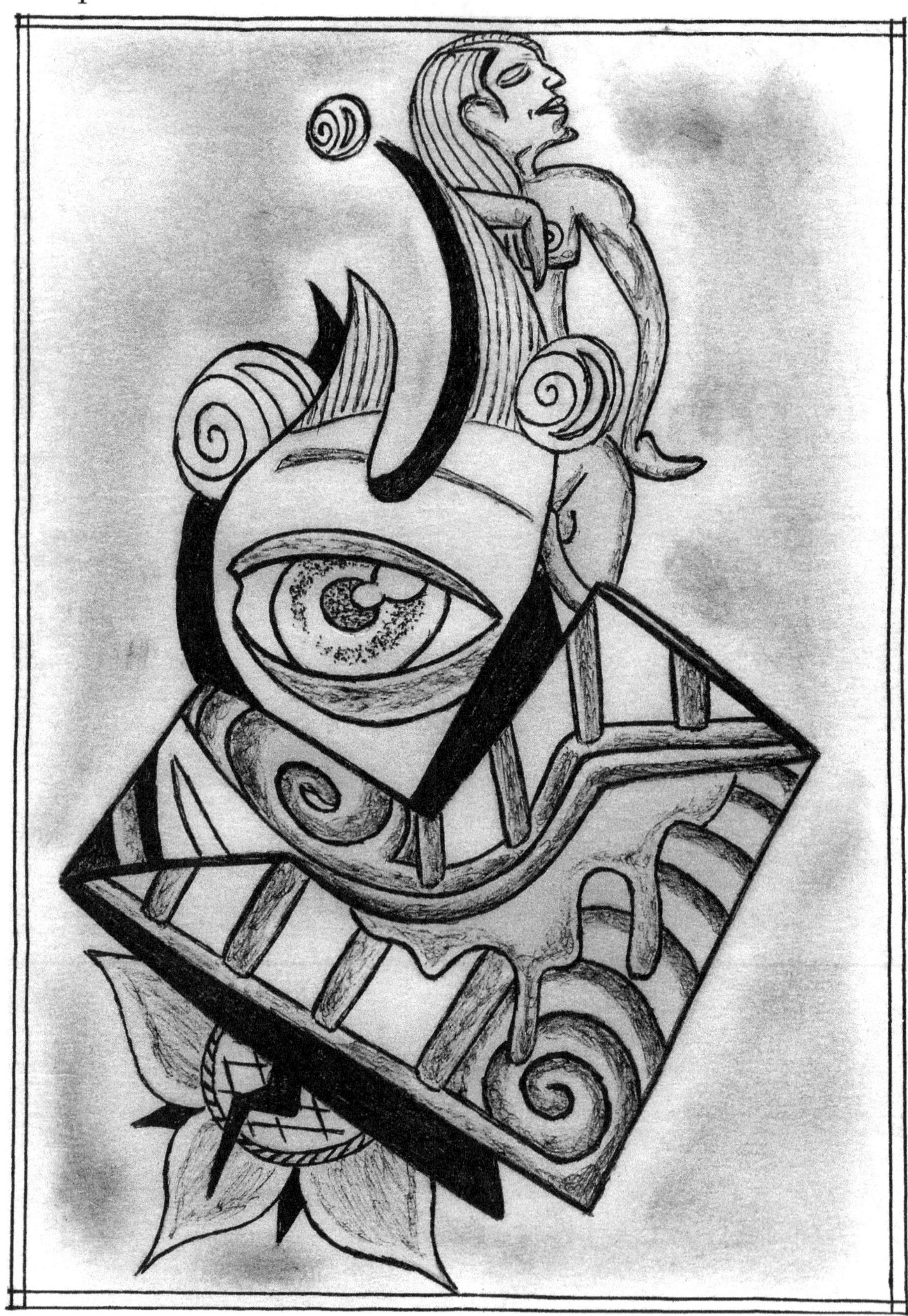

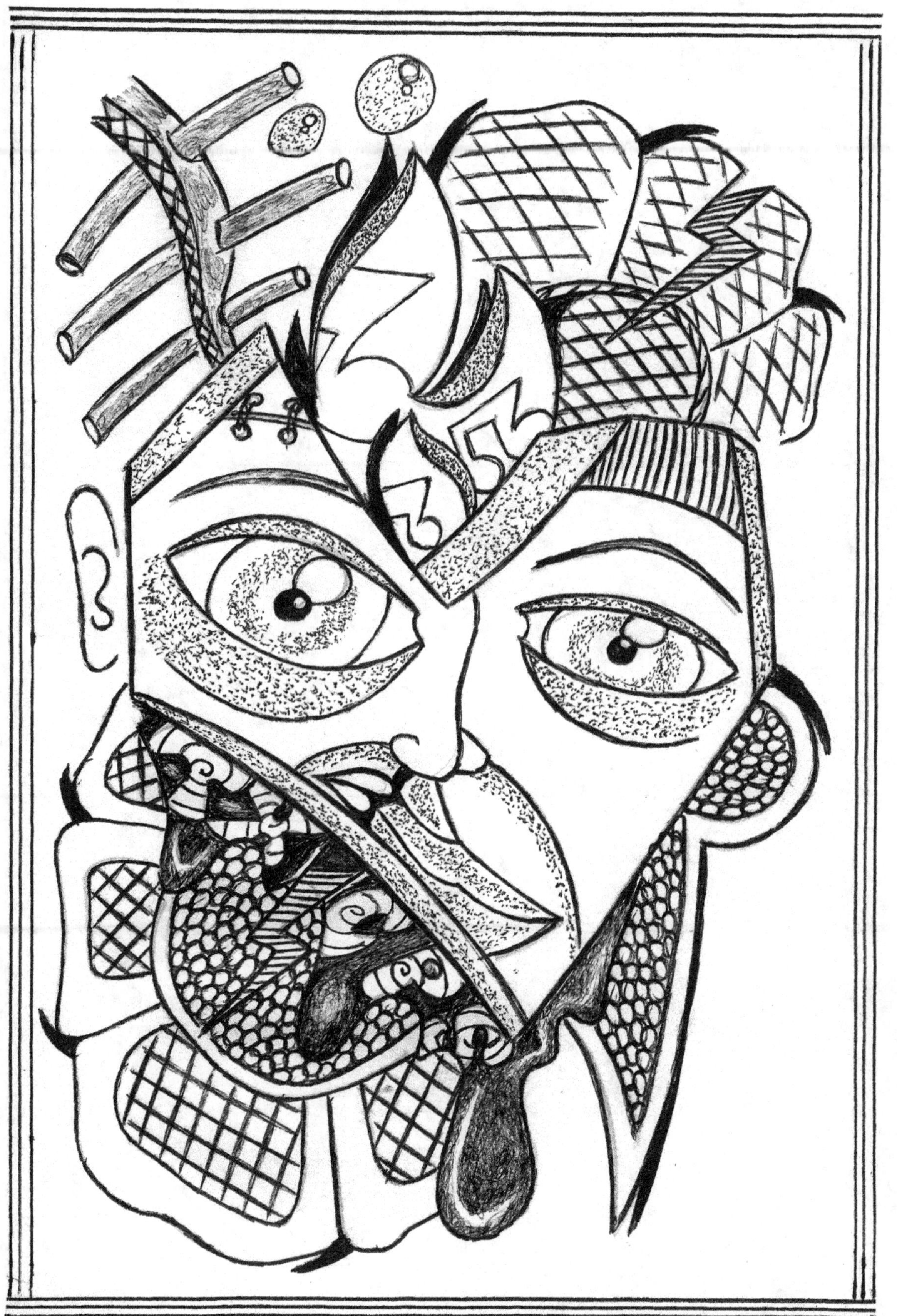

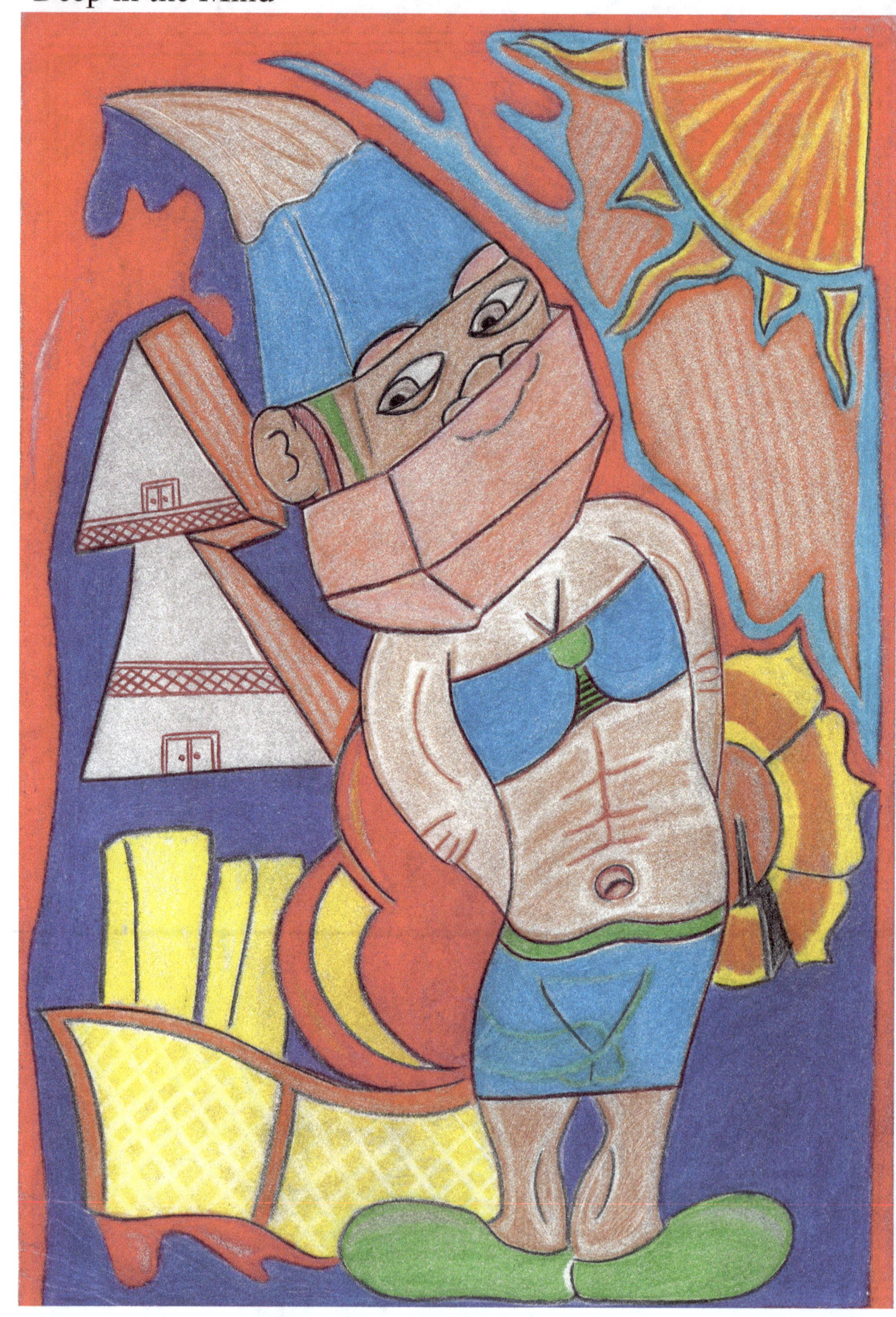

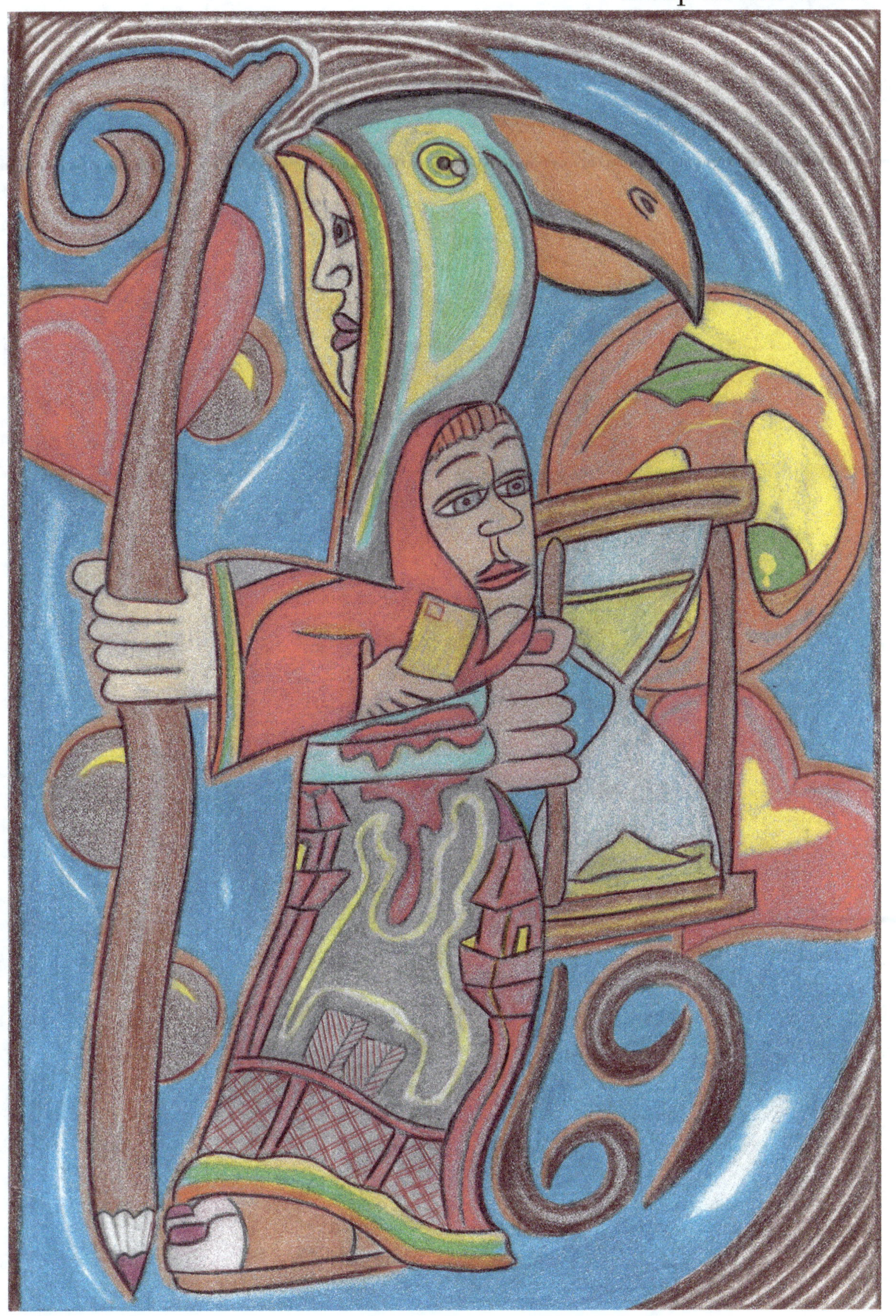

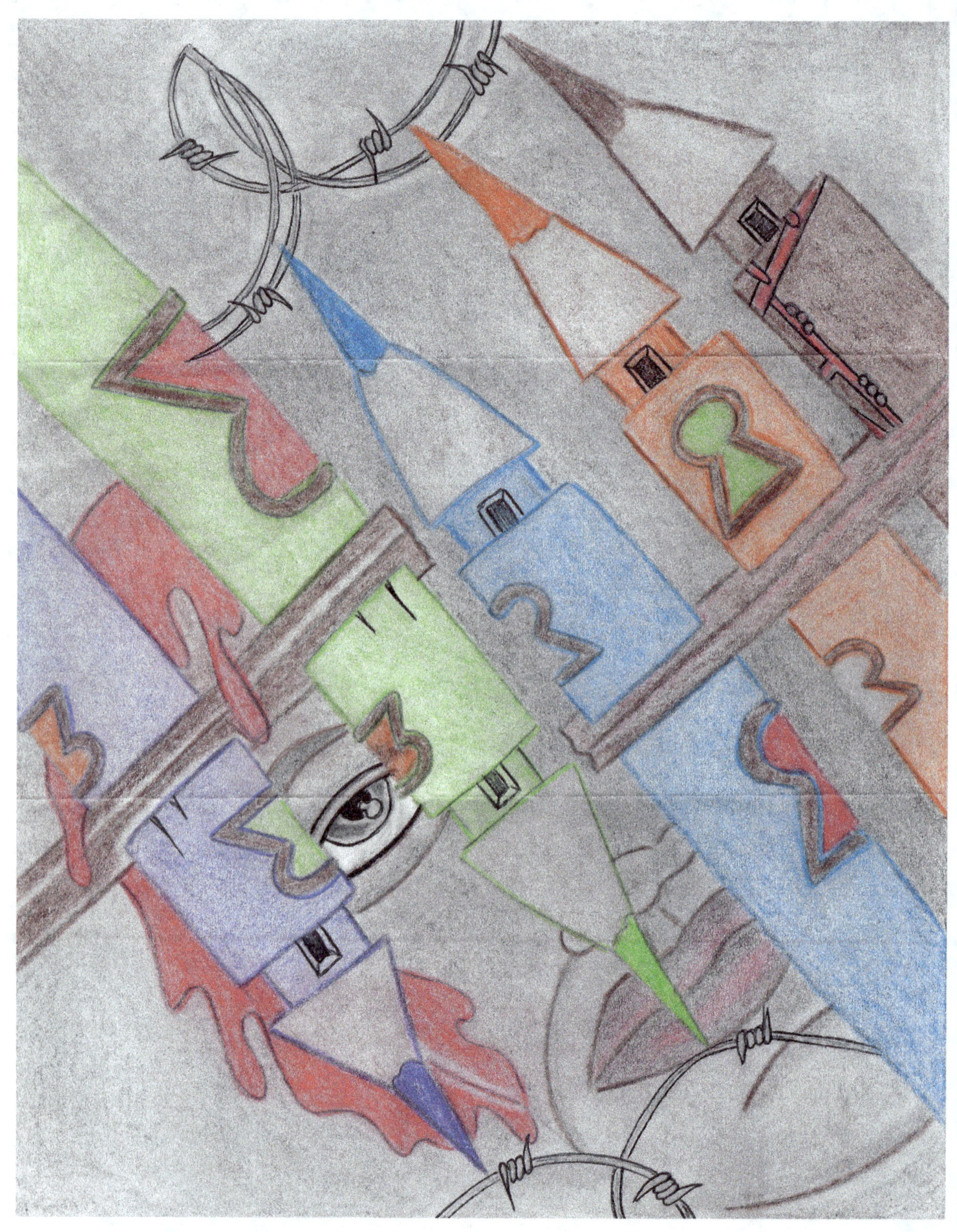

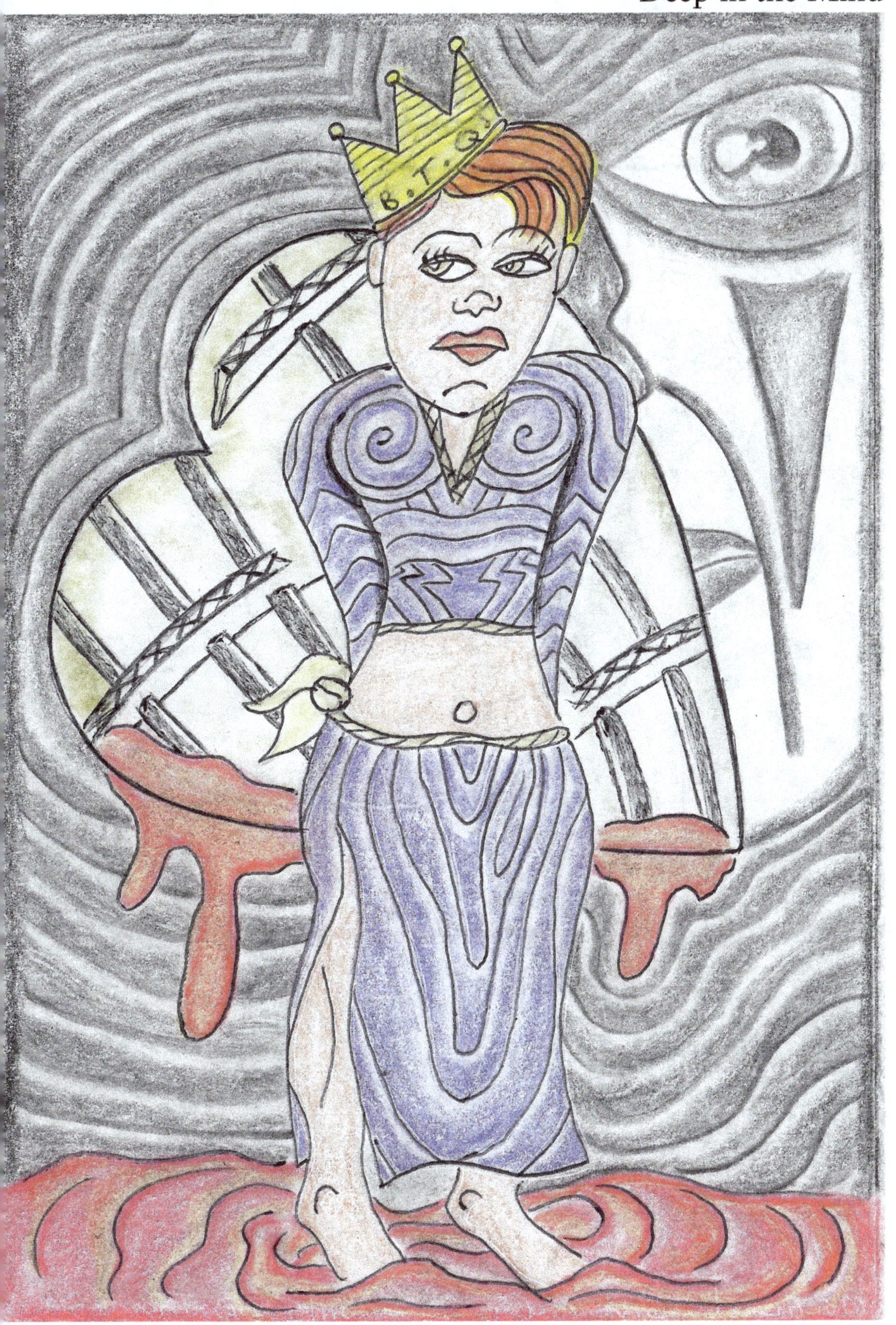

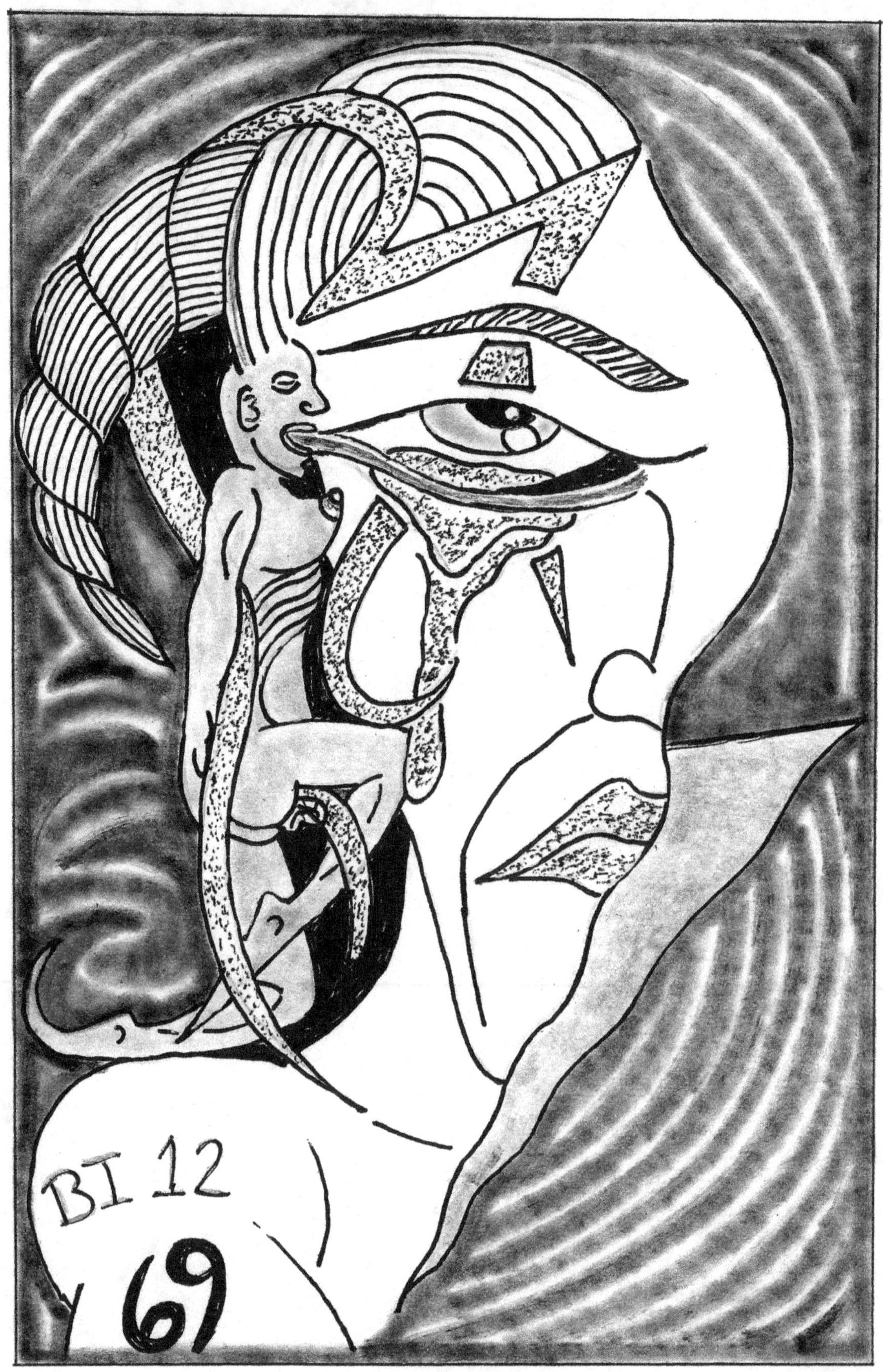
BI 12
69

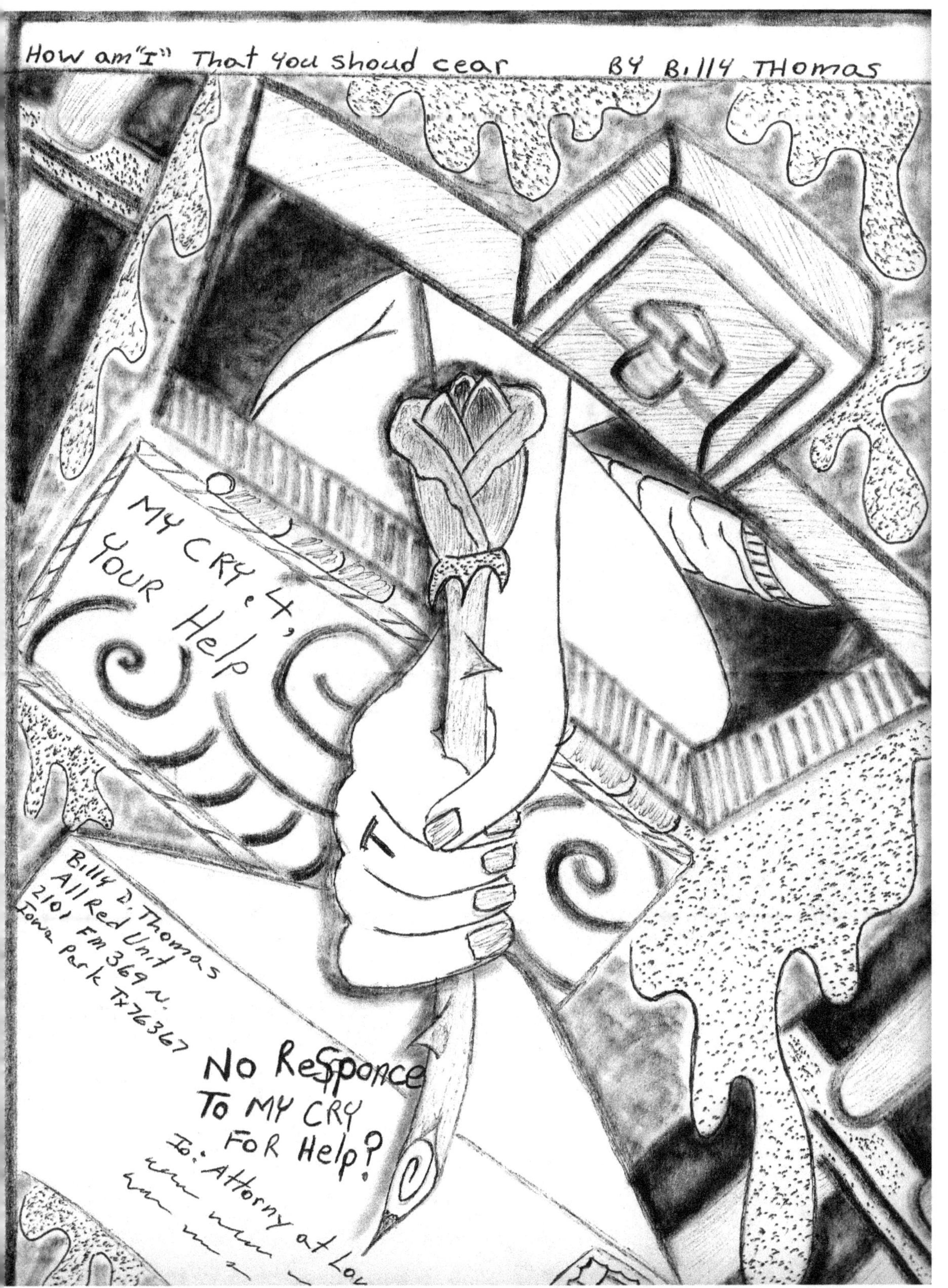
How am "I" That you shoud cear   BY Billy Thomas
MY CRY 4,
Your Help
Billy D. Thomas
All Red Unit
2101 FM 369 N.
Iowa Park TX 76367
No ReSponce
To MY CRY
FoR Help?
To: Attorny at Law

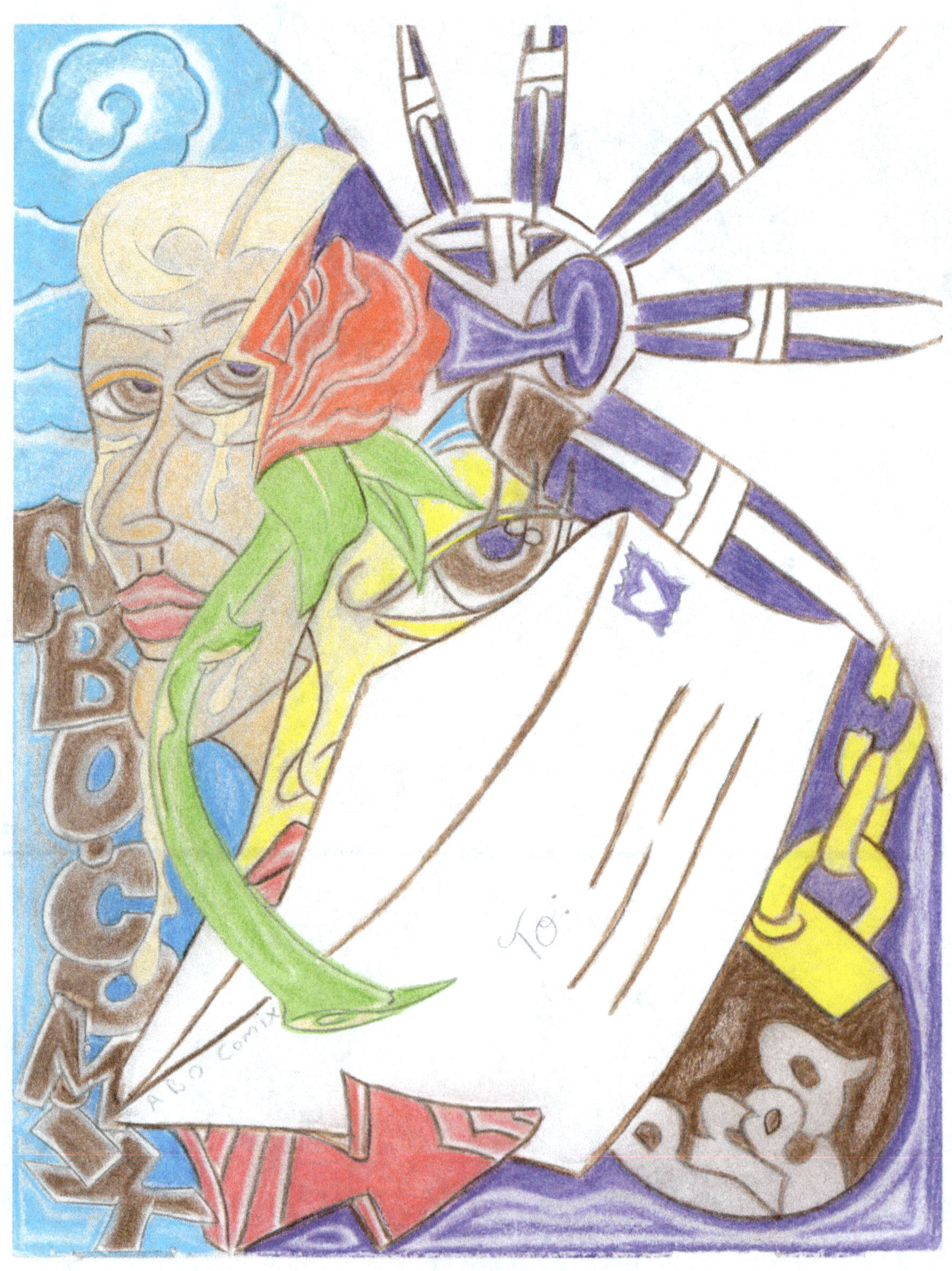

ABO Comix

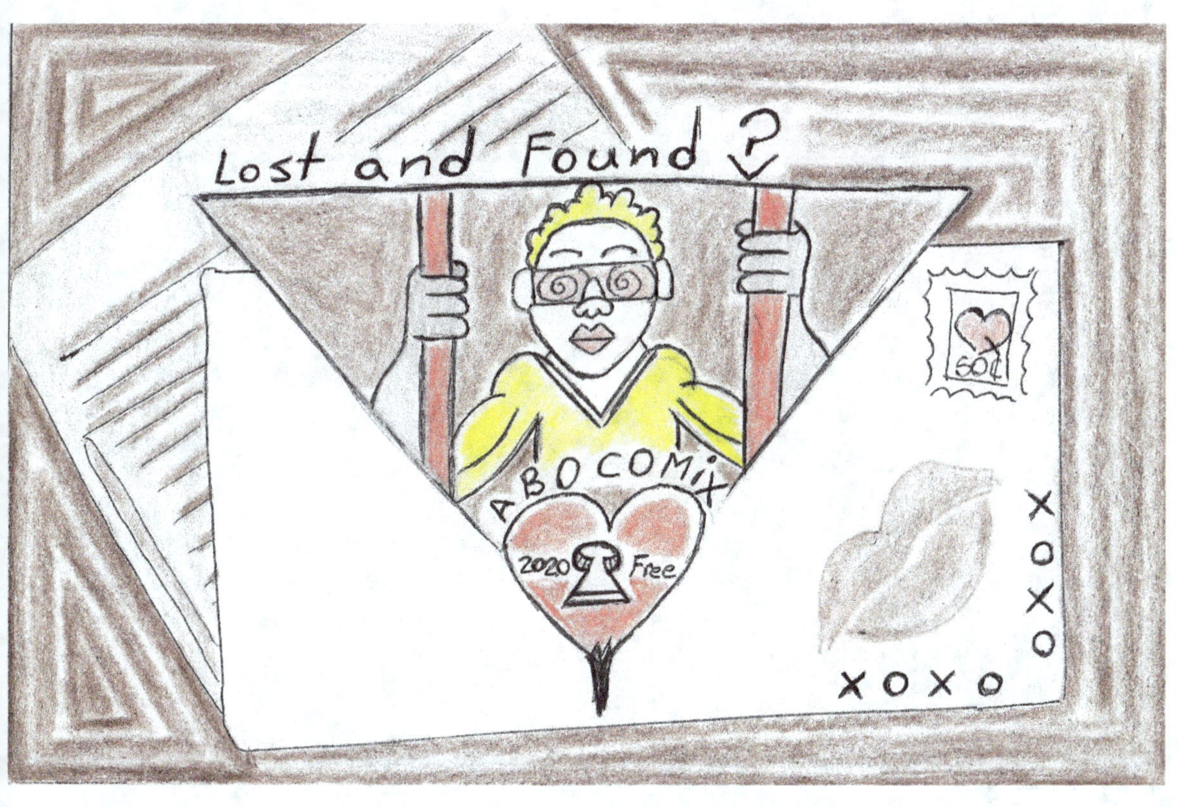
Lost and Found ?
ABO COMiX
2020 Free
XOXO
XOXO

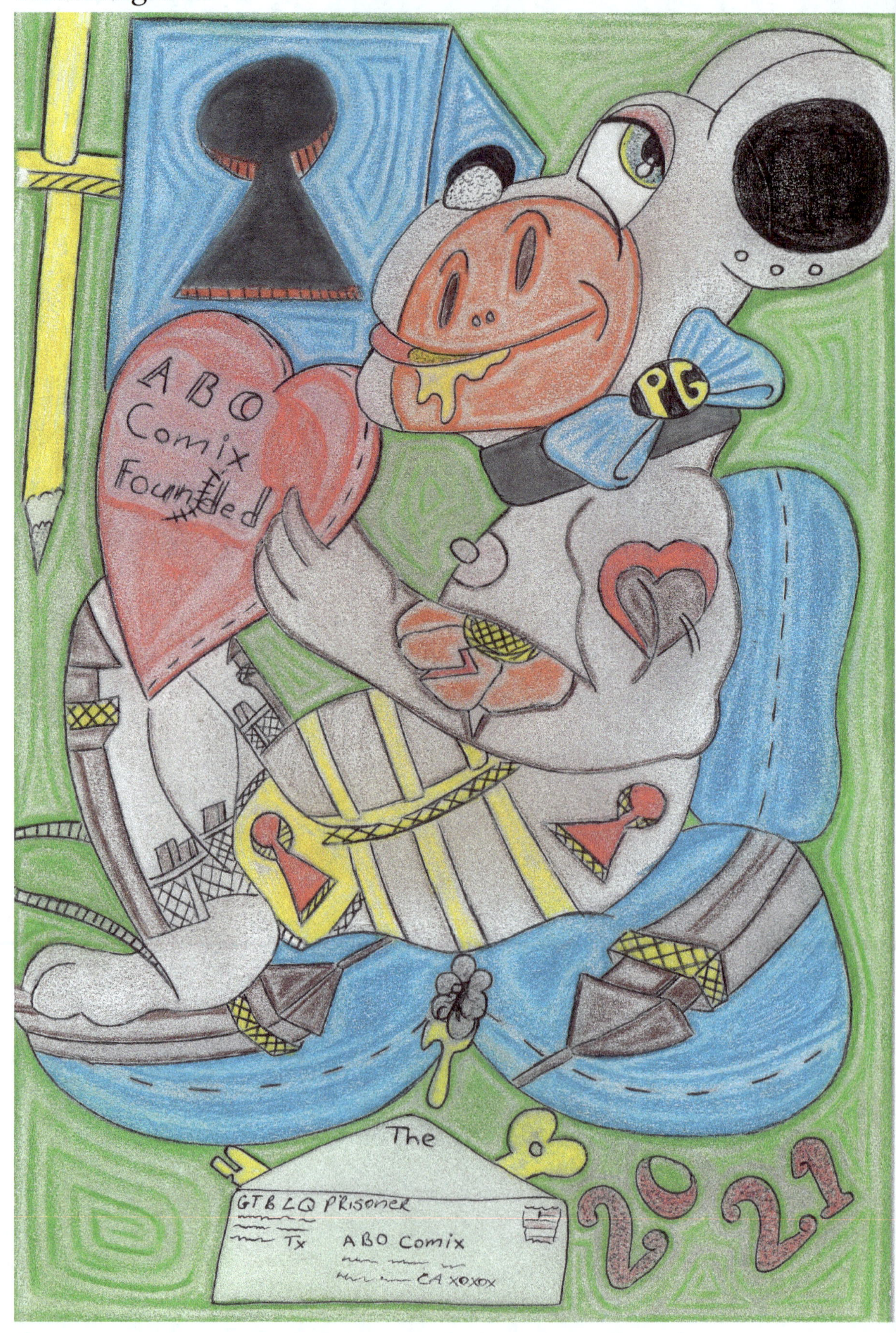
PG
ABO
Comix
Foun Filled
The
GTBLQ Prisoner
Tx
ABO Comix
CA XOXOX
2021

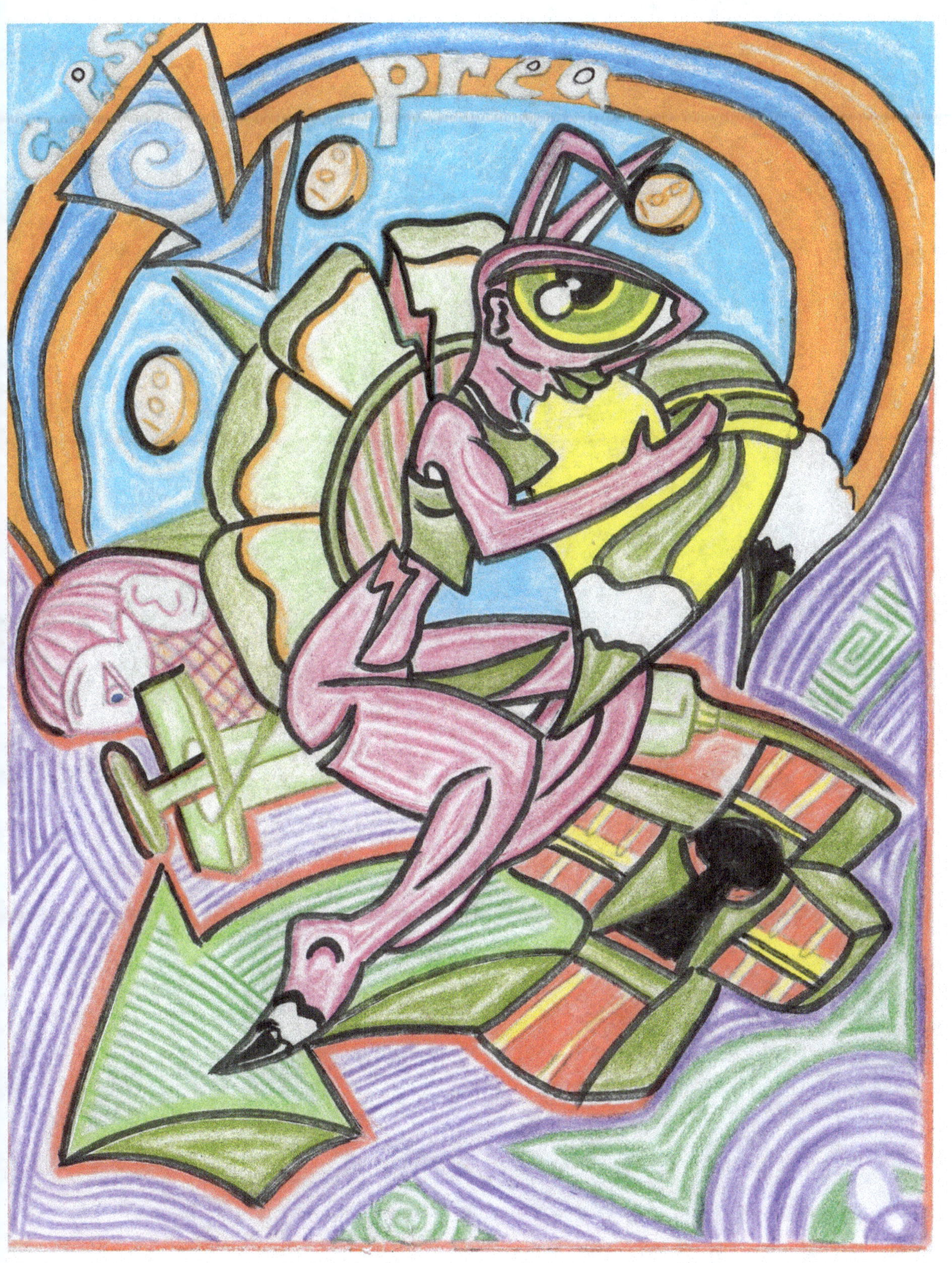
prea

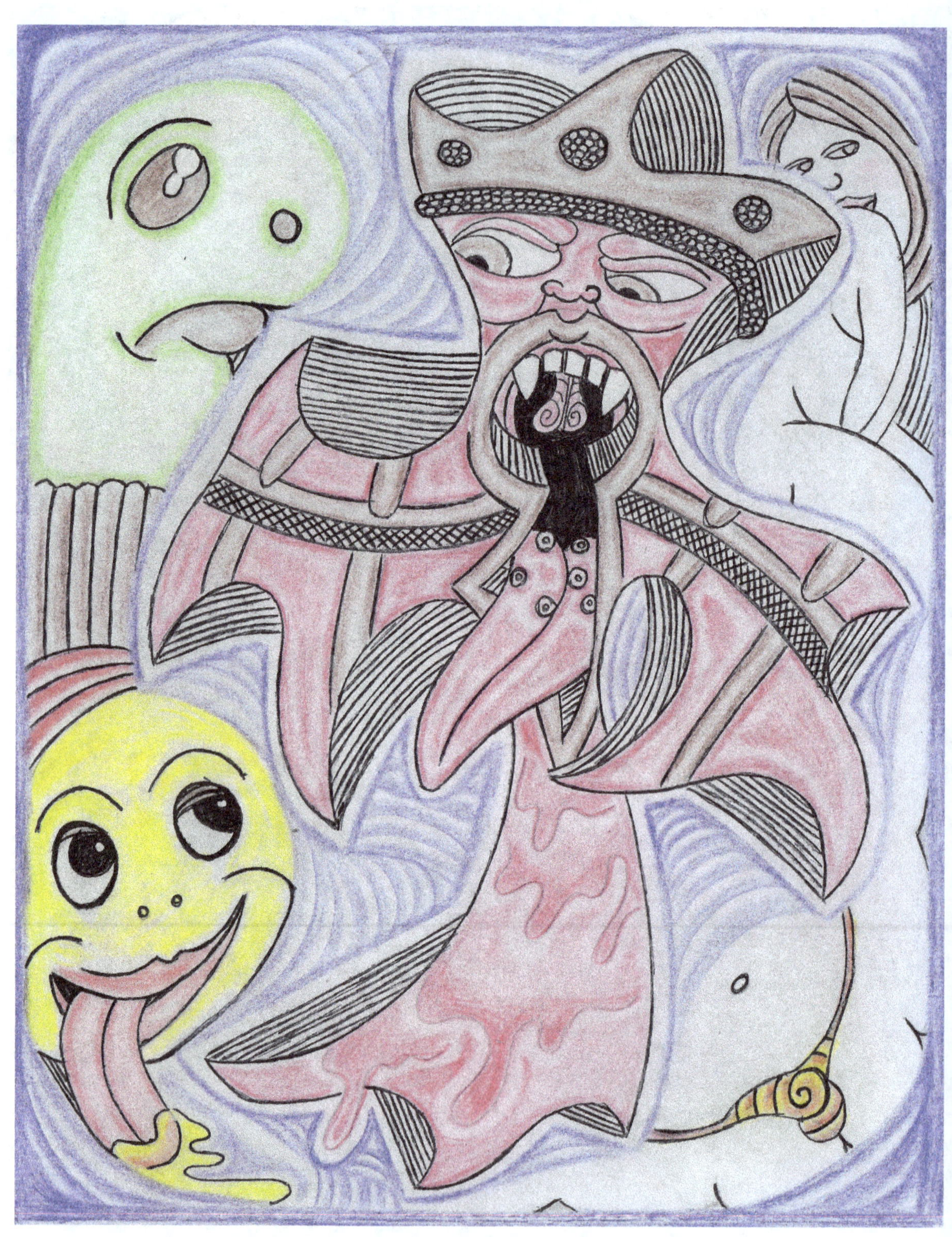

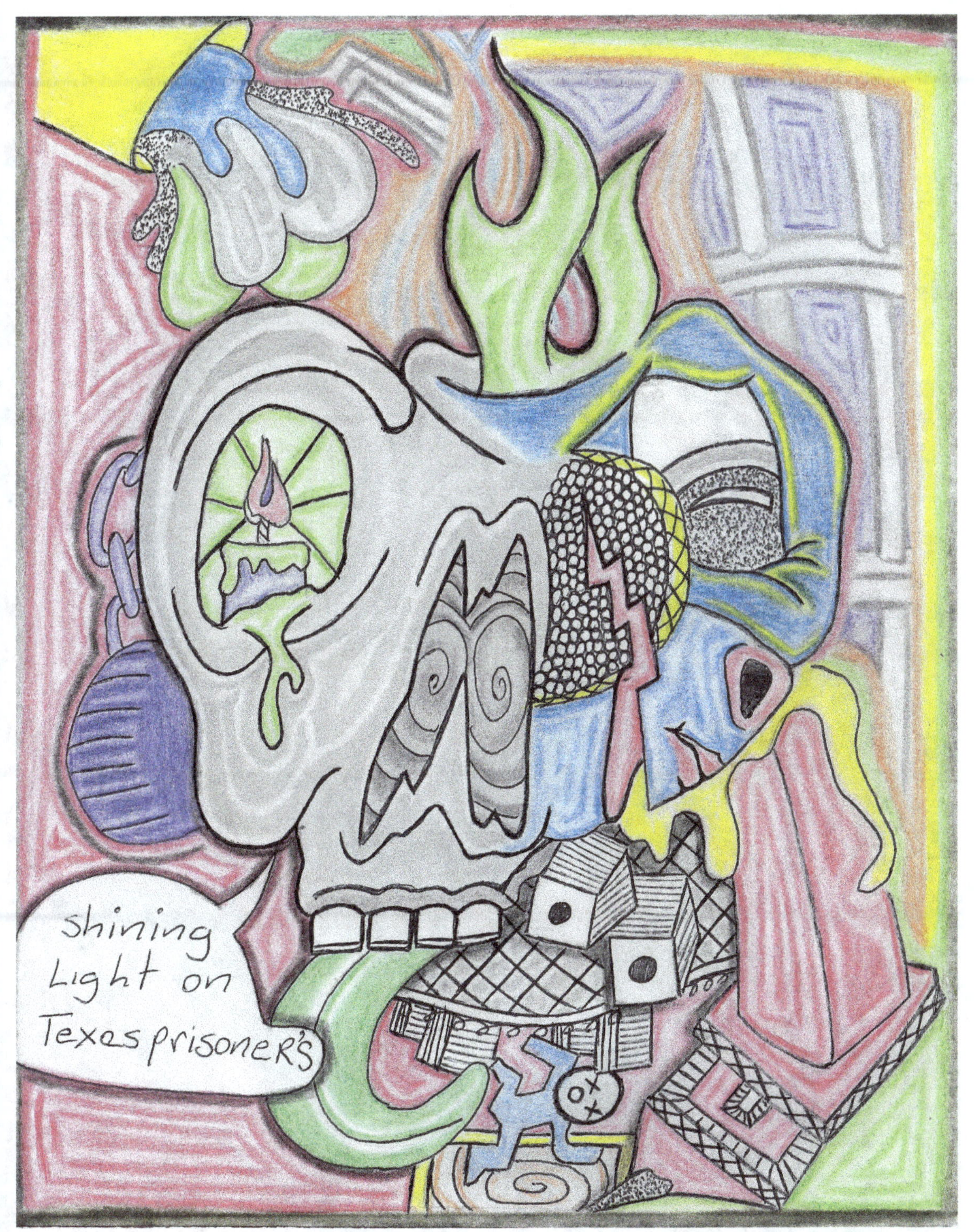
shining
Light on
Texas prisoners

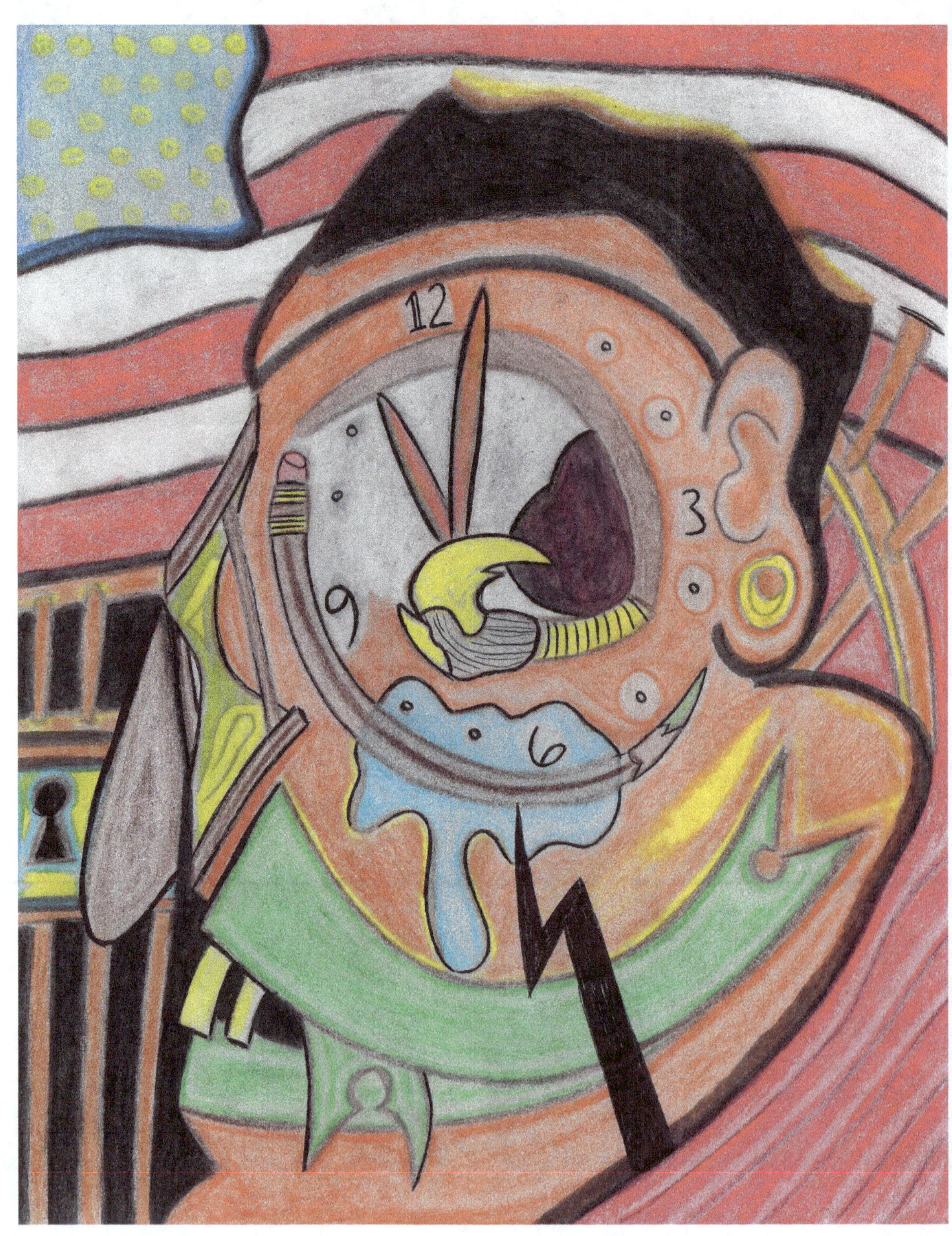

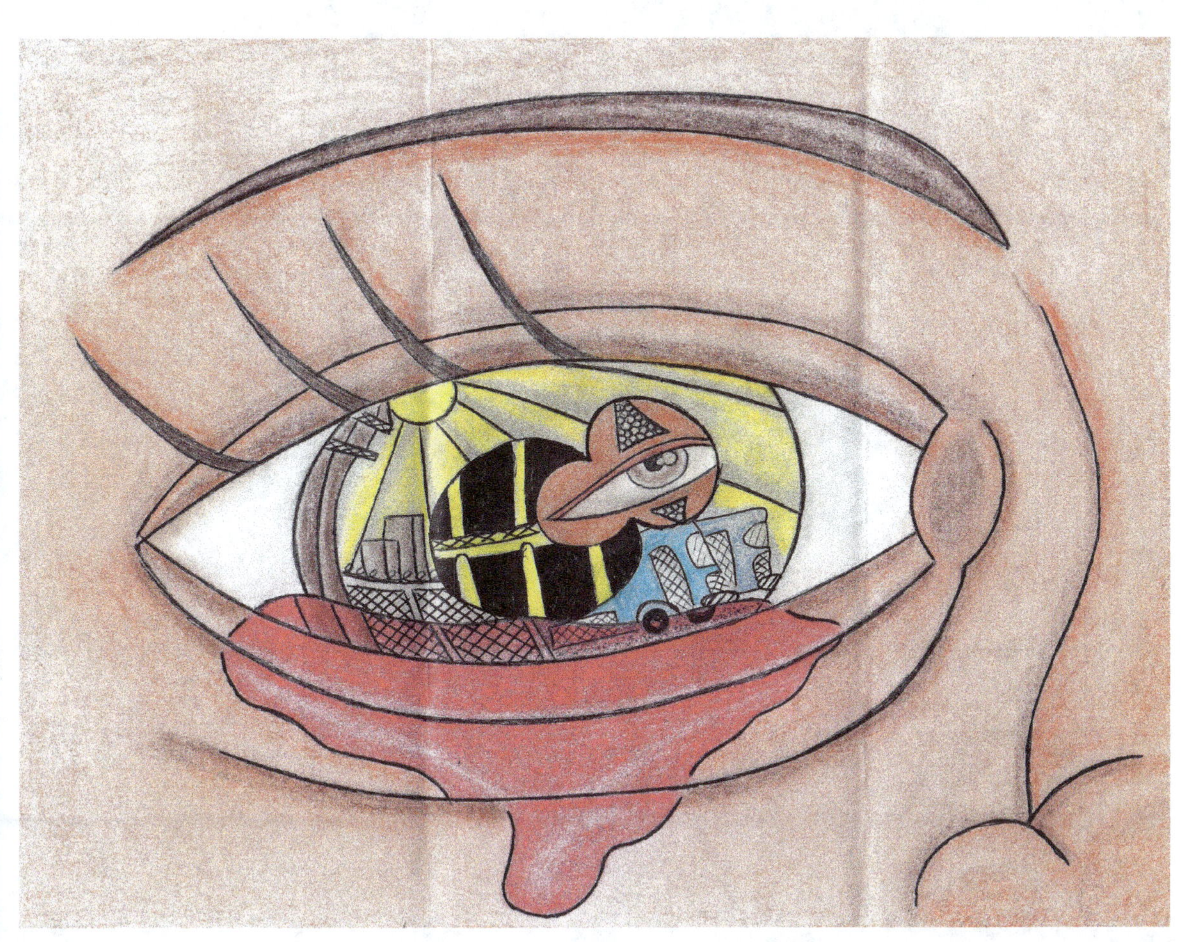

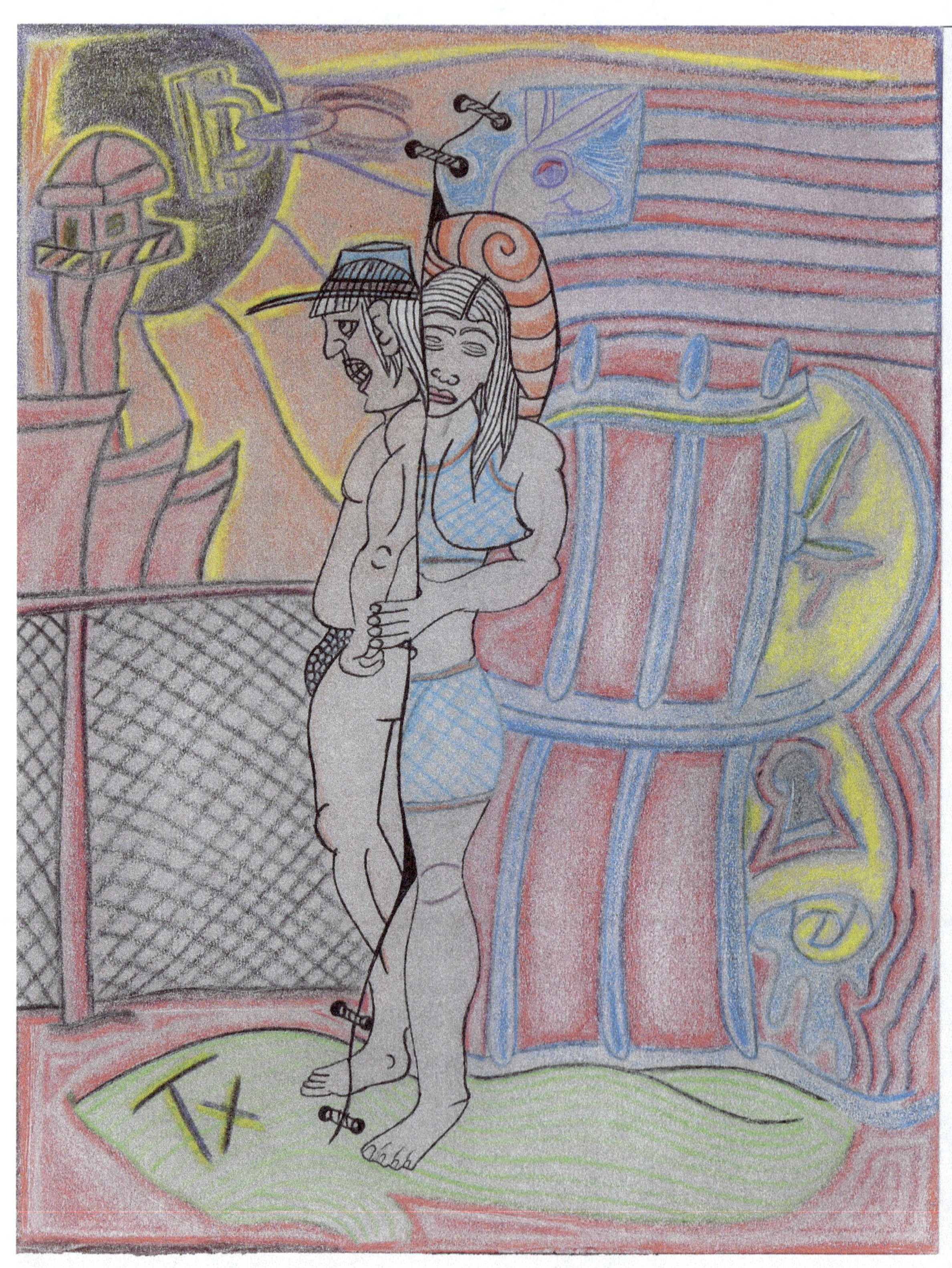

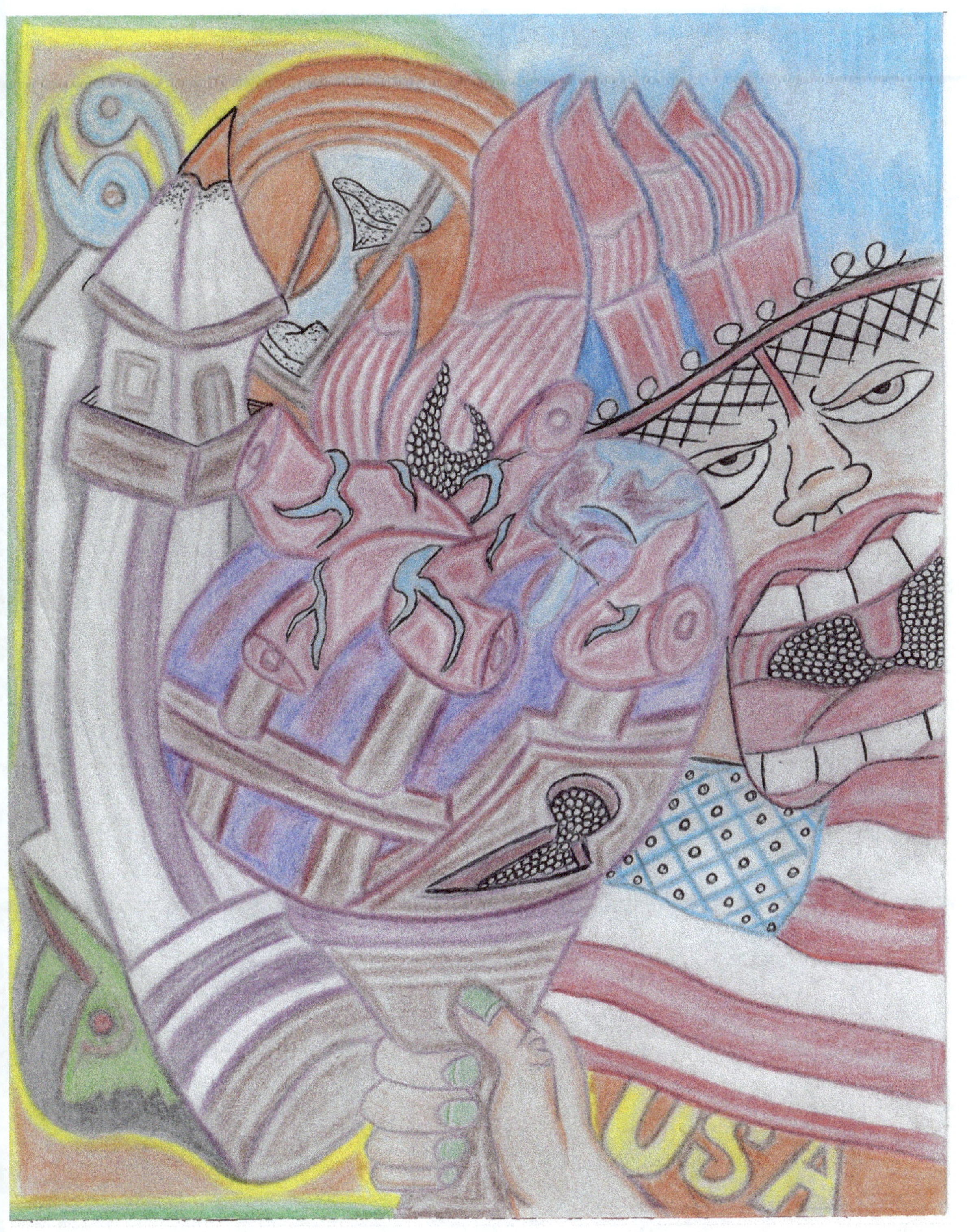
USA

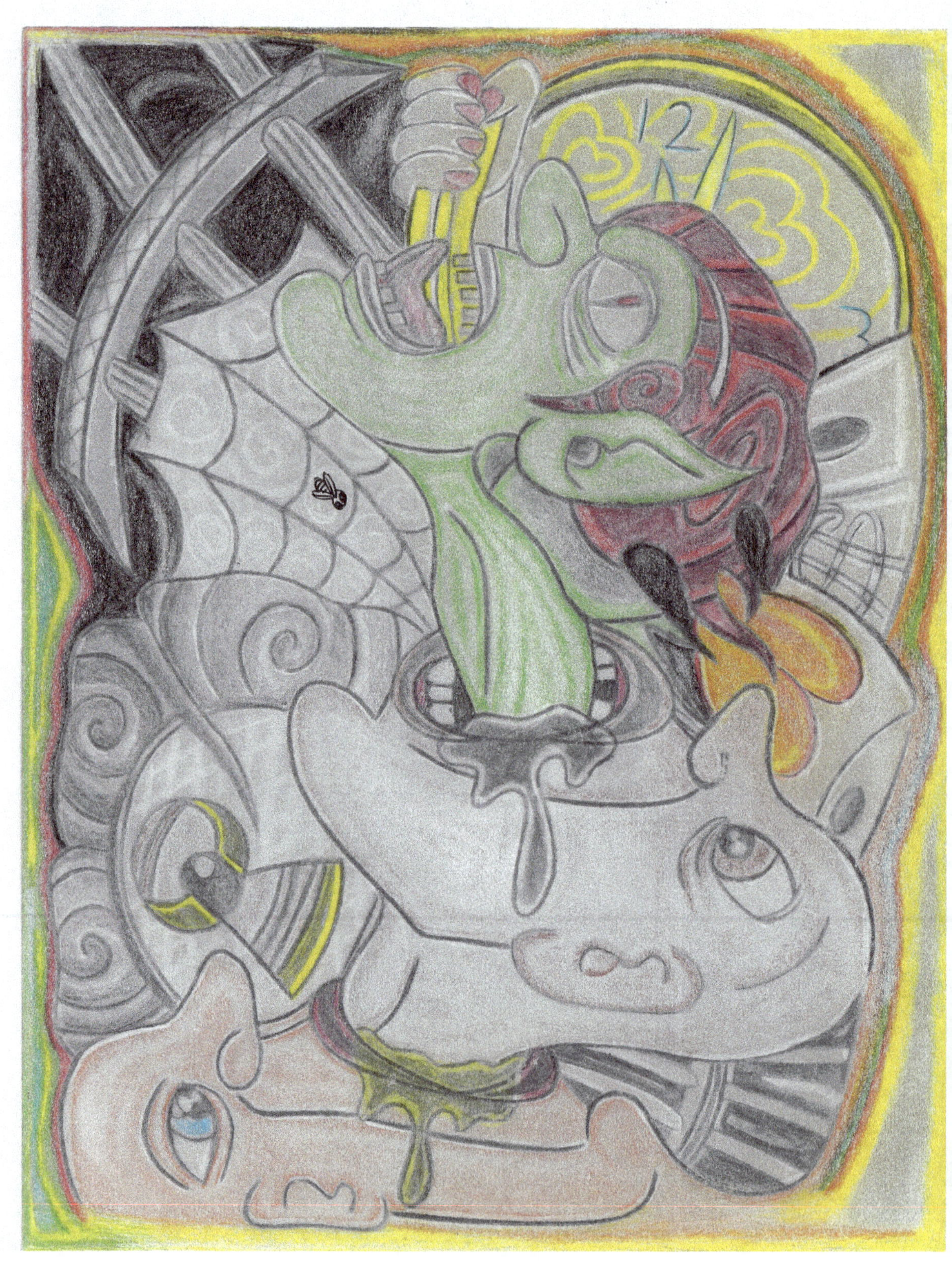

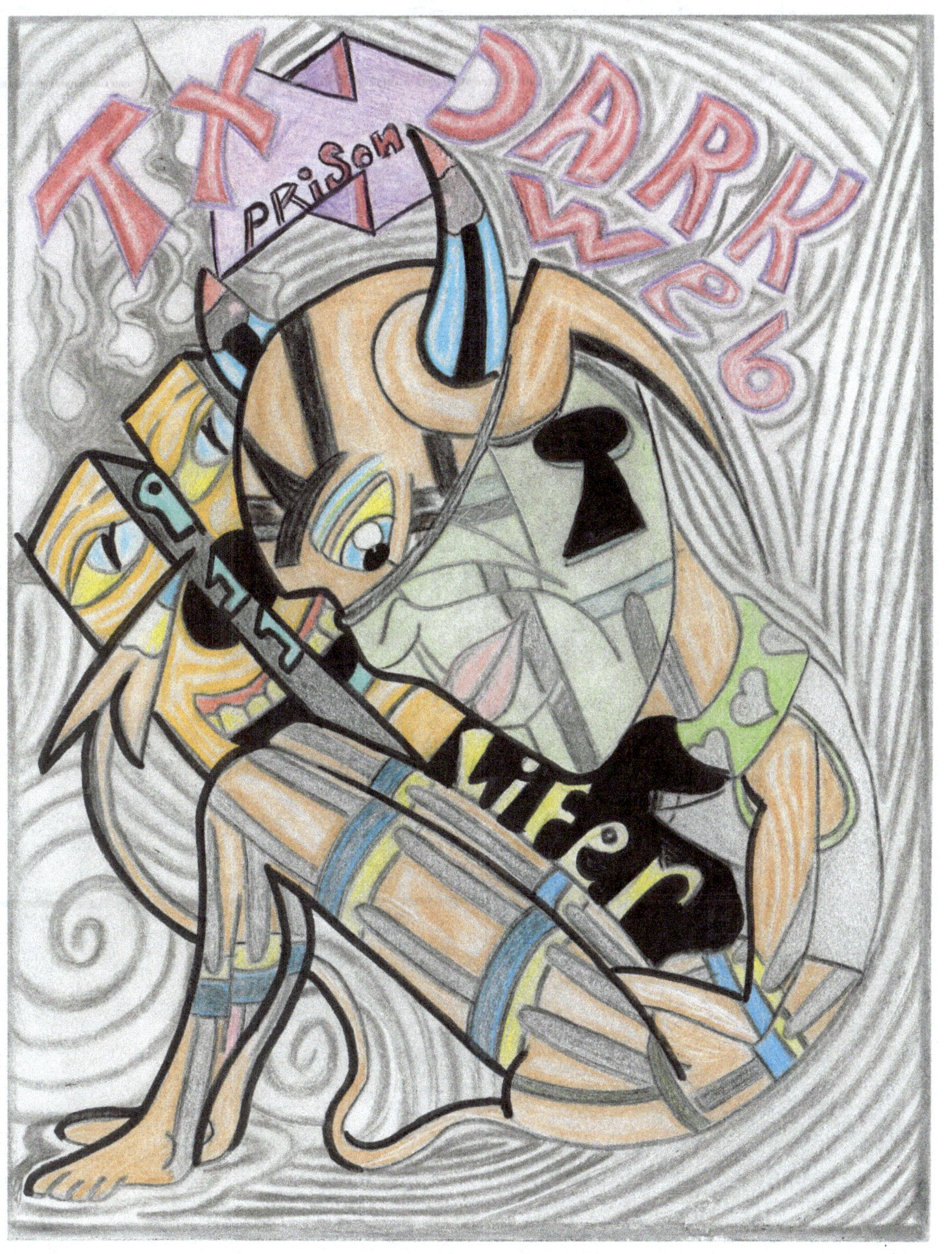

TX
DARK
PRiSon
web
LifeR

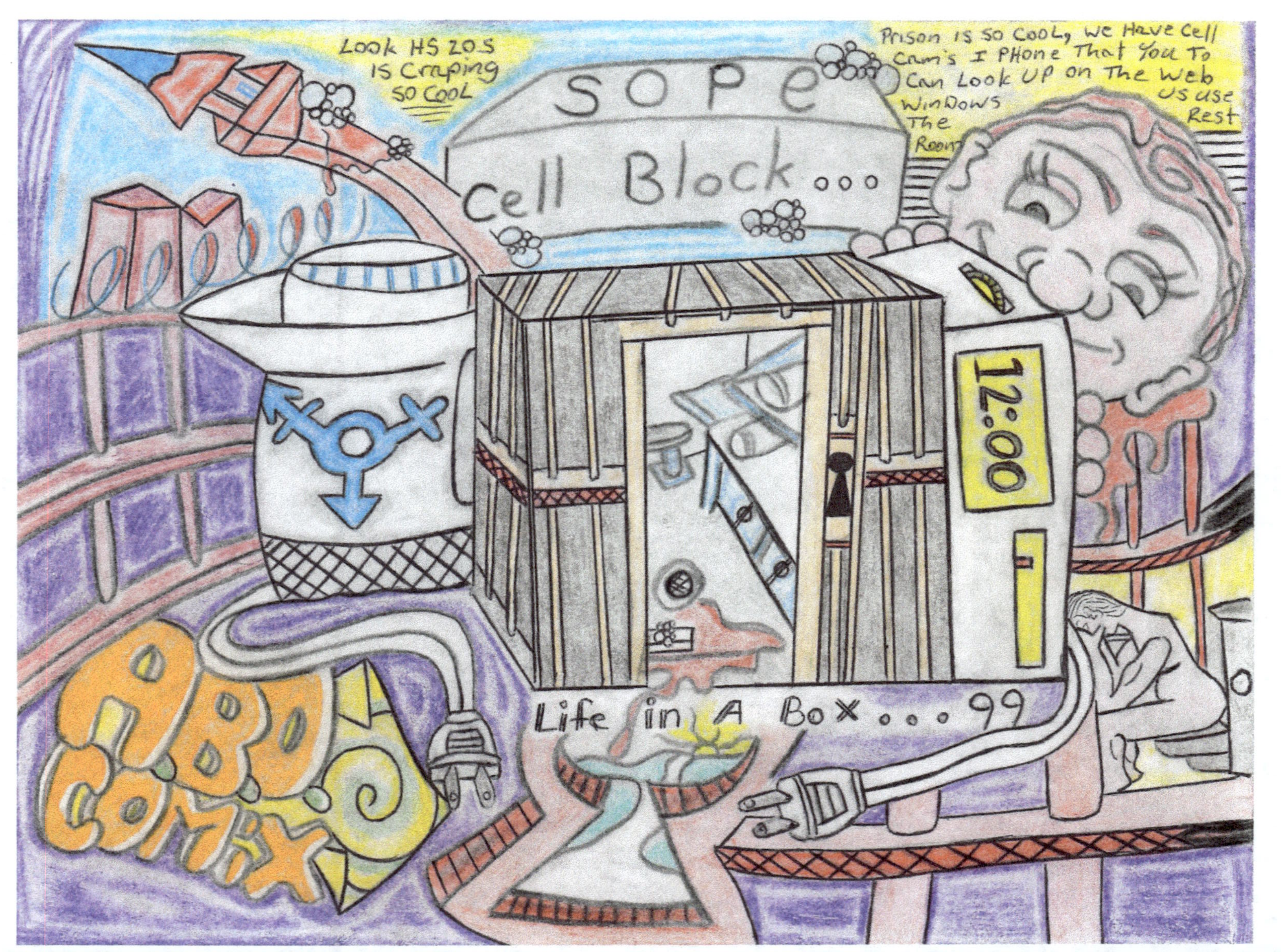
Look HS 205 is creeping so cool
SOPe
Cell Block ...
Prison is so cool, we have cell cam's i phone that you to can look up on the web windows the room us use rest
12:00
Life in a Box ... 99
ABO COMIX

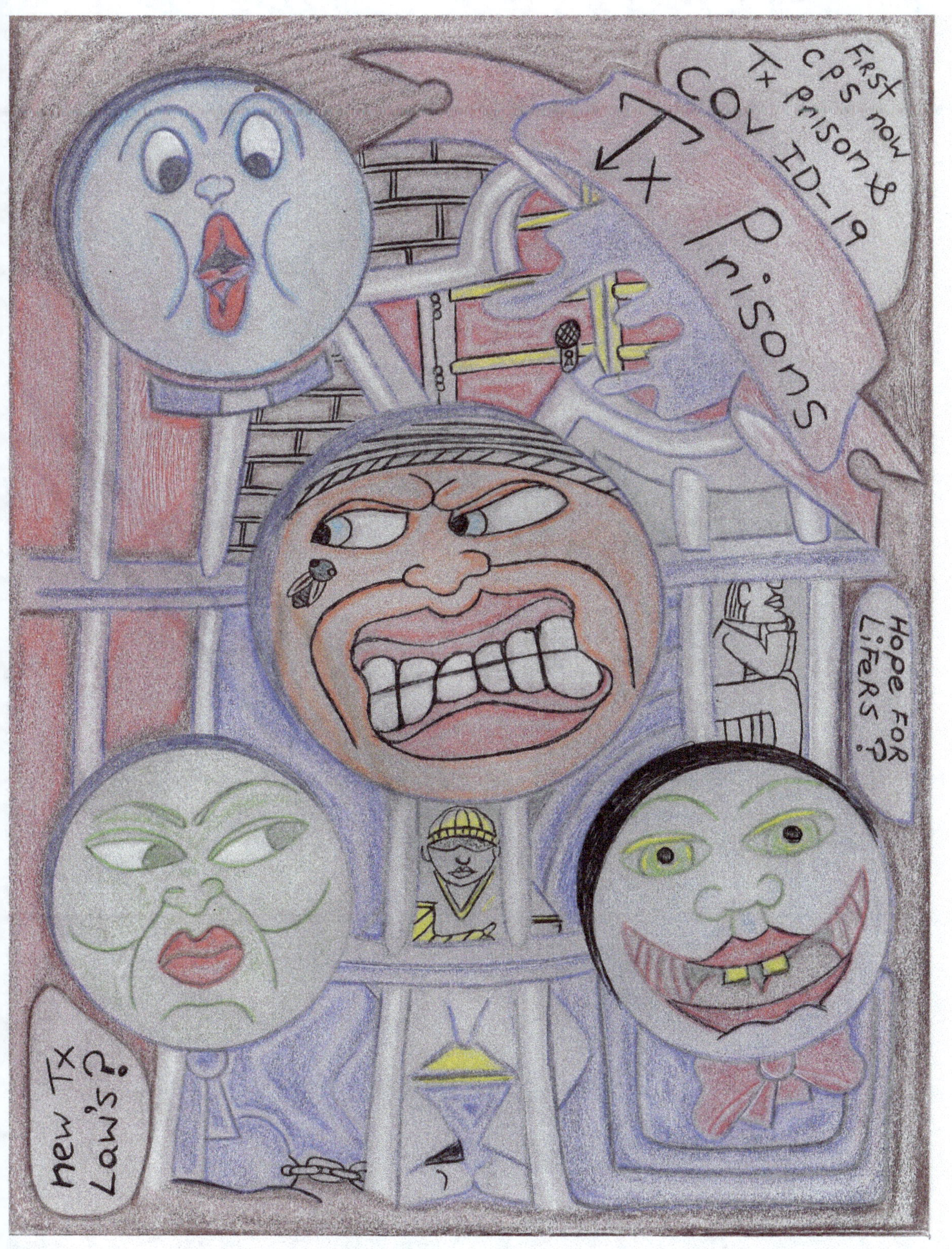
Tx Prisons
First now CPS Prison & Tx Prison & COVID-19
Hope for Lifers?
new Tx Law's?

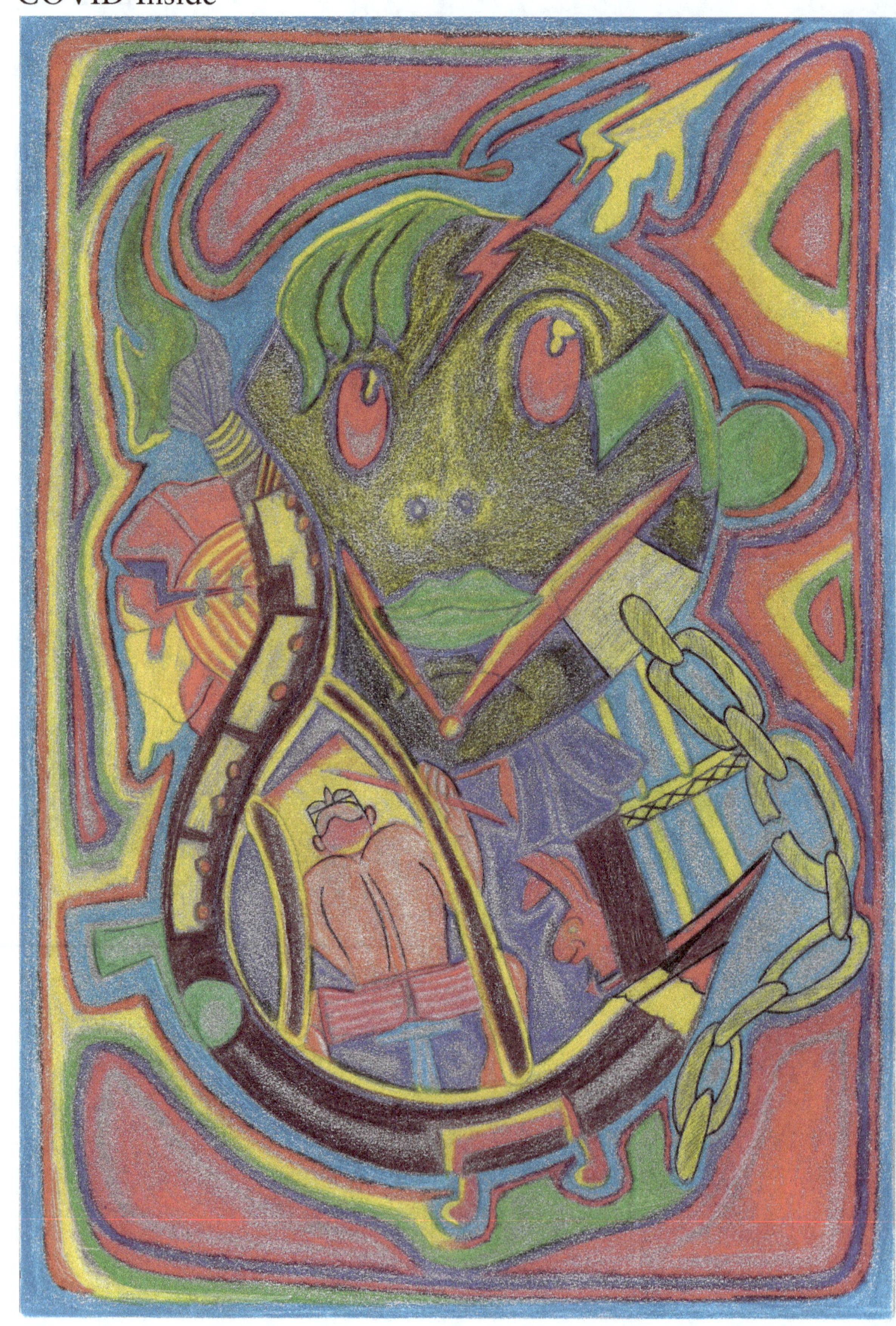

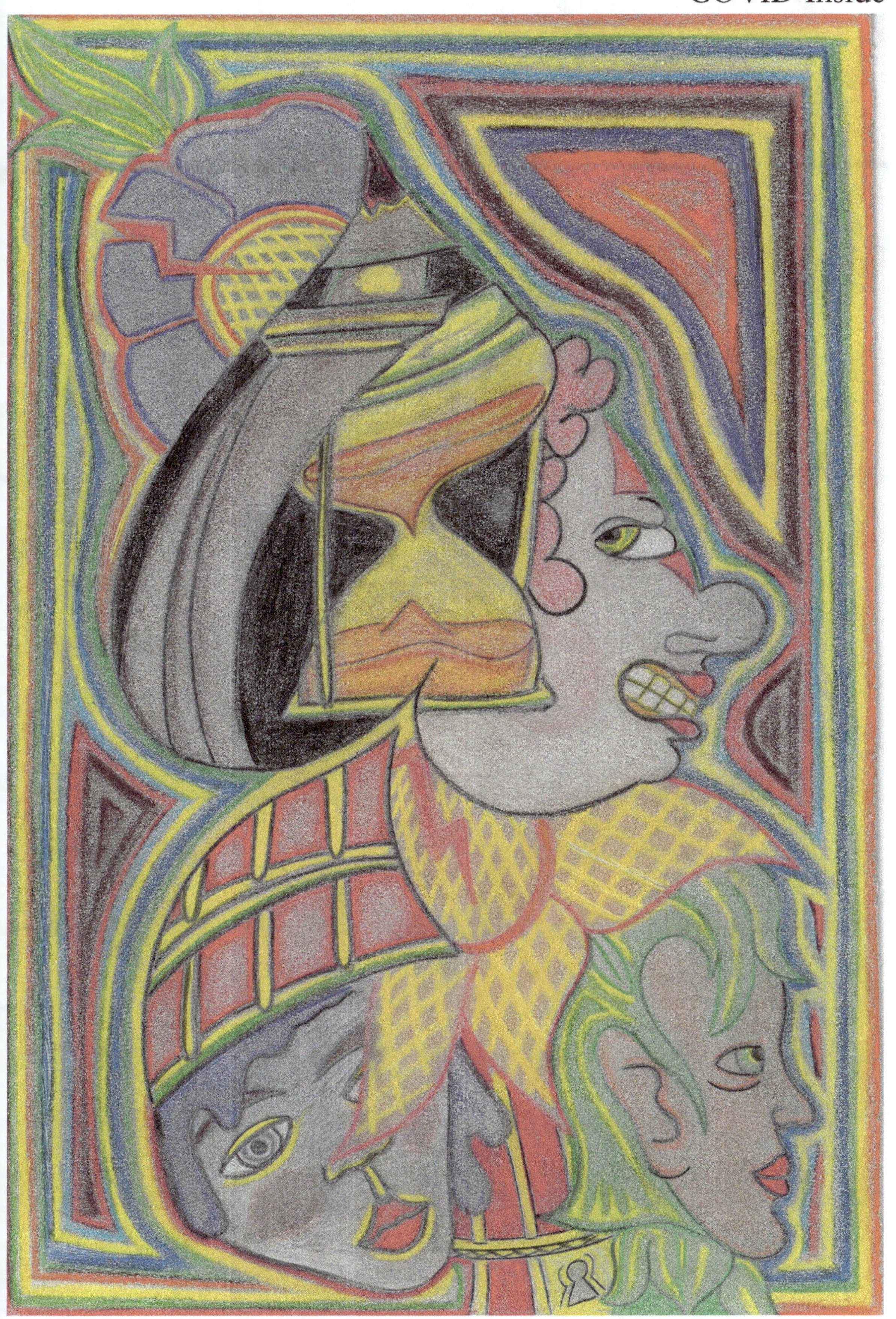

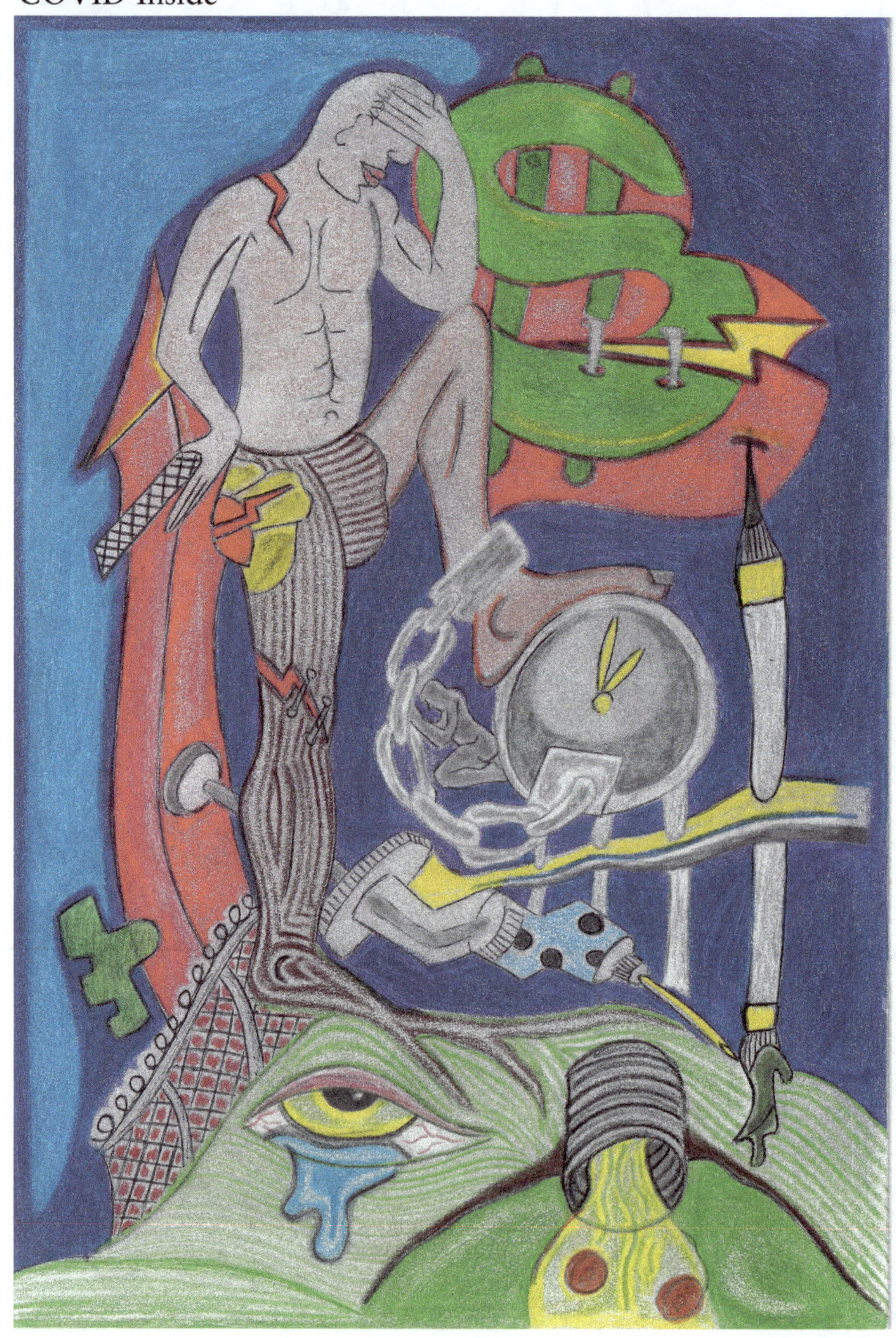

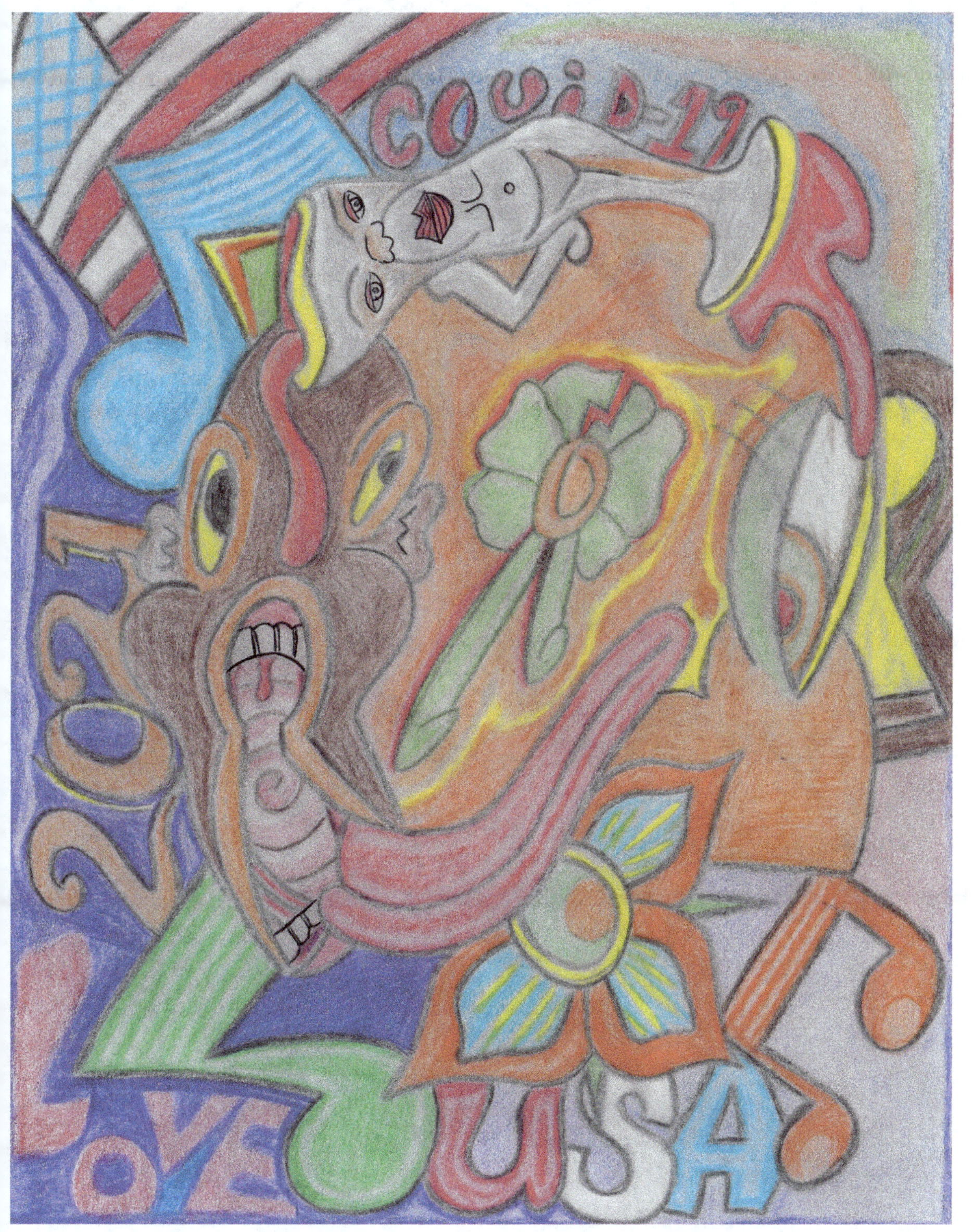

COVID-19
2021
LOVE
USA

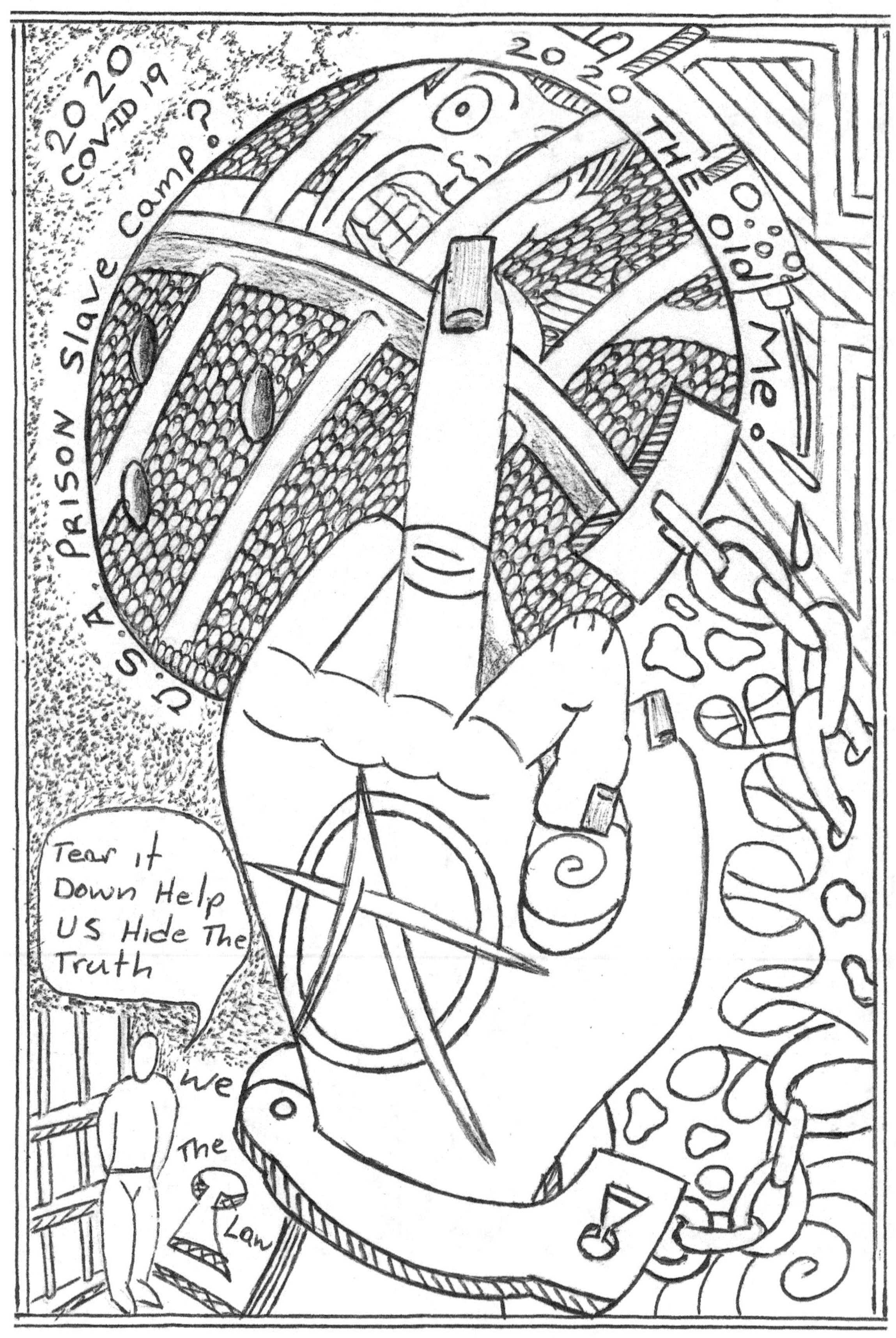

2020
COVID 19 ?
U.S.A. Prison Slave Camp ?
2020
THE Old Me!
Tear it Down Help US Hide The Truth
We The Law

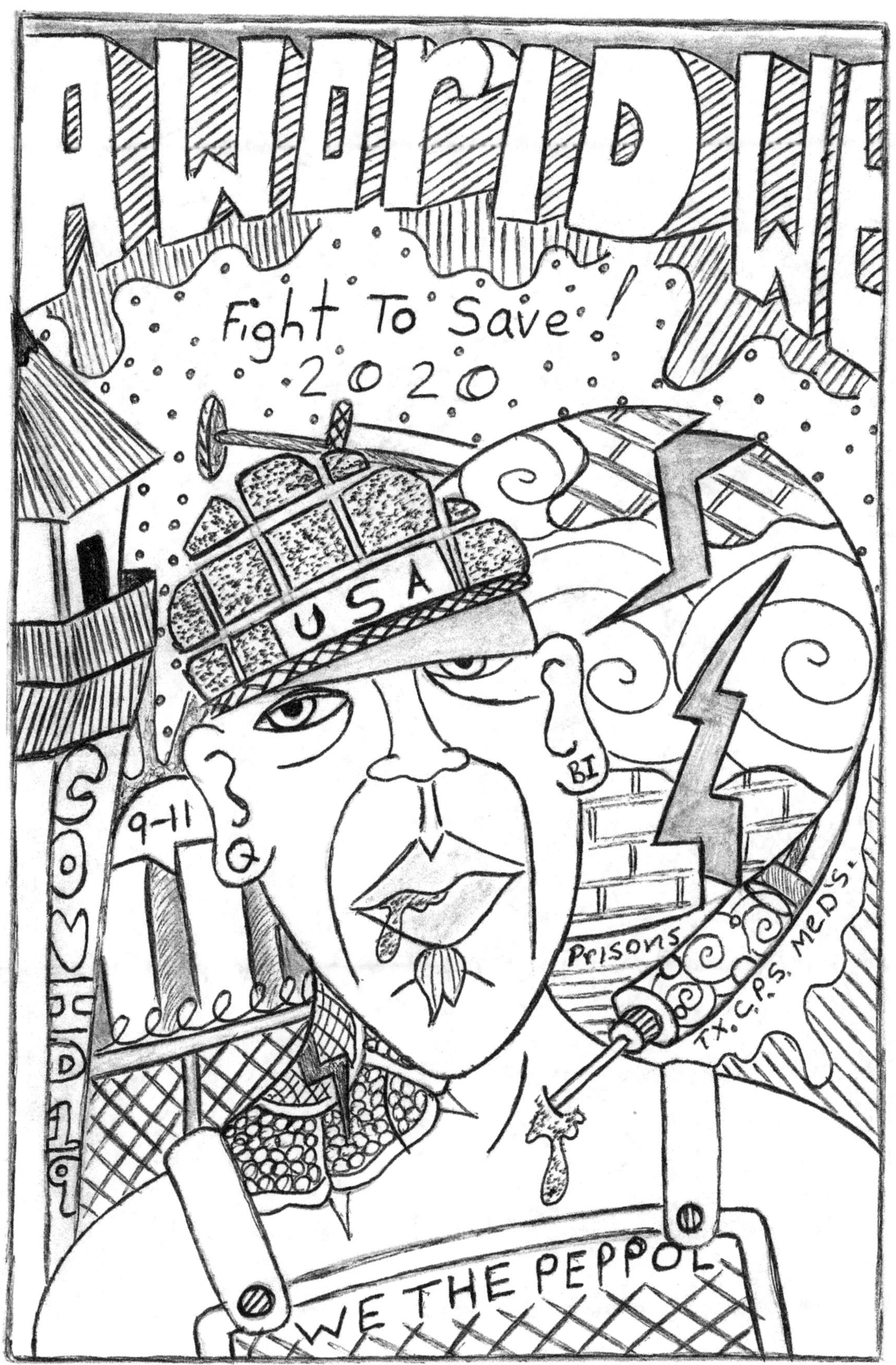
A WORLD WE
Fight To Save!
2020
USA
9-11
BI
COVID 19
Prisons
TX. C.P.S. MEDS.
WE THE PEPPOL

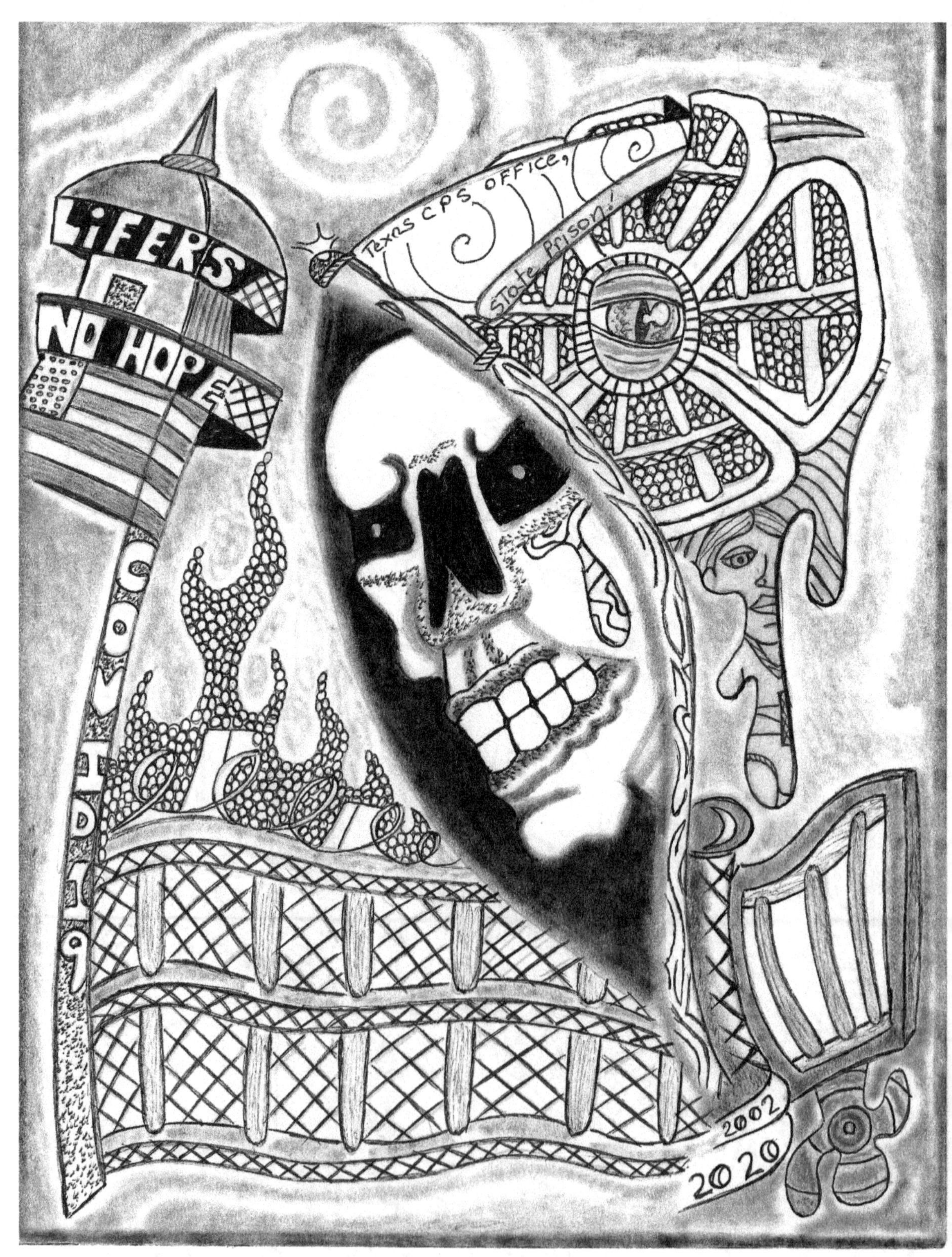
LiFERS
NO HOPE
COVID HOUSING
Texas CPS OFFICE,
STate Prison!
2002
2020

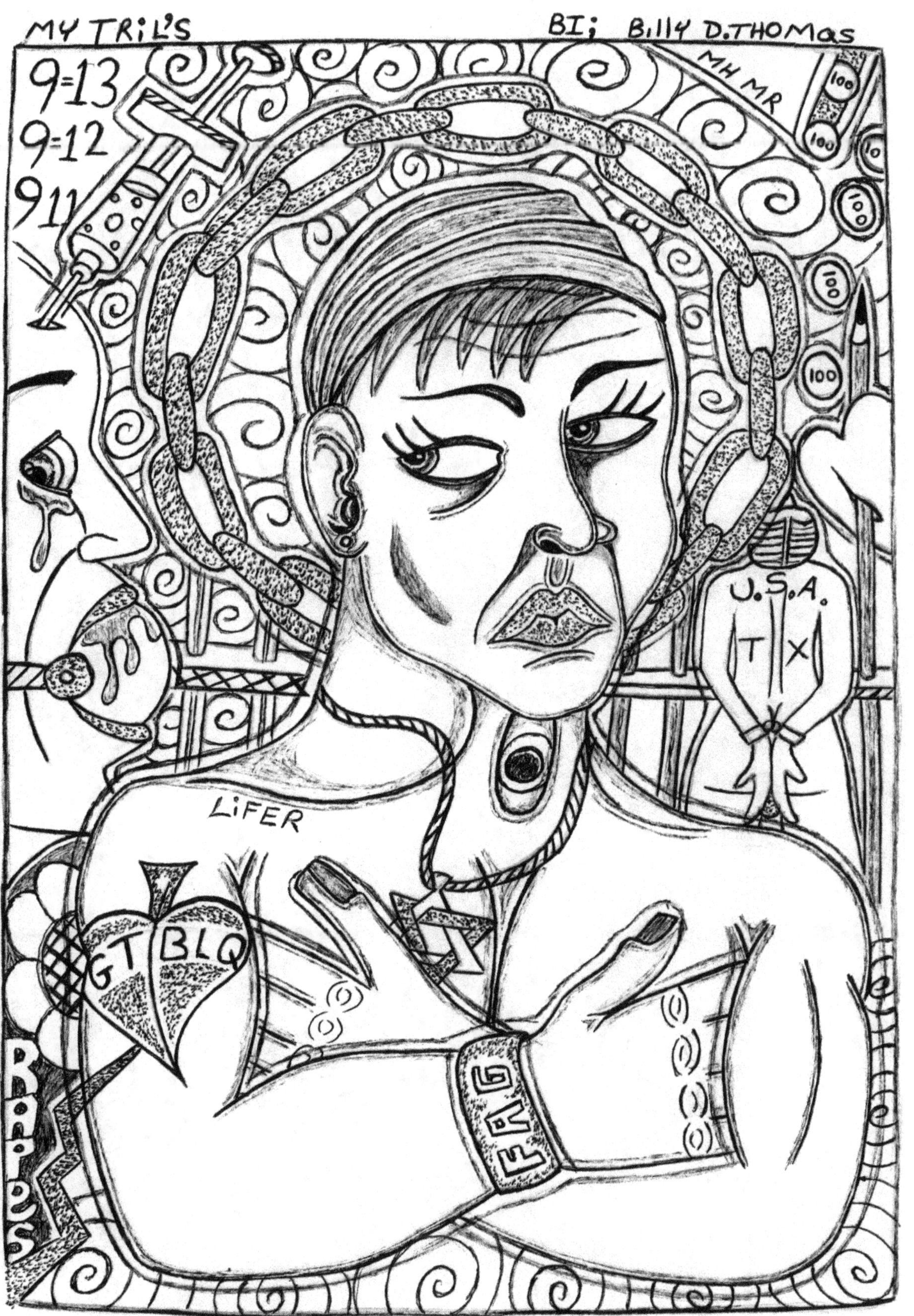
MY TRIL'S
9=13
9=12
911
BI; BILLY D.THOMAS
MH MR
100
100
10
100
100
100
LIFER
GT BLQ
U.S.A.
TX
FAG
RAPES

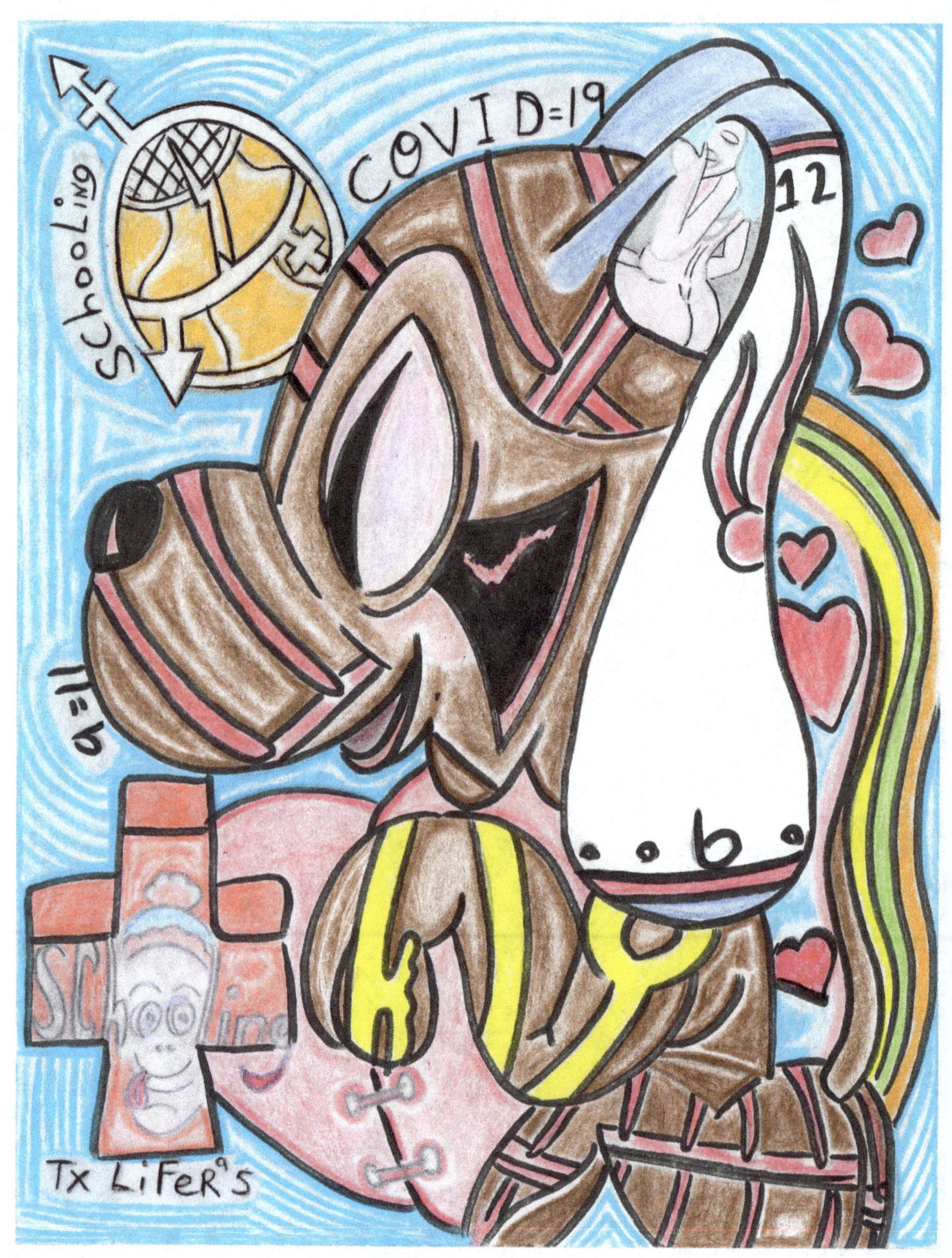

Schooling
COVID=19
12
9=11
Schooling
Tx LiFeR's

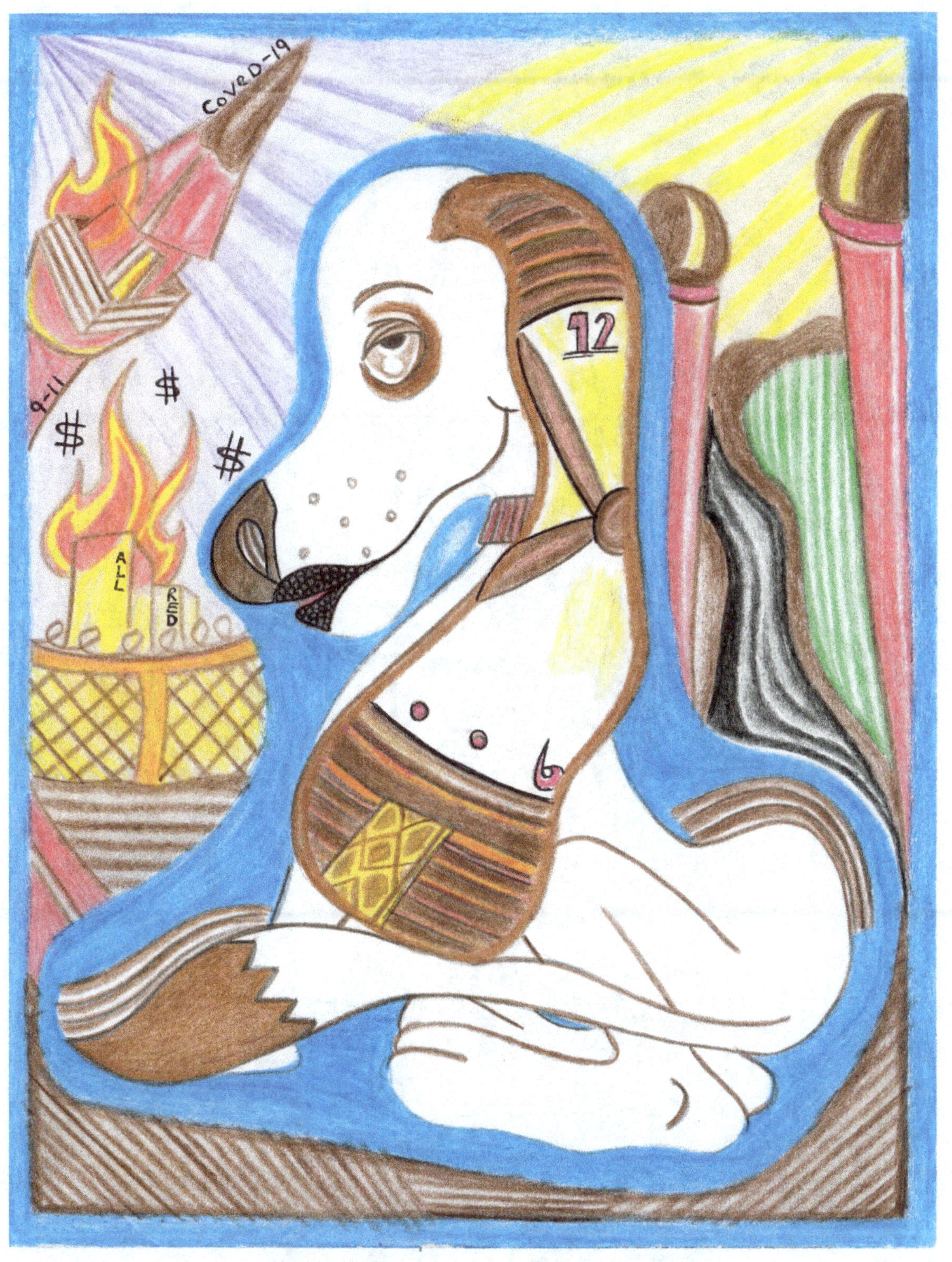
CoVeD-19
9-11
$ $ $
$
12
ALL
RED

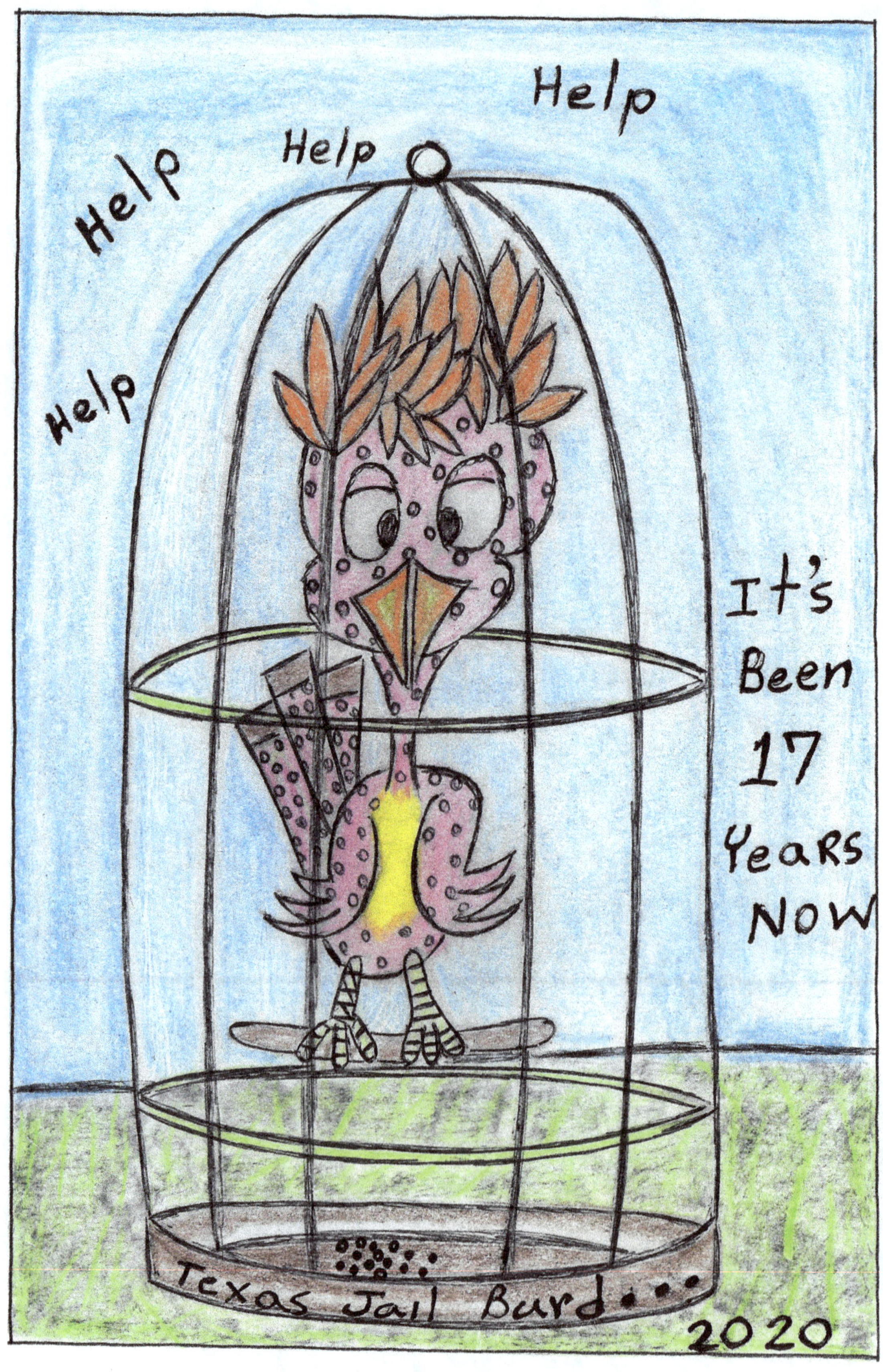
Help
Help
Help
Help
It's
Been
17
Years
Now
Texas Jail Burd...
2020

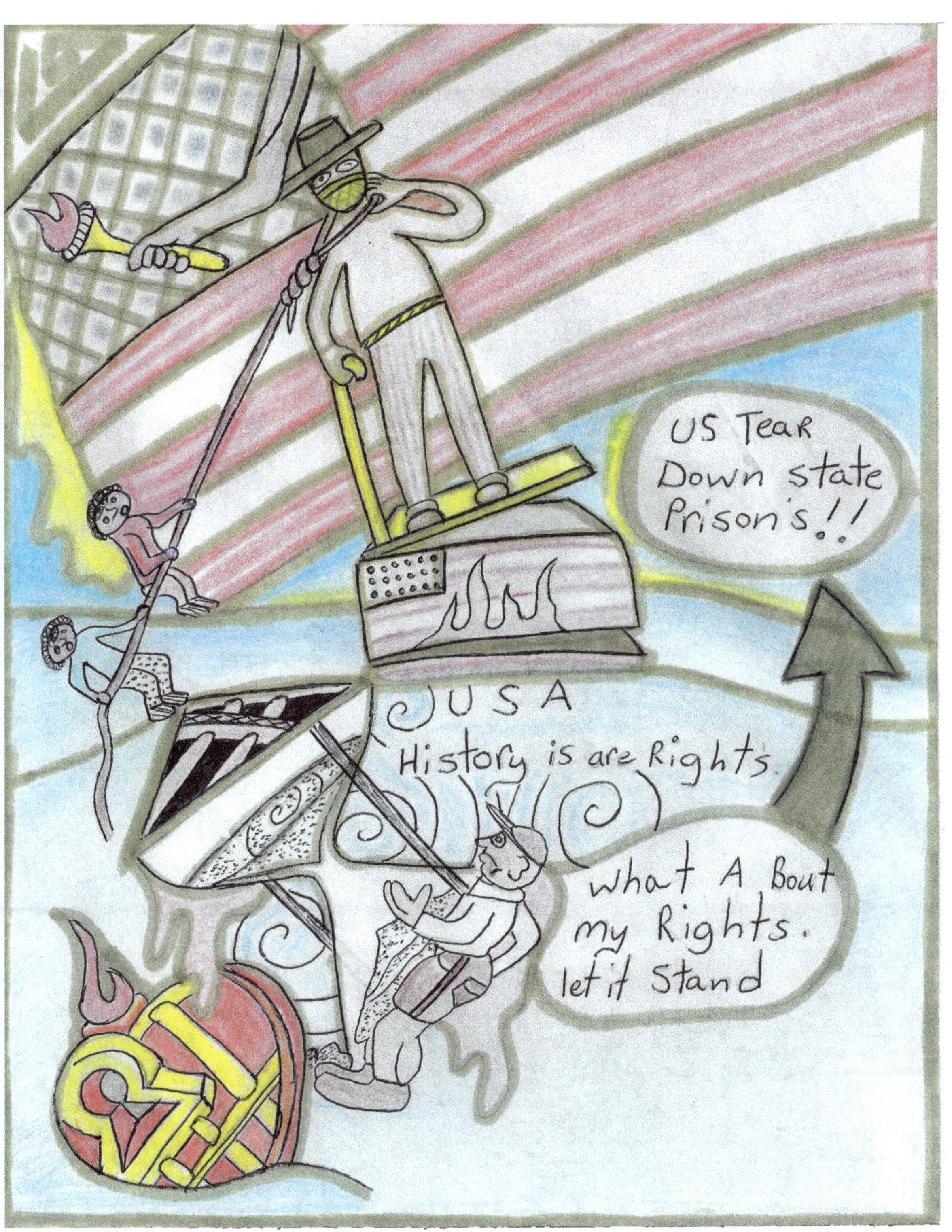
US Tear Down state Prison's!!
USA History is are Rights.
what A Bout my Rights. let it Stand

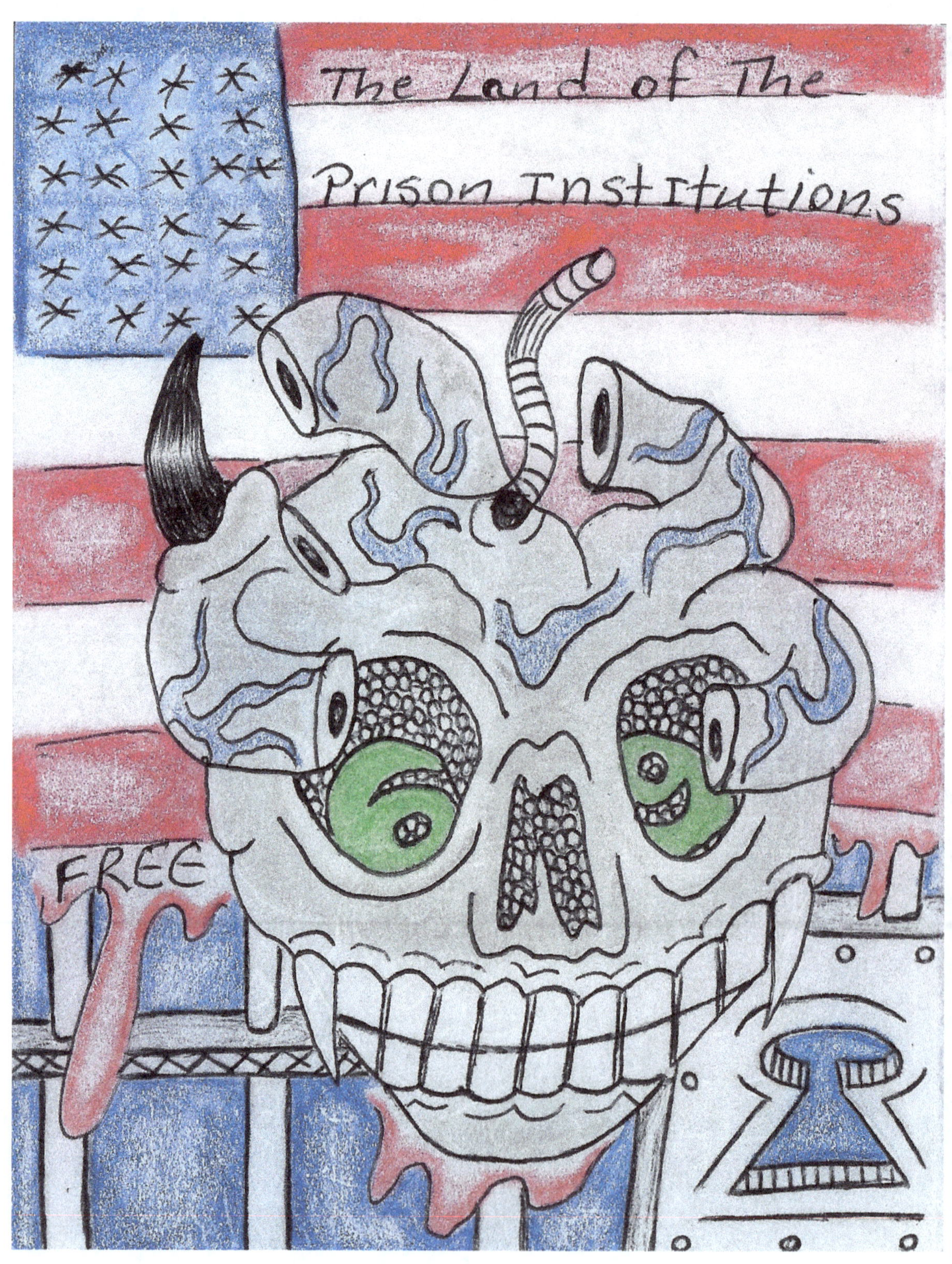
The Land of The
Prison Institutions
FREE

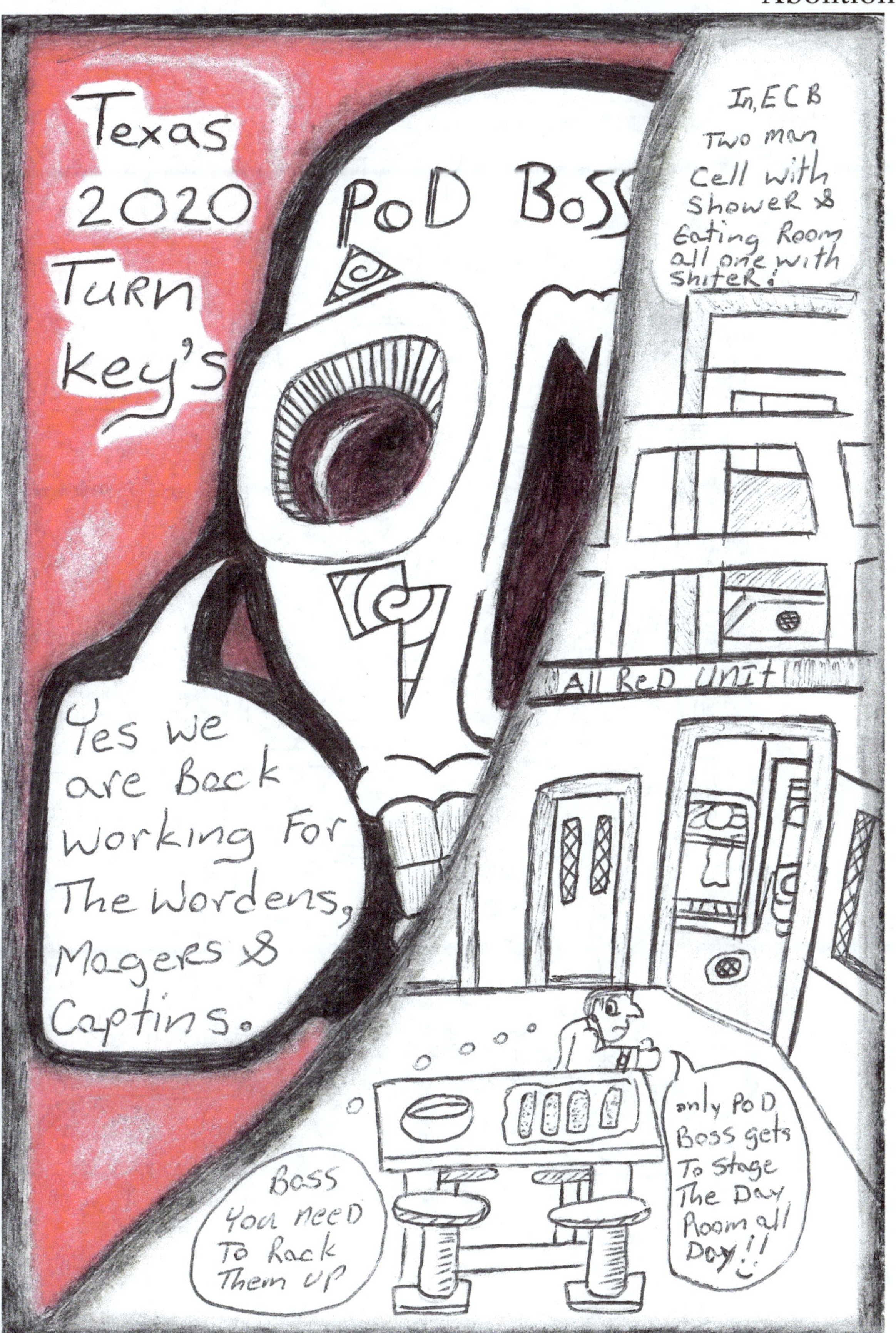
Texas 2020 Turn key's
PoD Boss
In, E C B two man Cell with shower & Eating Room all one with shiter!
Yes we are Back Working For The Wordens, Magers & Captins.
ALL RED UNIT
only PoD Boss gets To Stage The Day Room all Day!!
Boss You neeD To Rack Them up

Abolition

Texas Prison
Bands Inmats
From, in Prison
Art.!

and stops in
Prison # # #
Macking ??

The NO HoPe FoR ?

LiFERS

TRAINS

Texas keeping US Down!
When Will You Take A STand?
The Rights of mentalill!

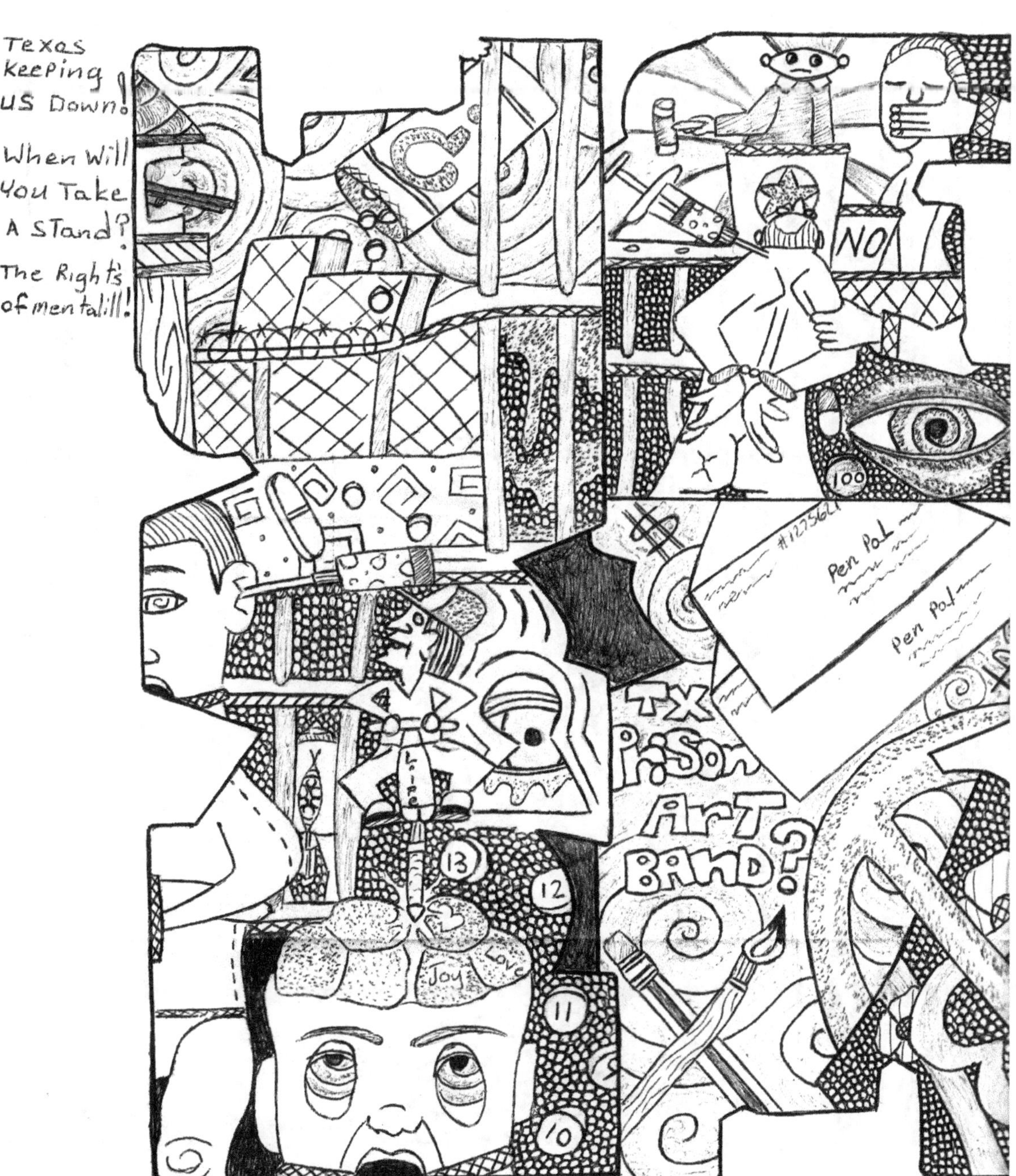

NO
Pen Pal
Pen Pal
TX Prison Art Band?

Abolition

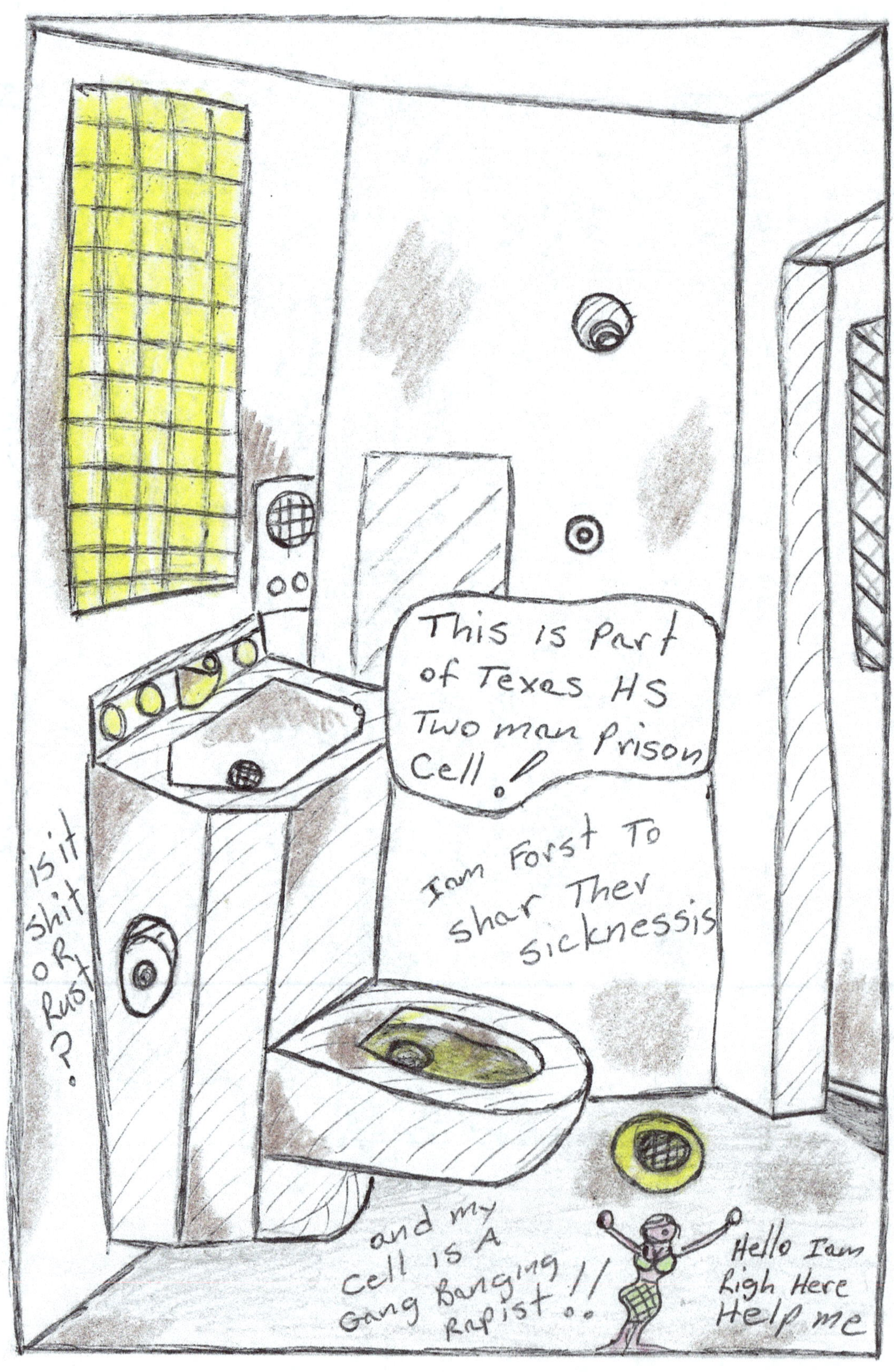

This is Part of Texas HS Two man Prison Cell!
Iam Forst To shar Ther Sicknessis
is it shit oR Rust ?
and my cell is A Gang Banging Rapist !!
Hello Iam Righ Here Help me

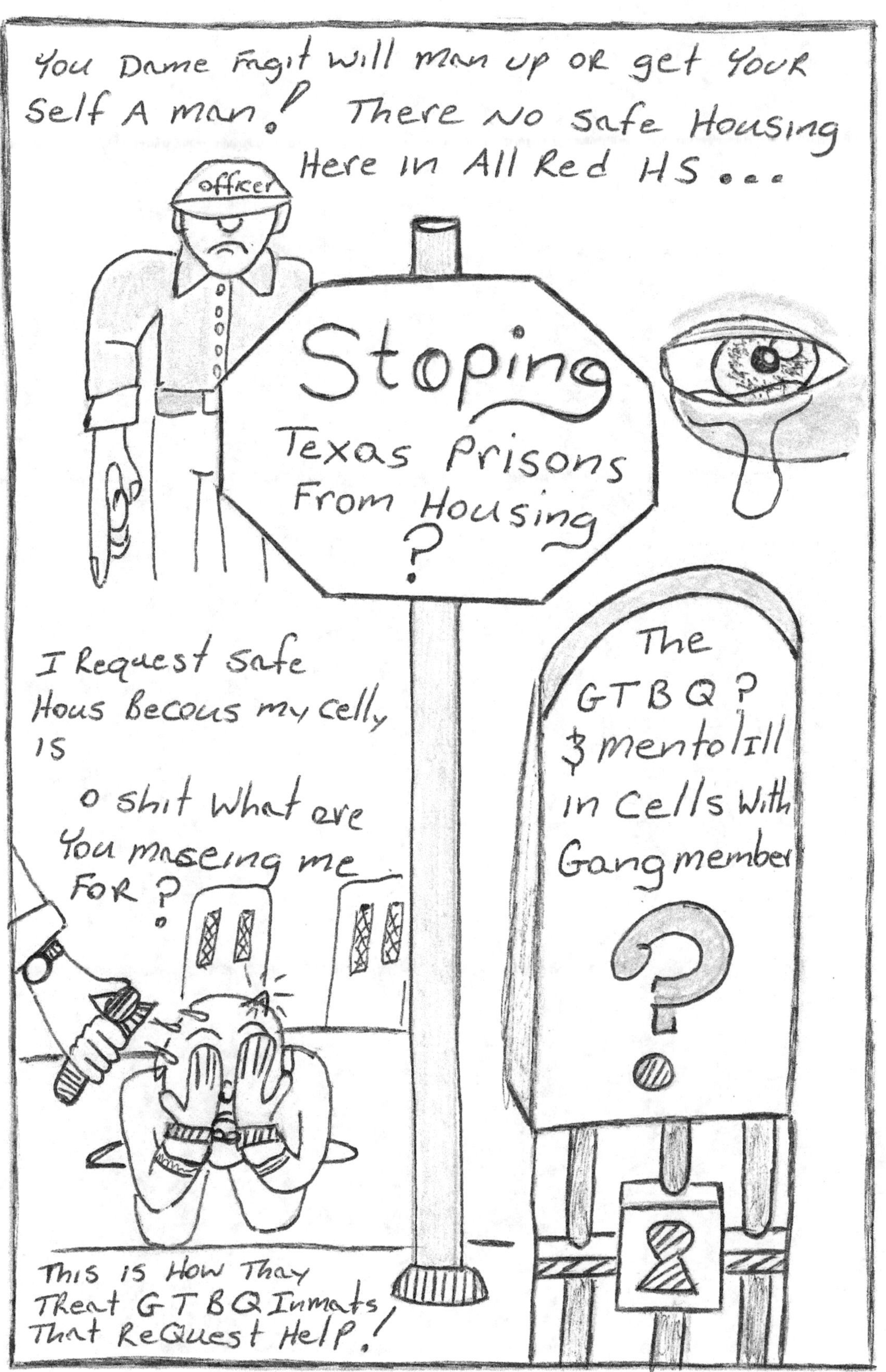
You Dame Fagit will man up or get Your Self A man! There No Safe Housing Here in All Red HS...
officer
Stoping Texas Prisons From Housing ?
I Request Safe Hous Becous my celly is
o shit What are You maseing me For ?
The GTBQ ? & mentoIll in Cells With Gang member ?
This is How Thay Treat GTBQ Inmats, That ReQuest HelP !

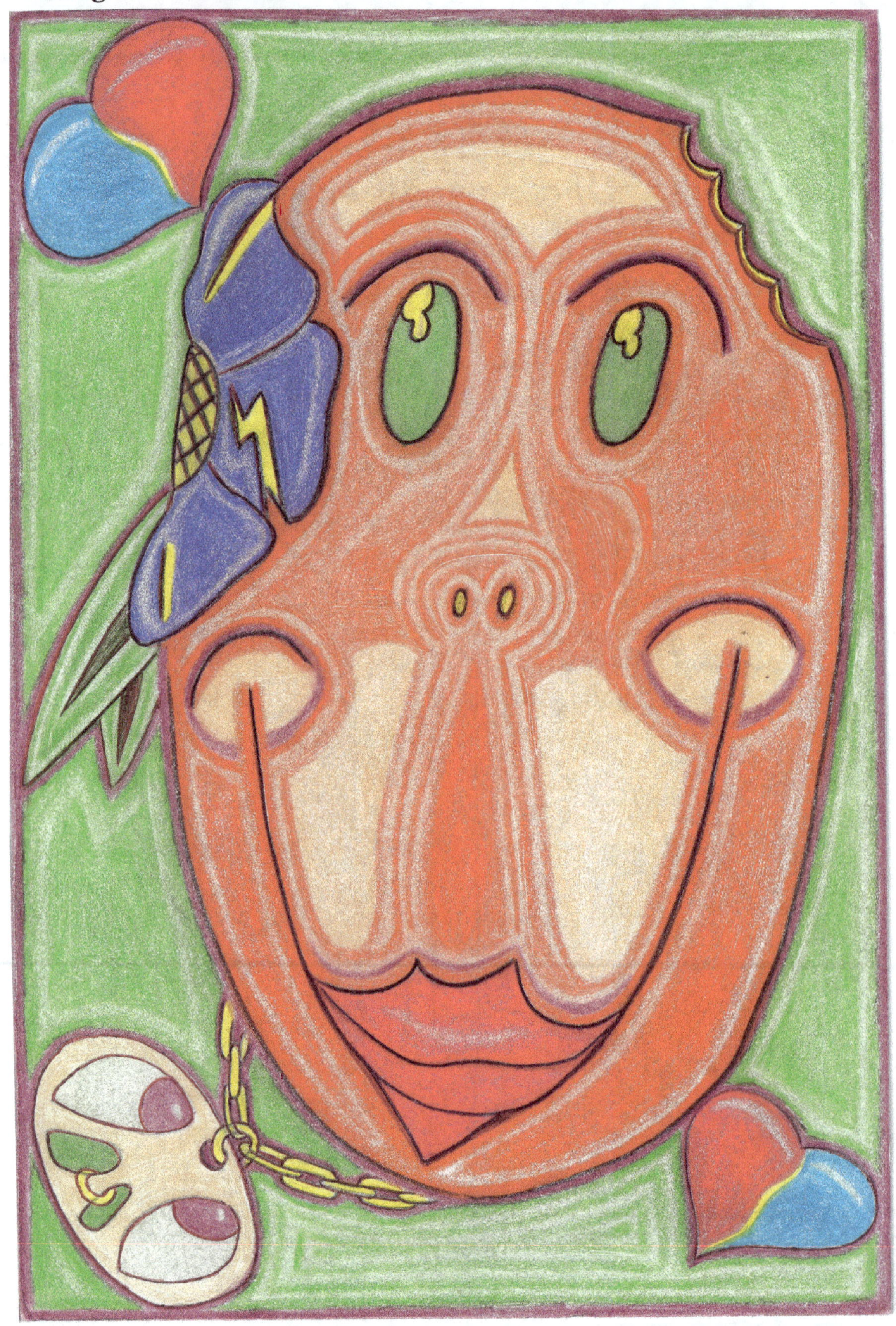

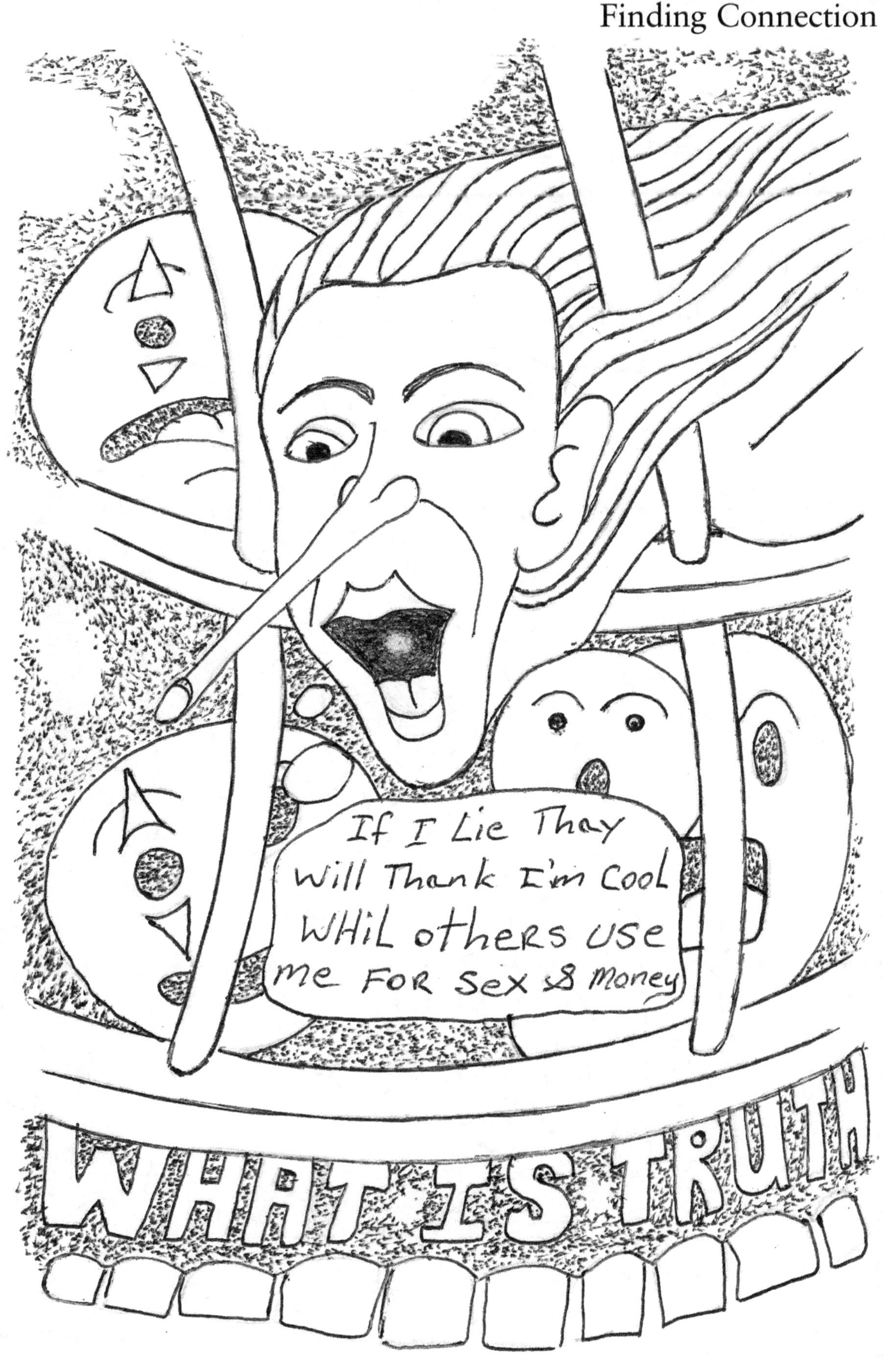

If I Lie Thay will Thank I'm Cool WHiL others use me For Sex & Money
WHAT IS TRUTH

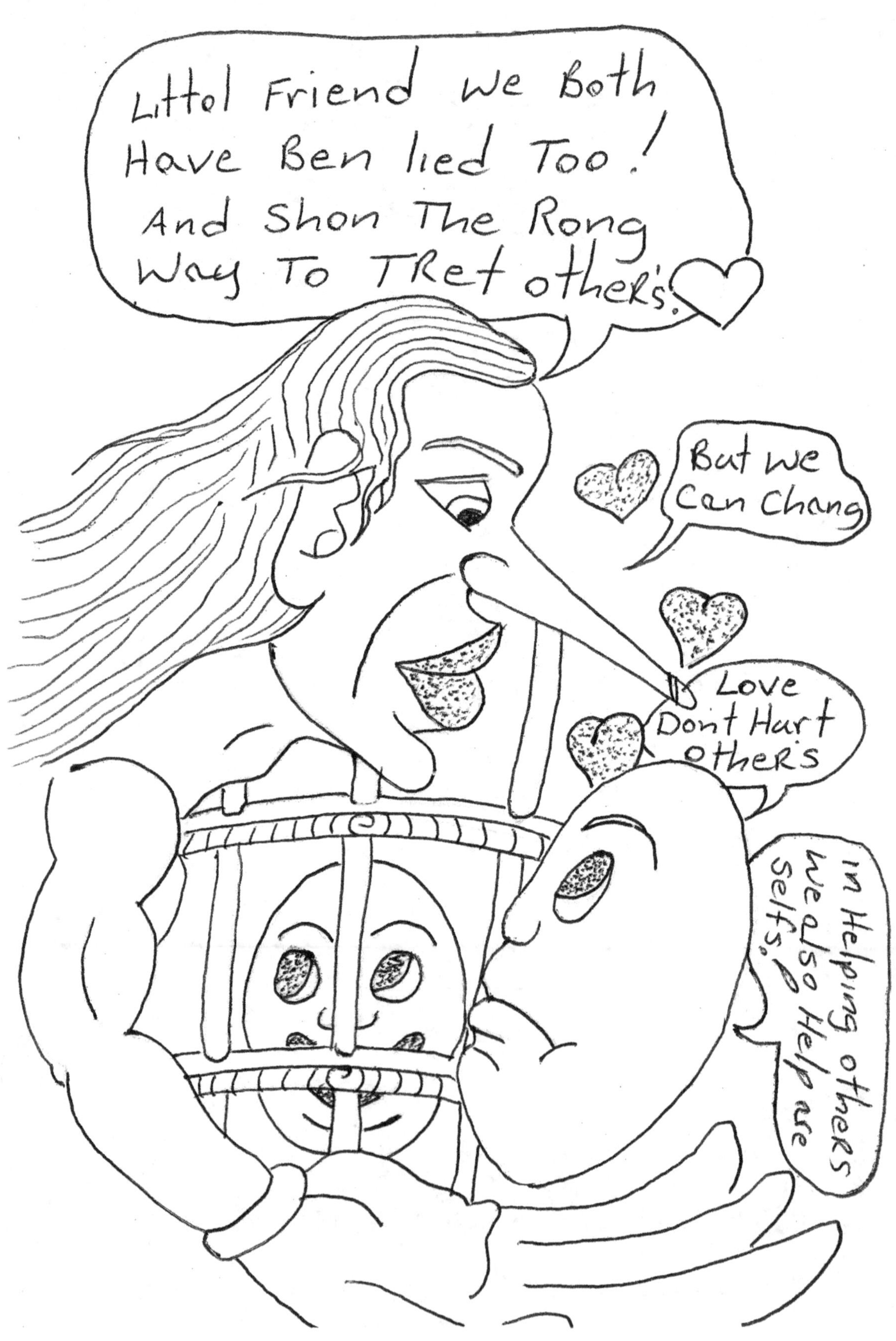
Littol Friend we Both Have Ben lied Too! And Shon The Rong Way To TRet other's.
But we Can Chang
Love Dont Hart other's
in Helping others we also Help our selfs.

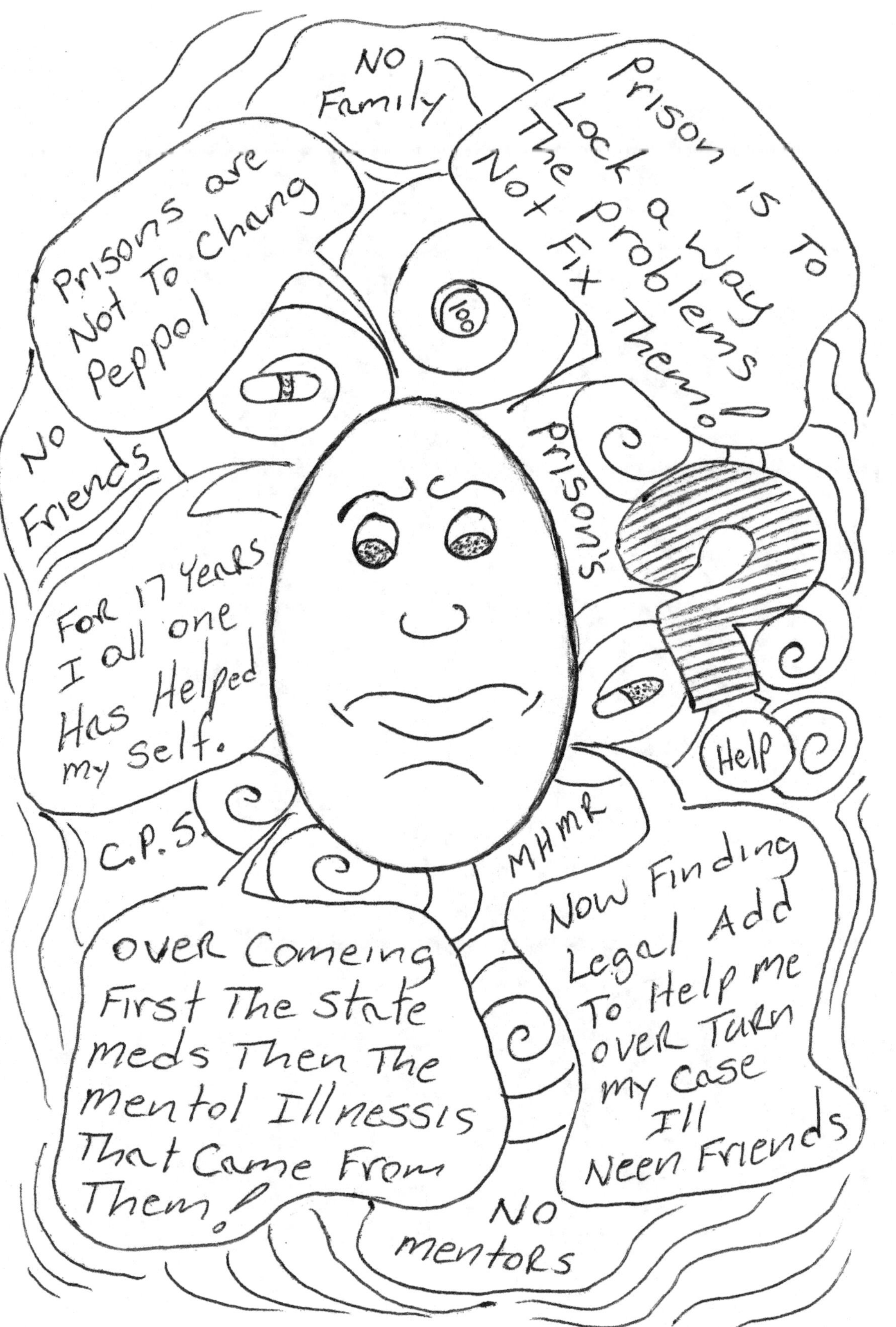

No Family
Prisons are Not To chang Peppol
Prison is To Lock a way The problems! Not Fix Them!
No Friends
For 17 Years I all one Has Helped my Self.
Prison's
Help
C.P.S.
MHMR
over Comeing First The State meds Then The mentol Illnessis That Came From Them!
Now Finding Legal Add To Help me over Turn my Case Ill Neen Friends
No mentors

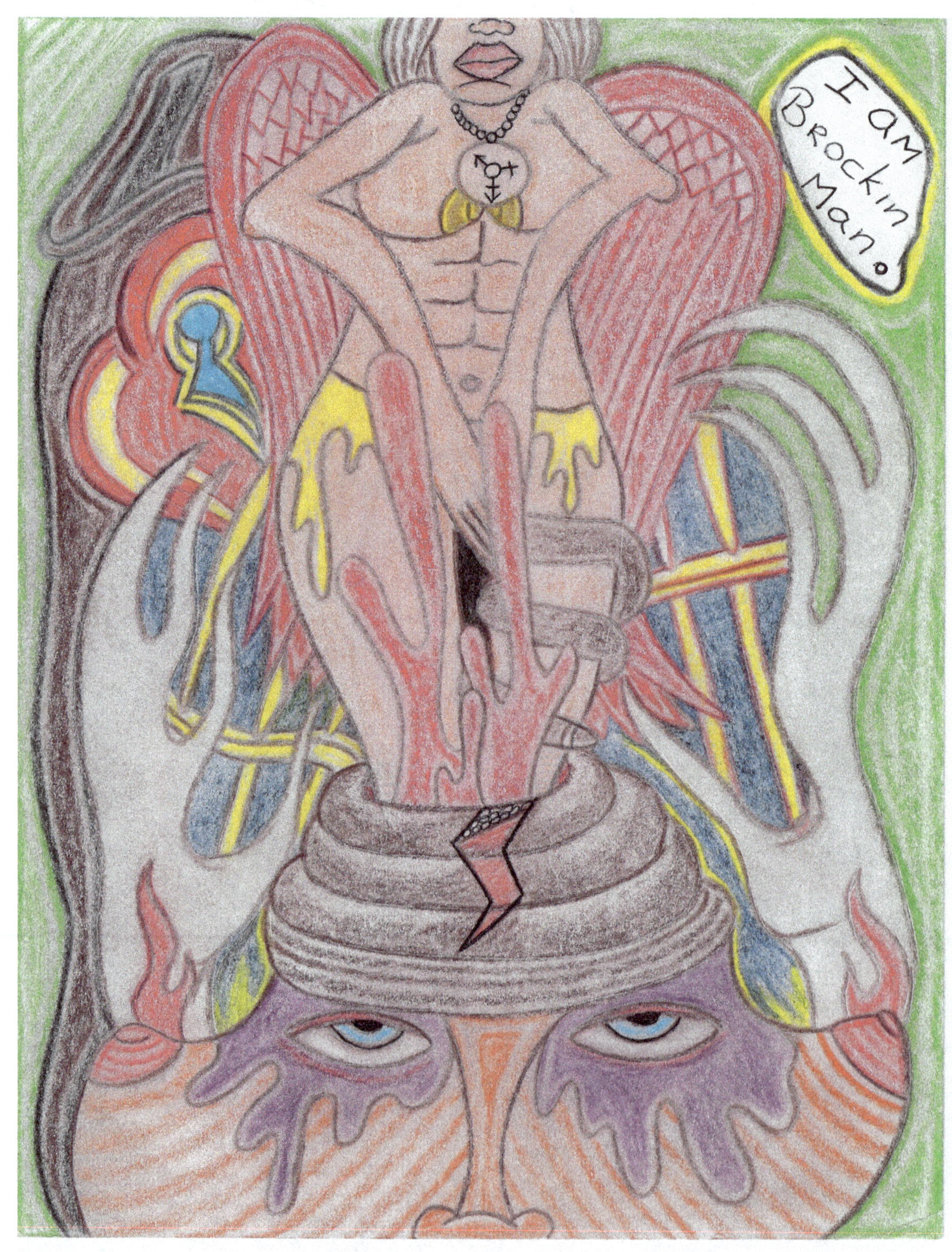
I am
Brockin
Man.

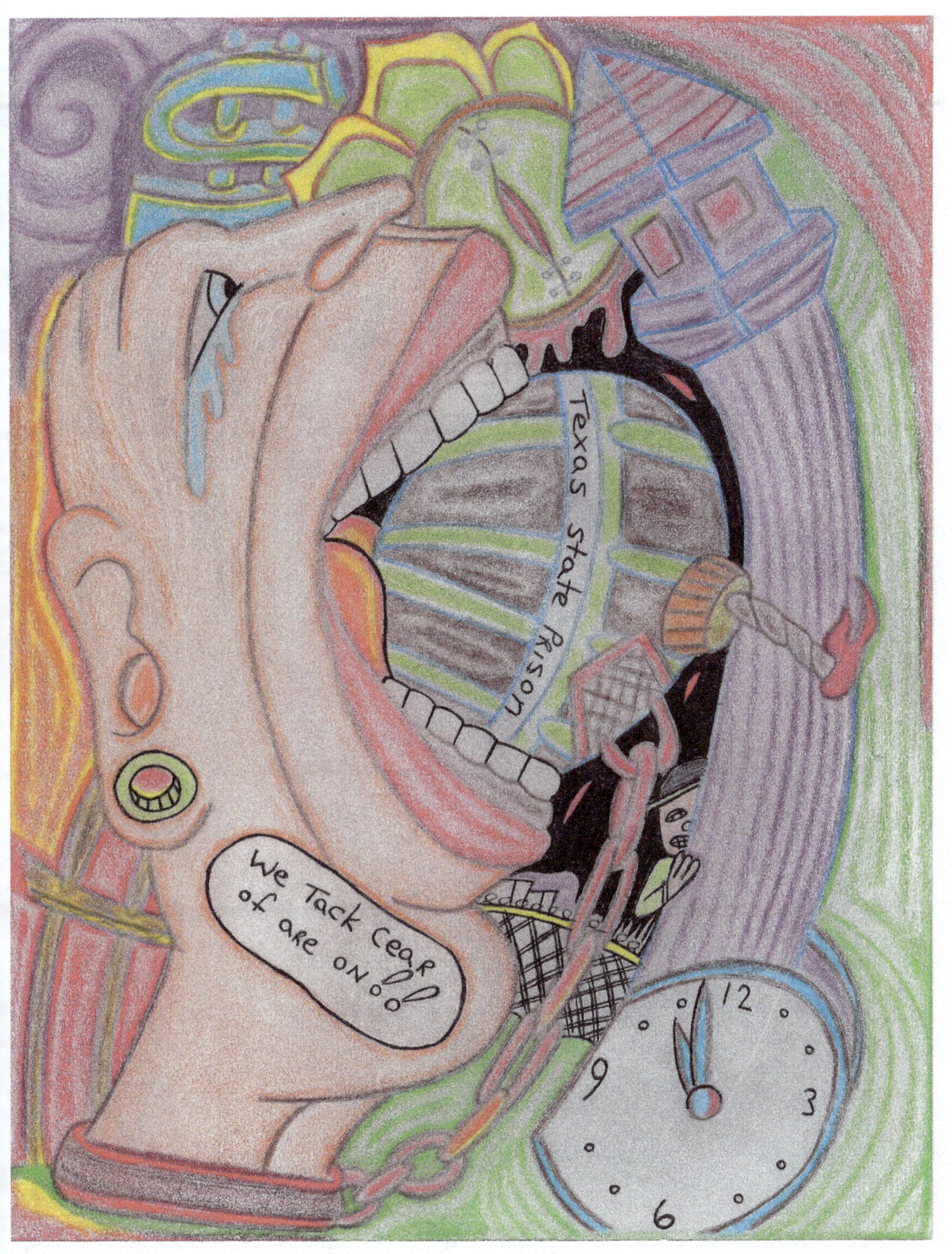
Texas State Prison
We Tack CeaR of are on
12
9
3
6

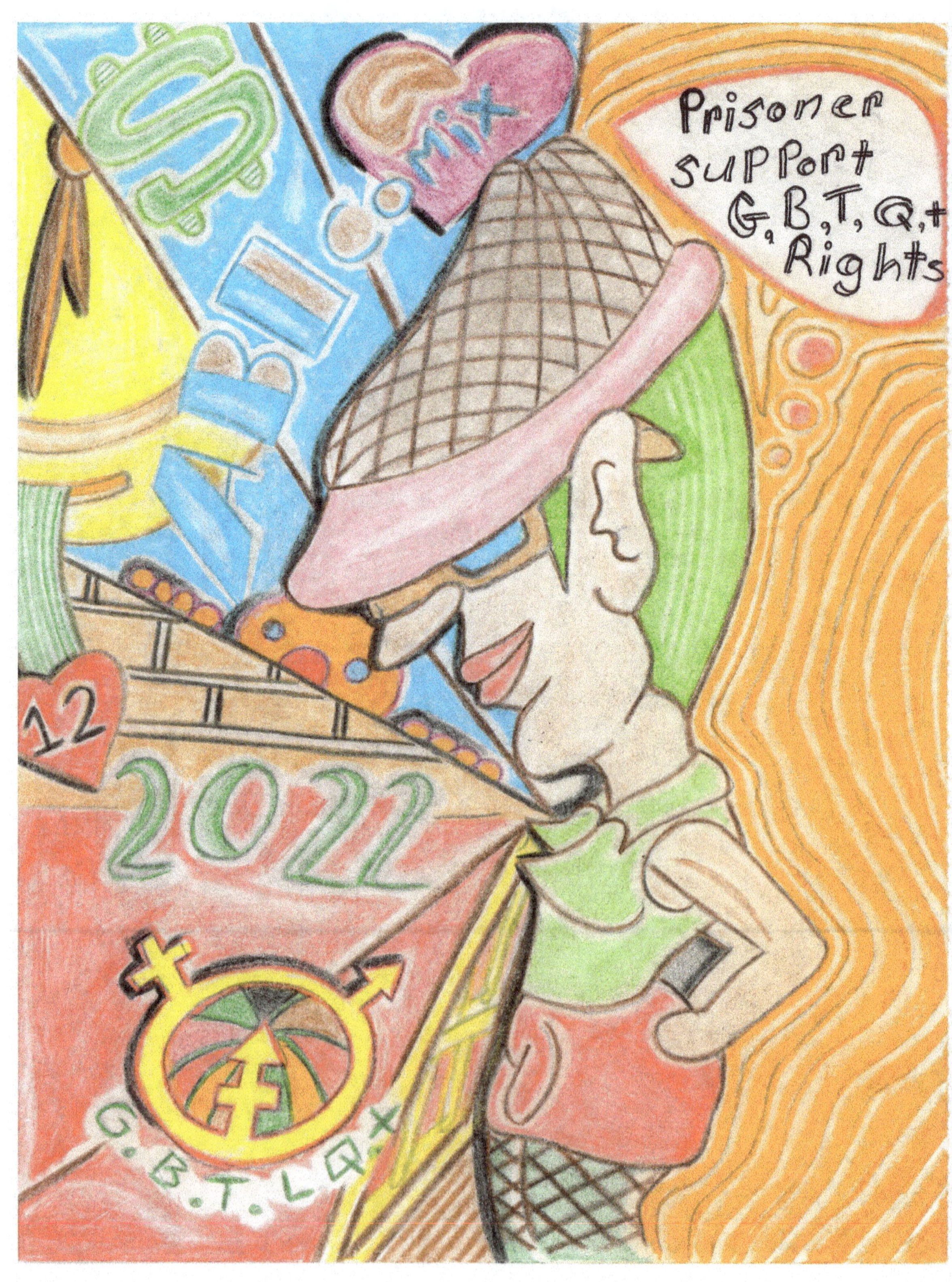
$
mix
ABI
Prisoner
suPPort
G,B,T,Q,+
Rights
12
2022
G.B.T.LQ+

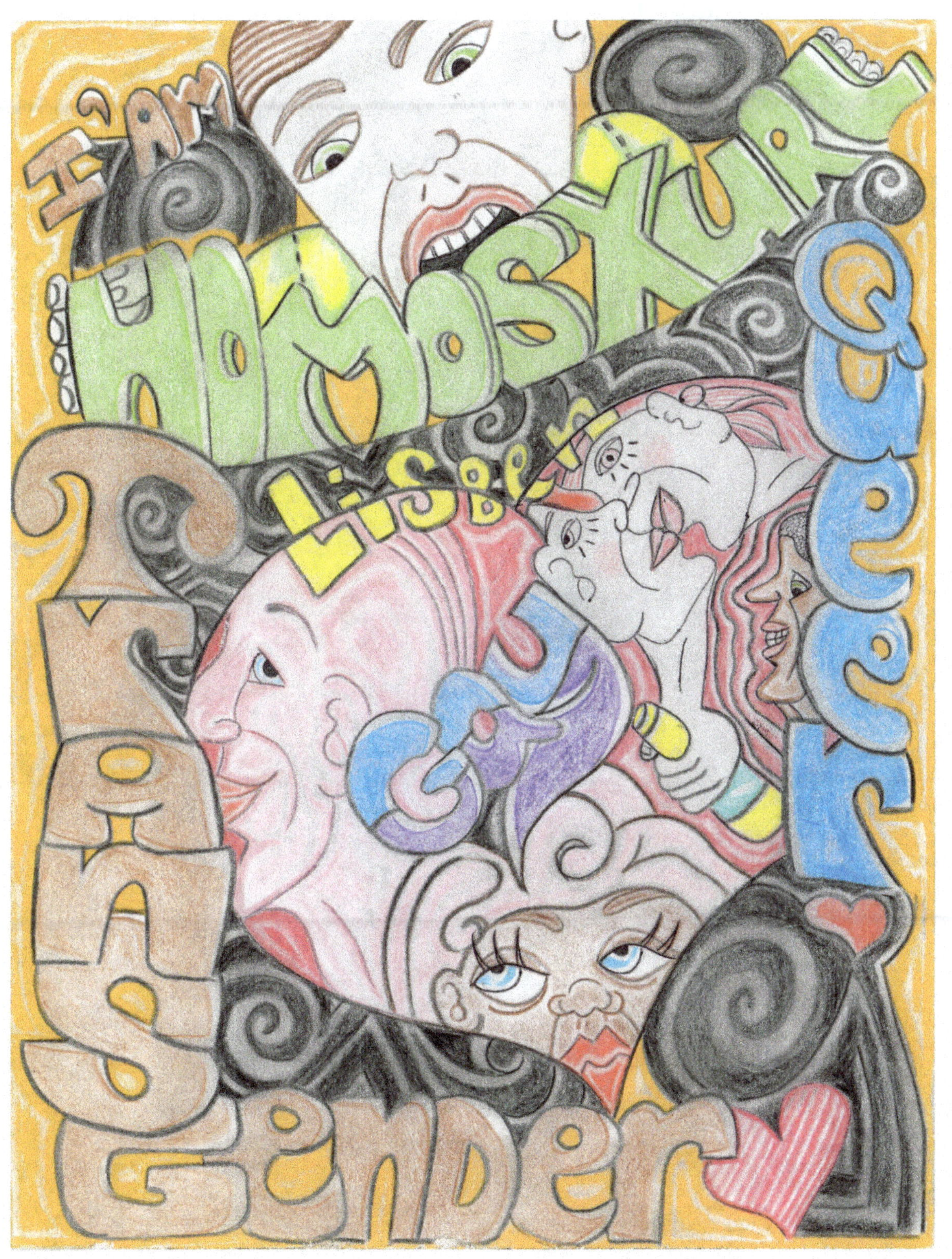
I AM
HOMOSXUR
QUEER
LISBEN
TRANS
GENDER

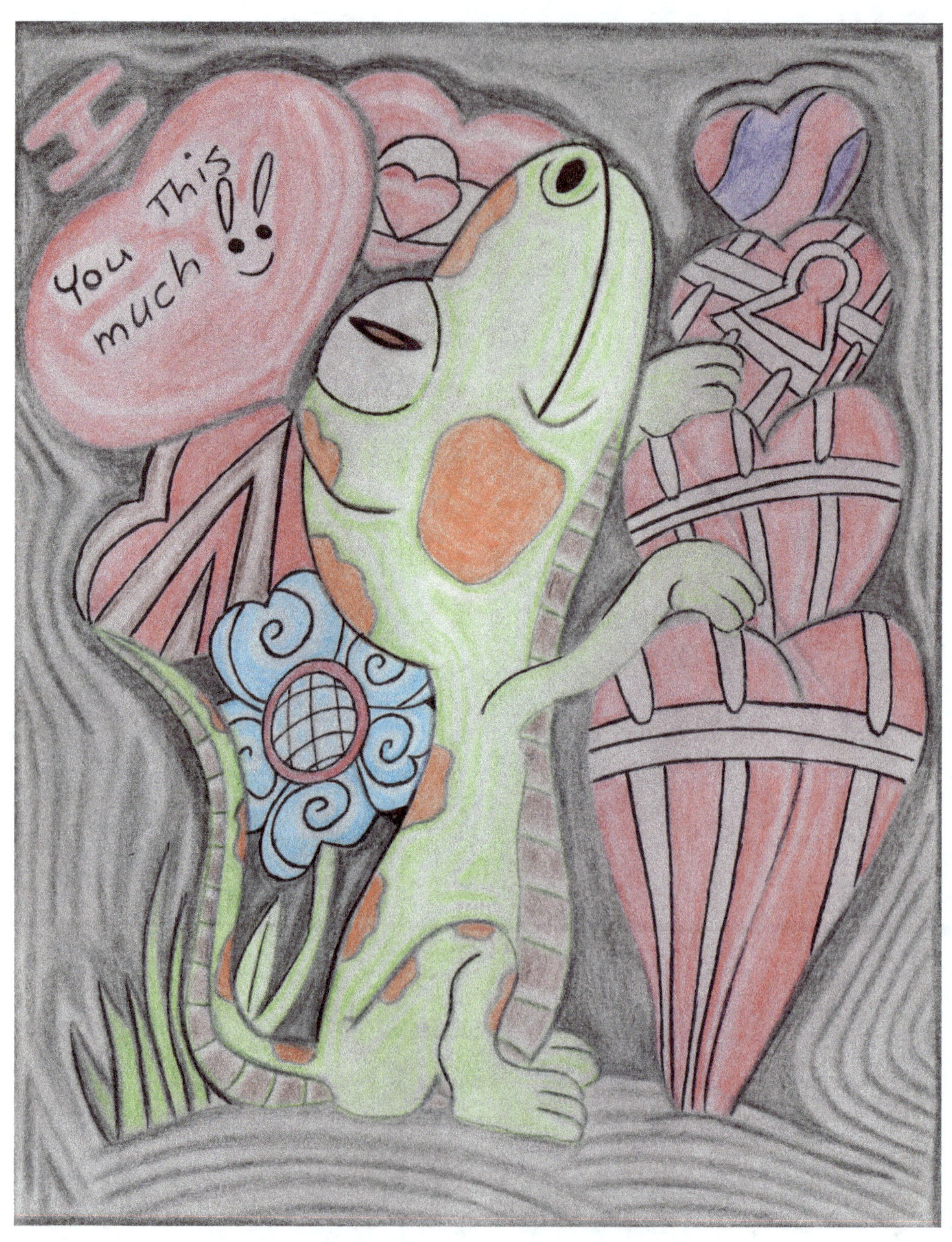
I
You This
much !!

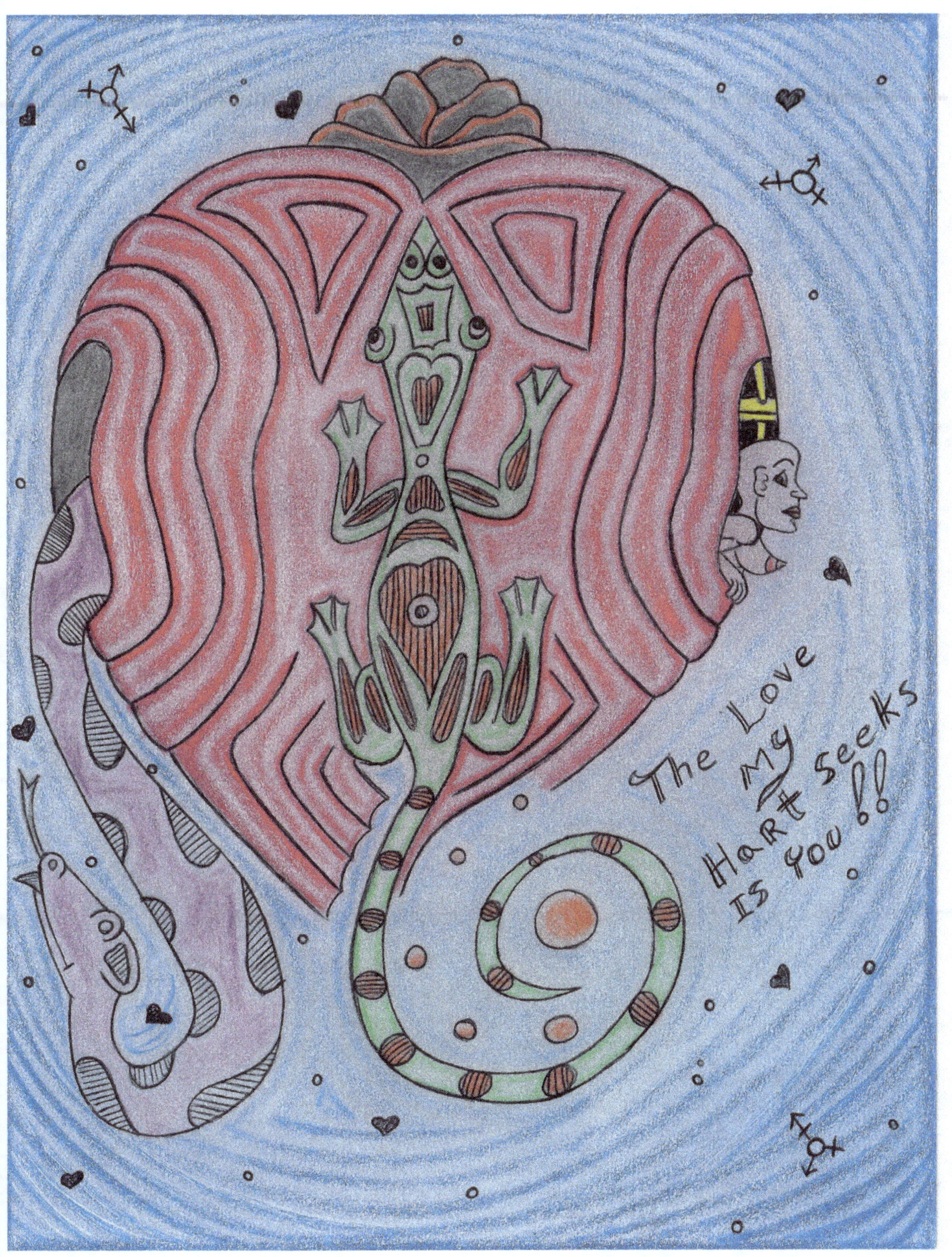
The Love My Hart Seeks IS You!!

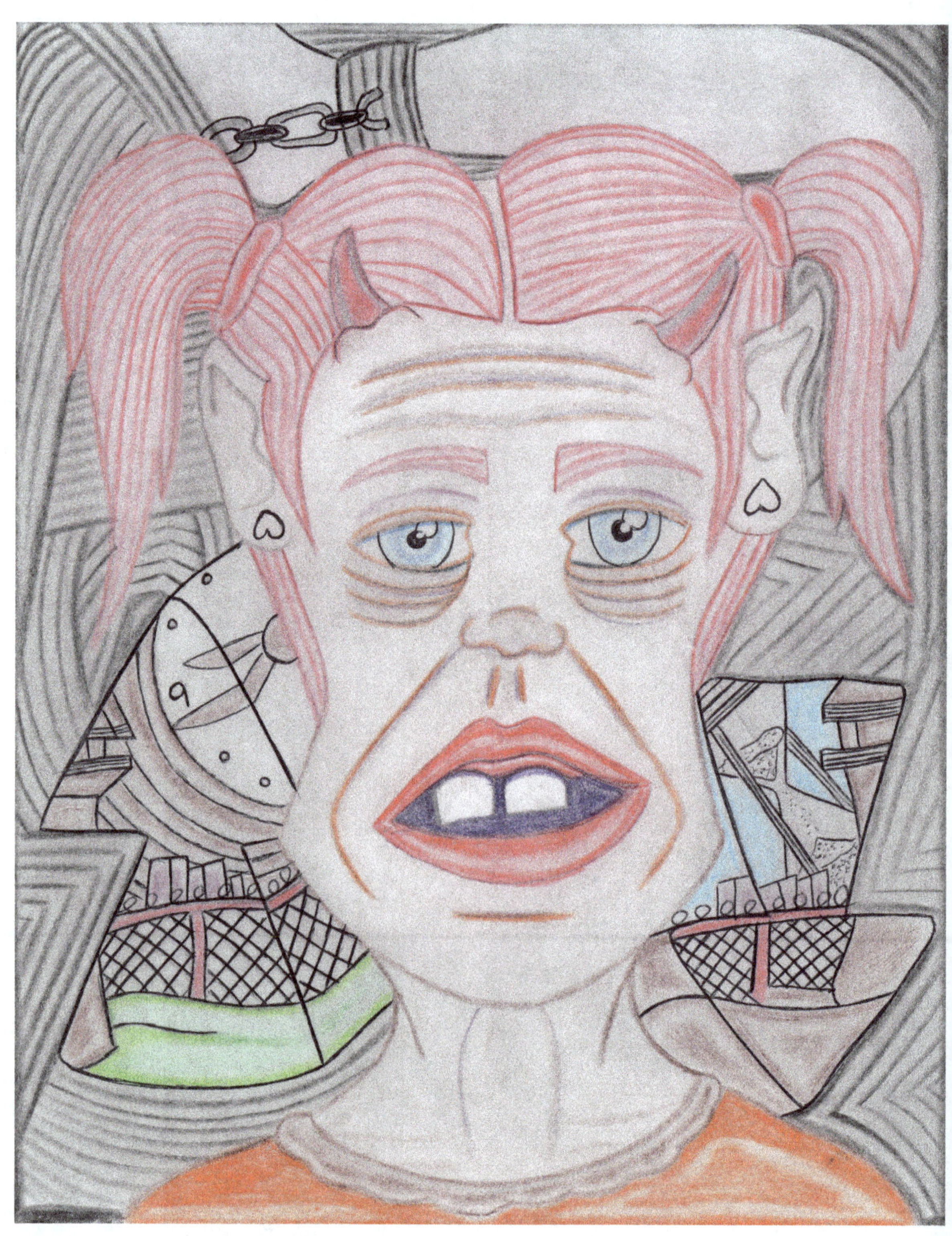

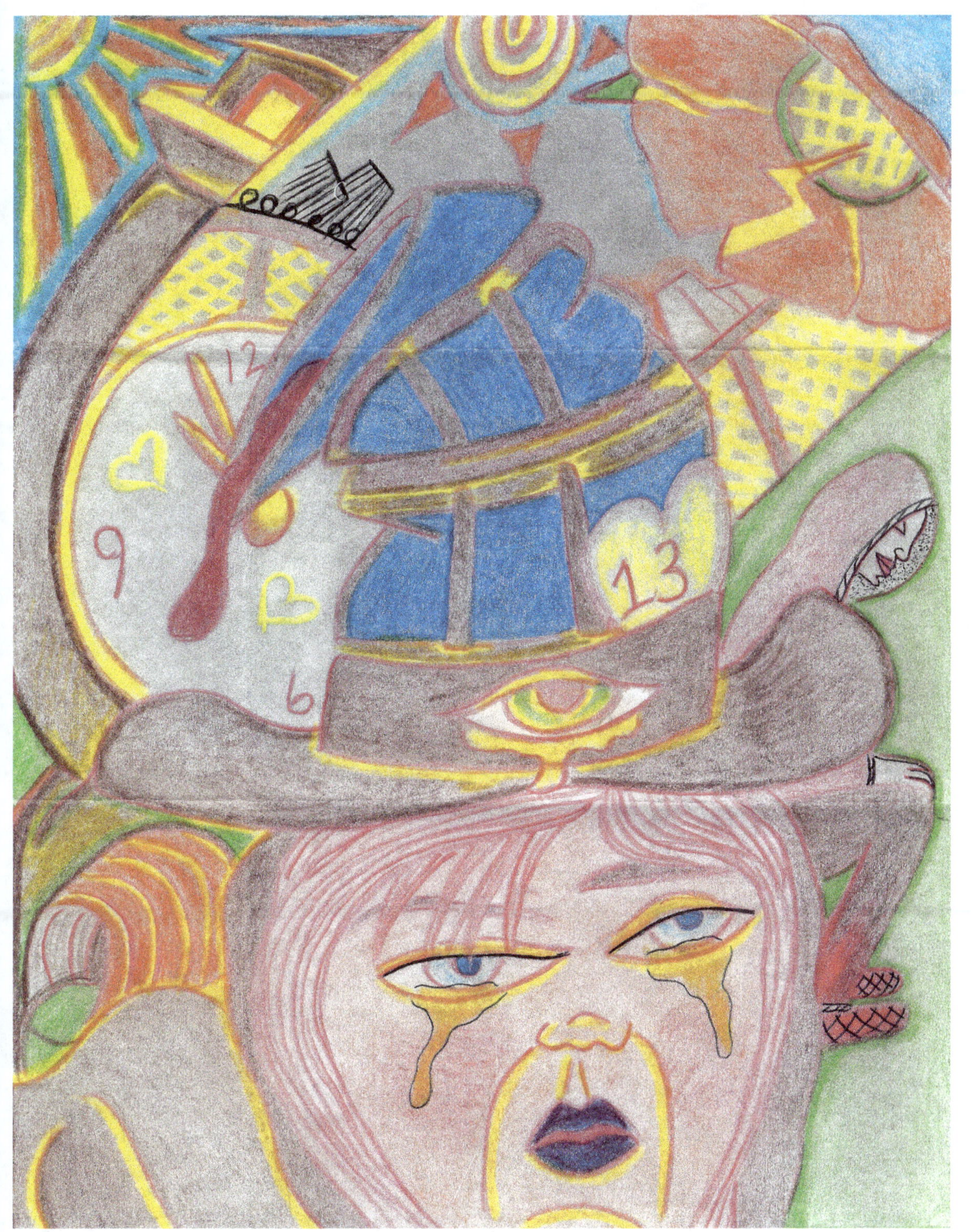
12
9
6
13

Lonsome Billy

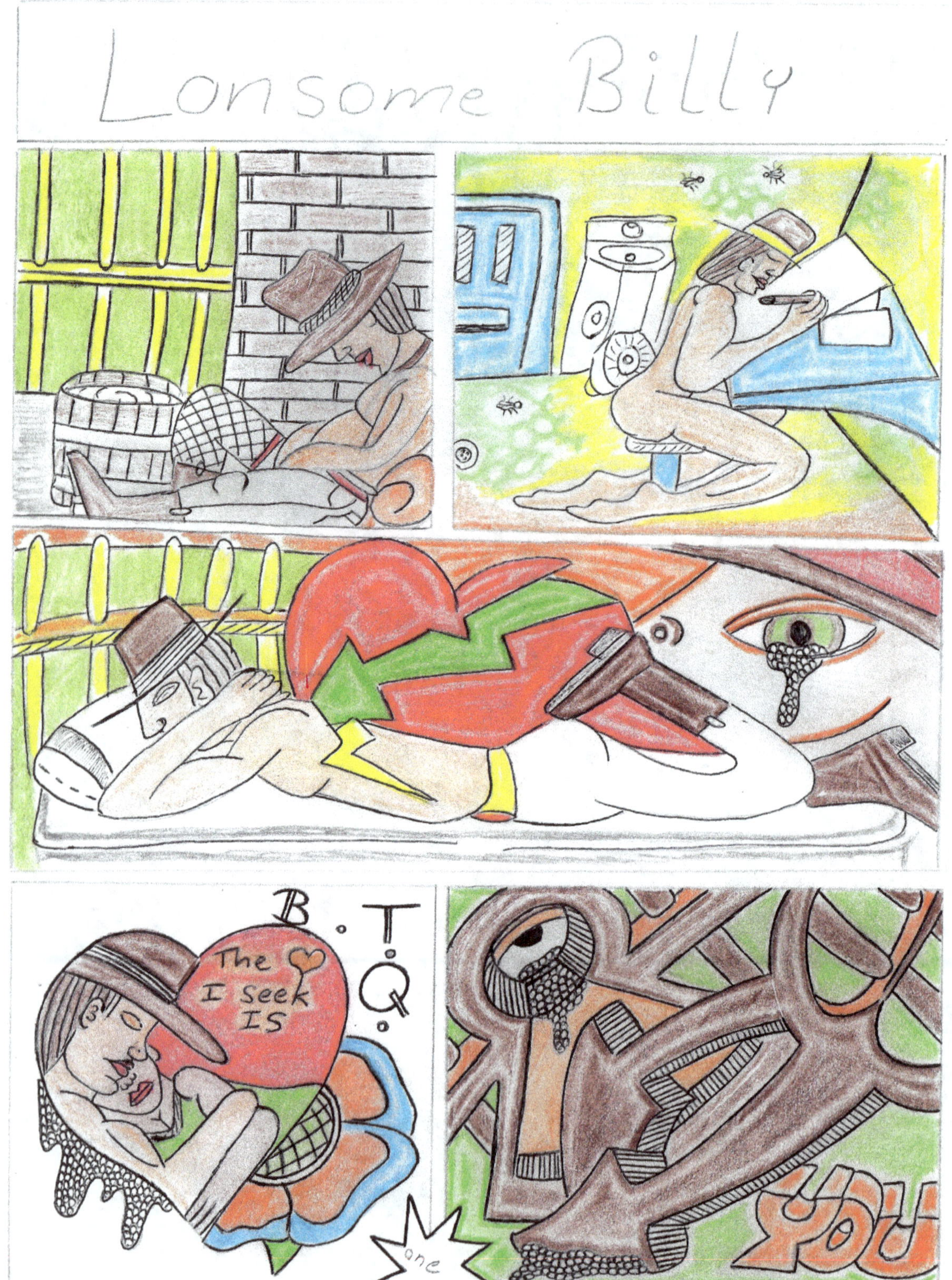

Lonsome Billy

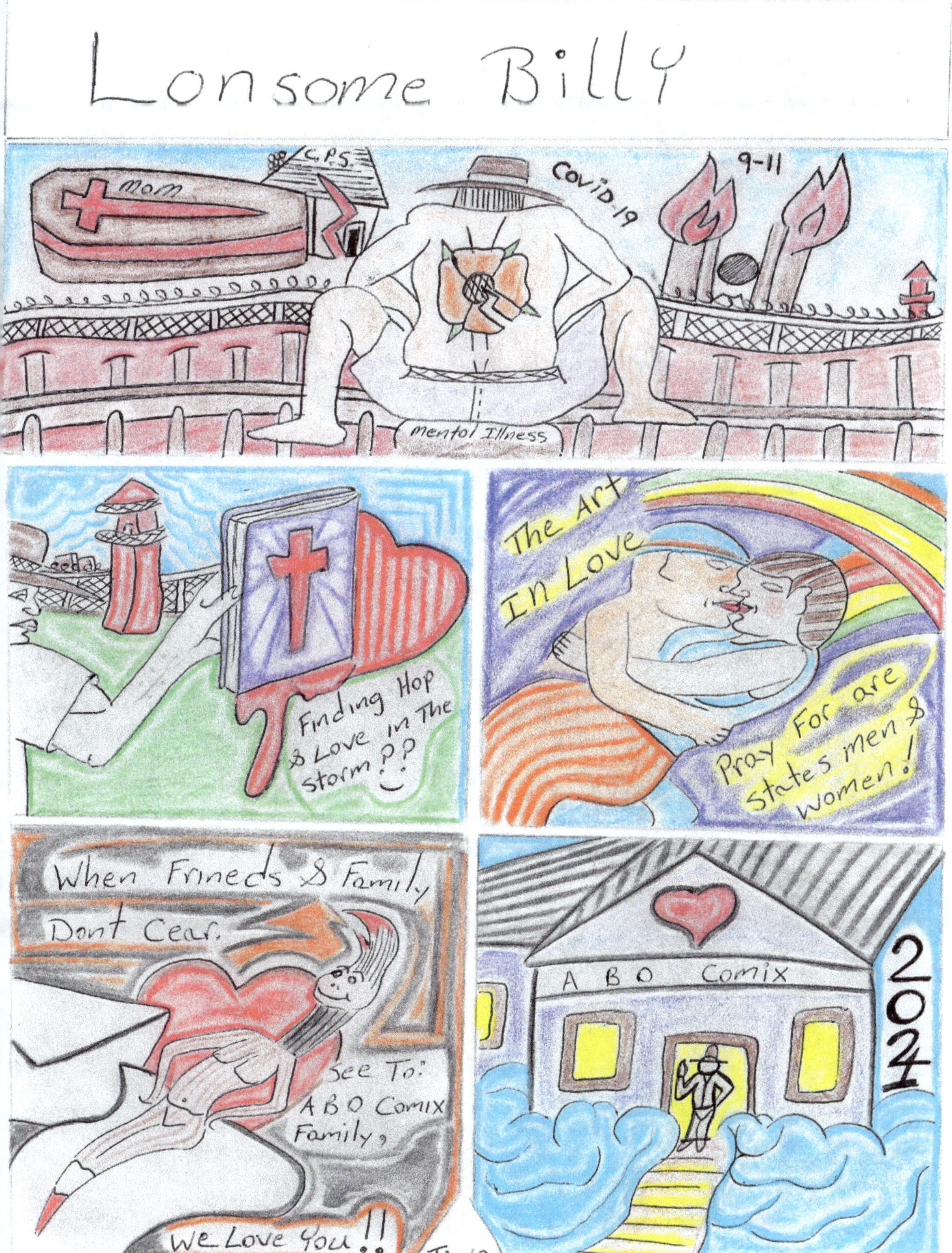

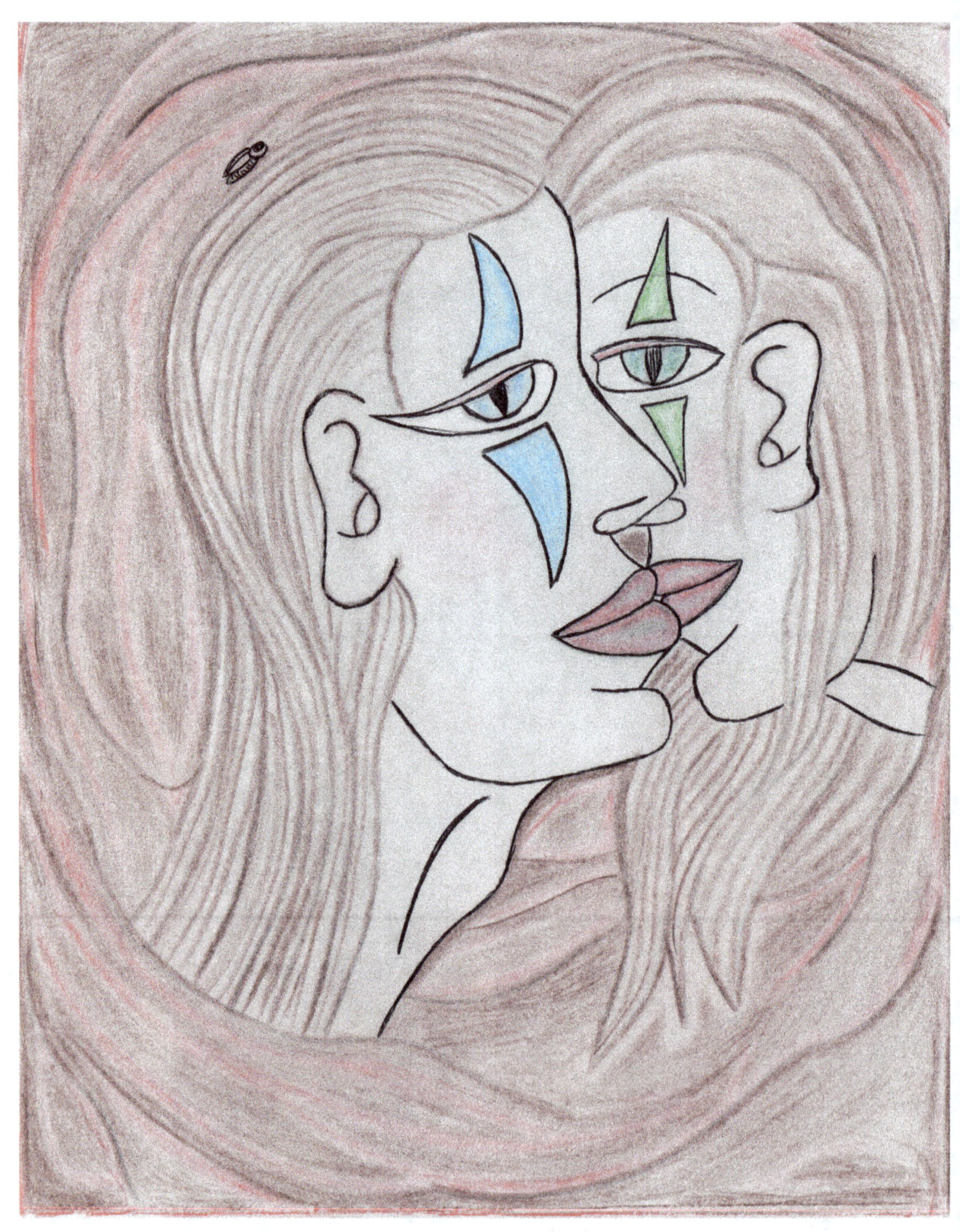

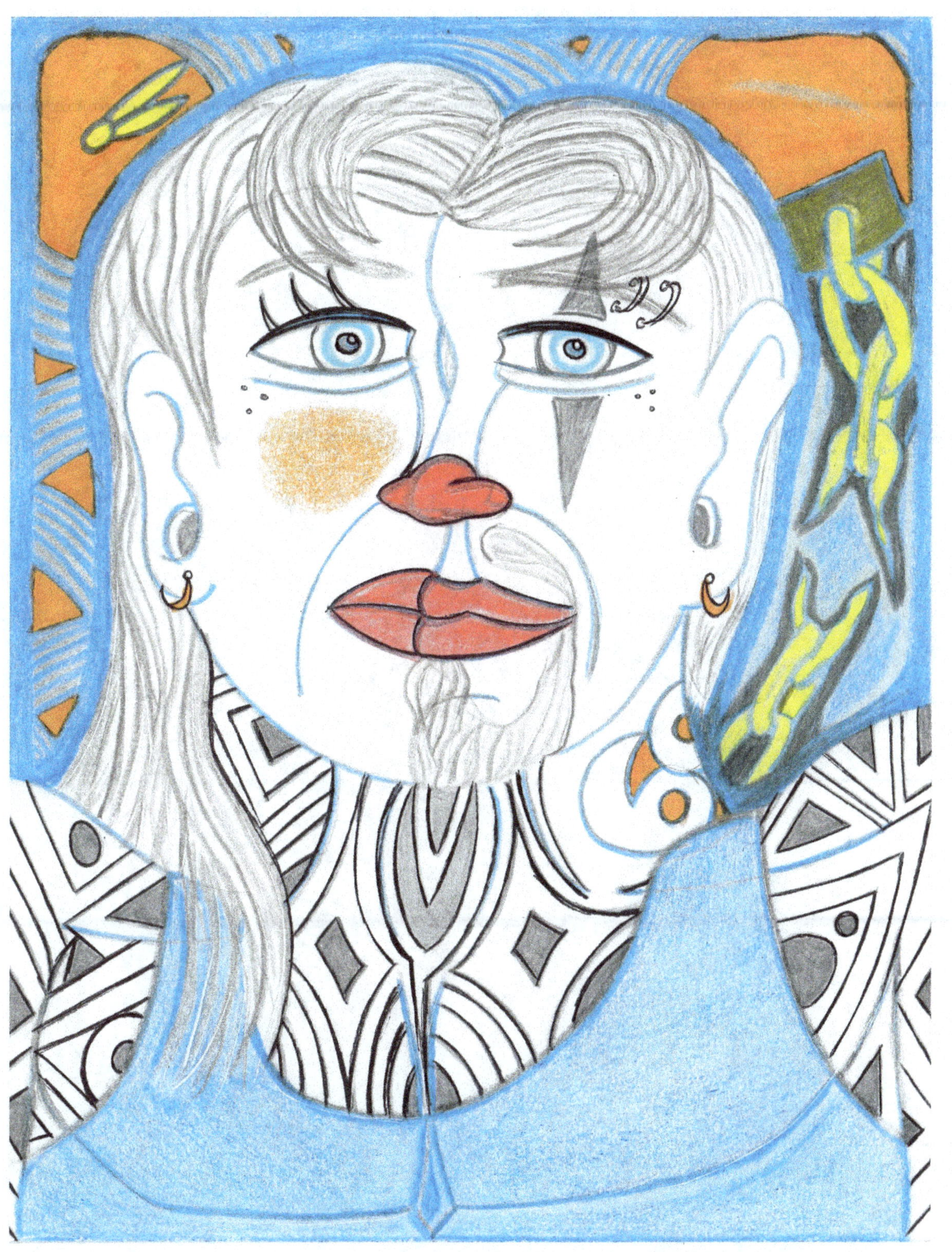

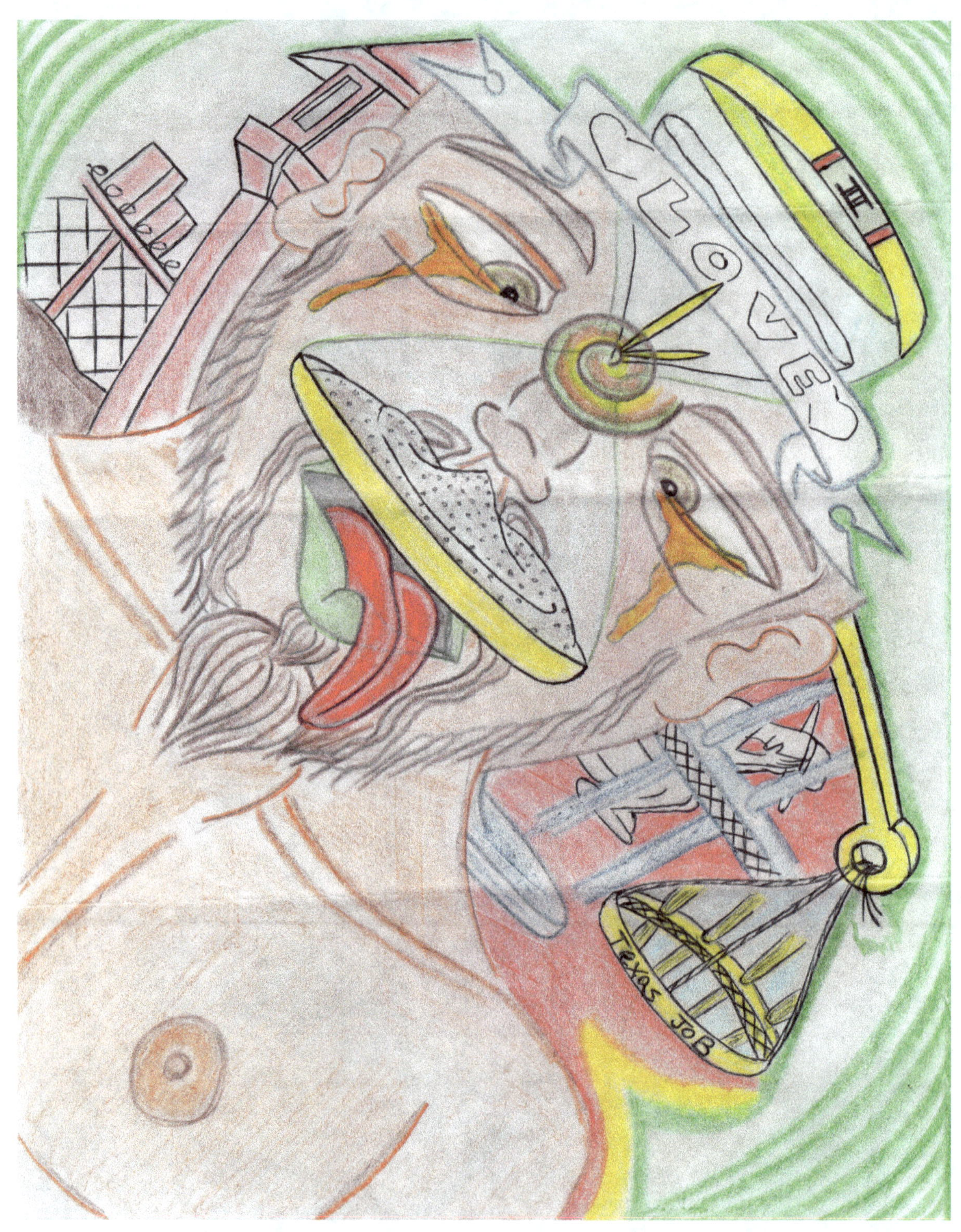
LOVE
Texas Job

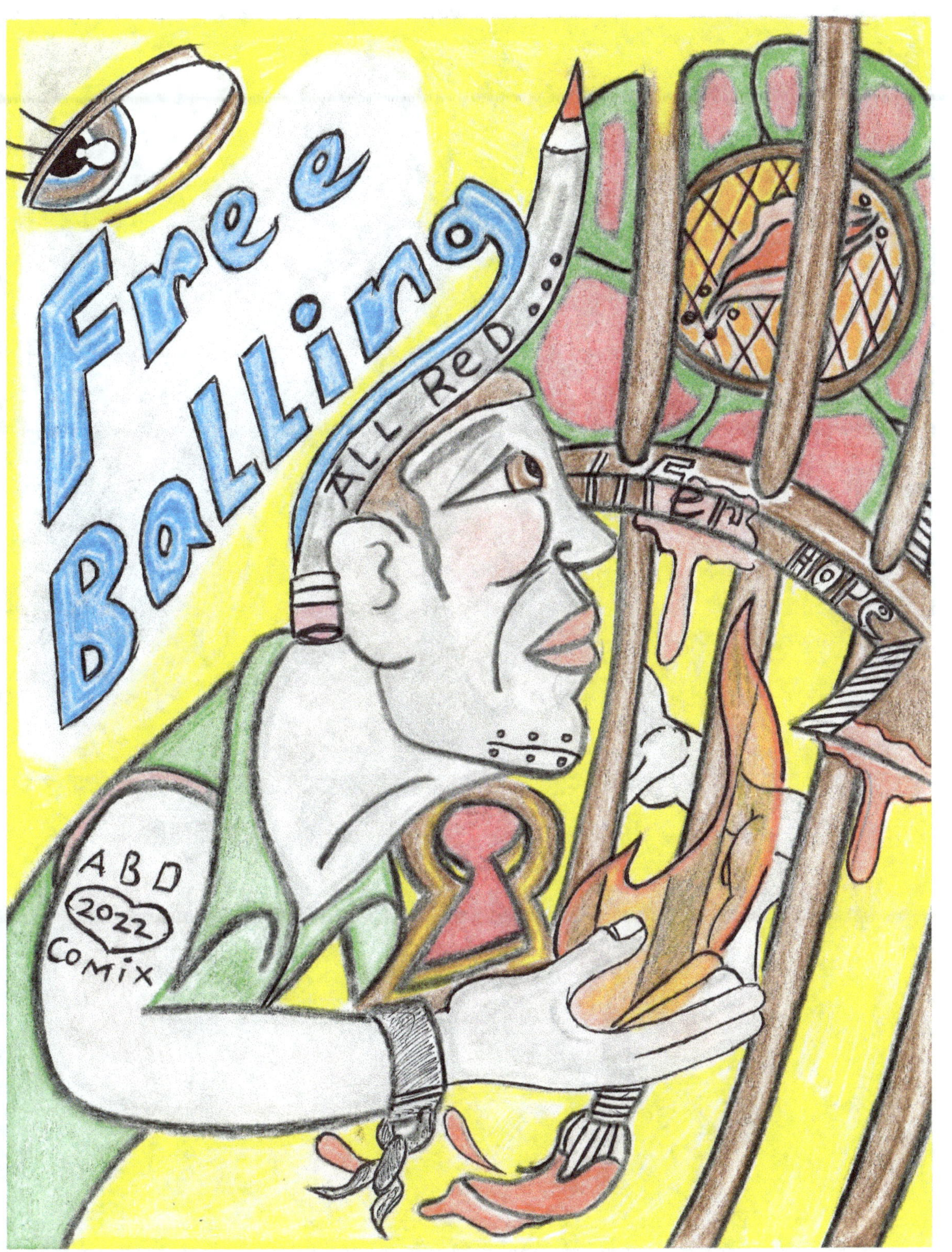
Free Balling
ALL ReD
EEN HopE
ABD
2022
CoMiX

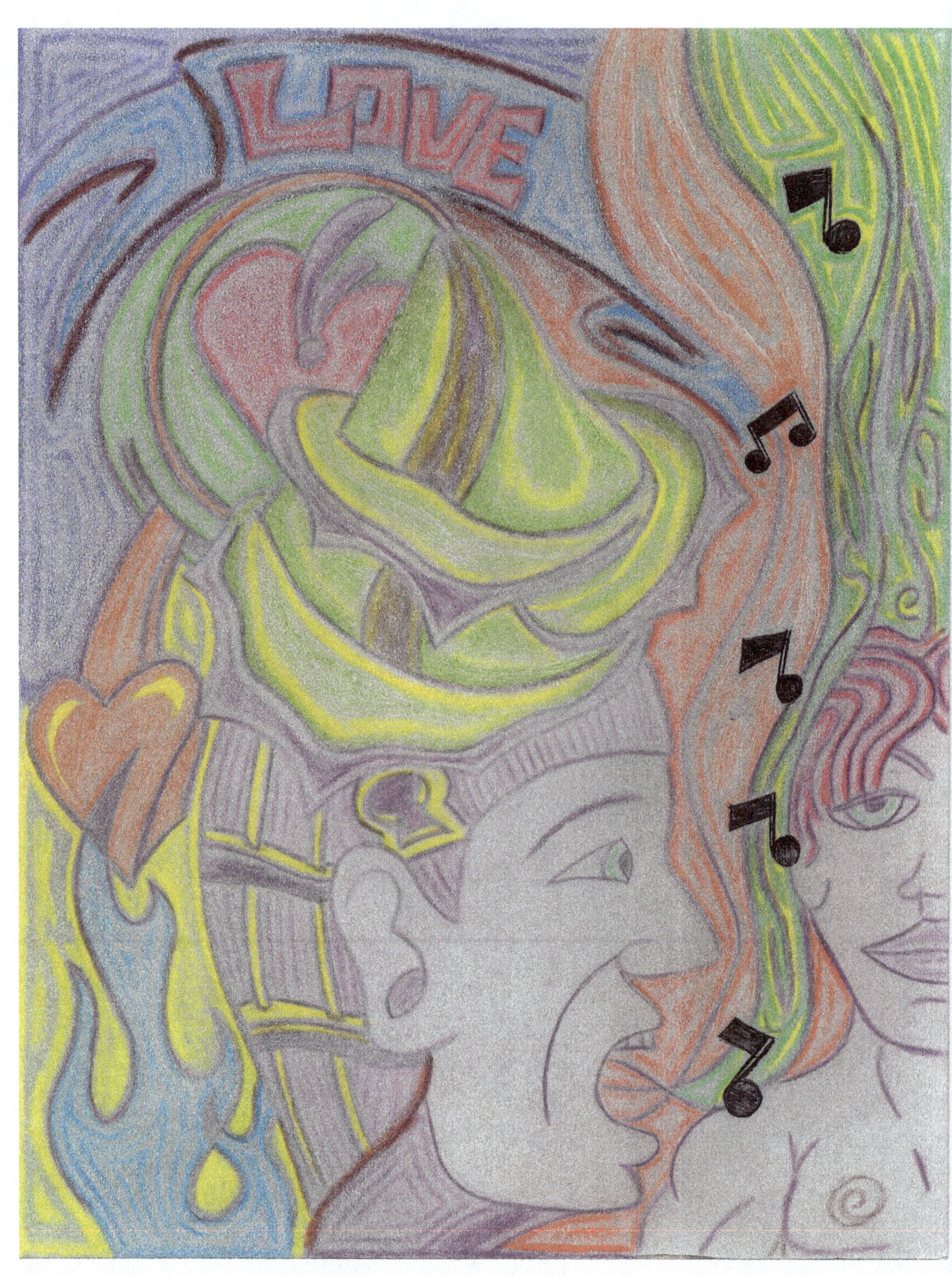

LOVE

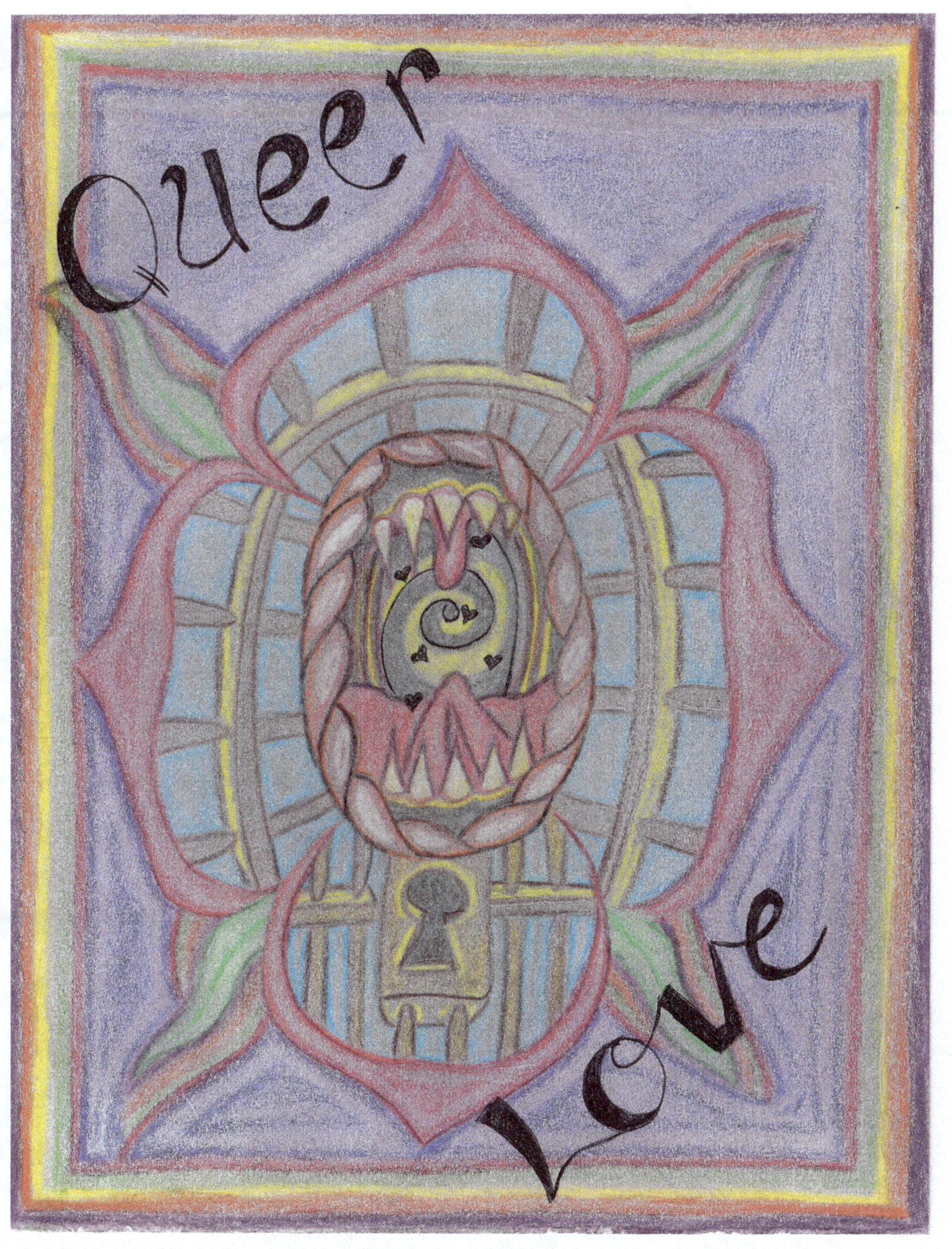

Queer
Love

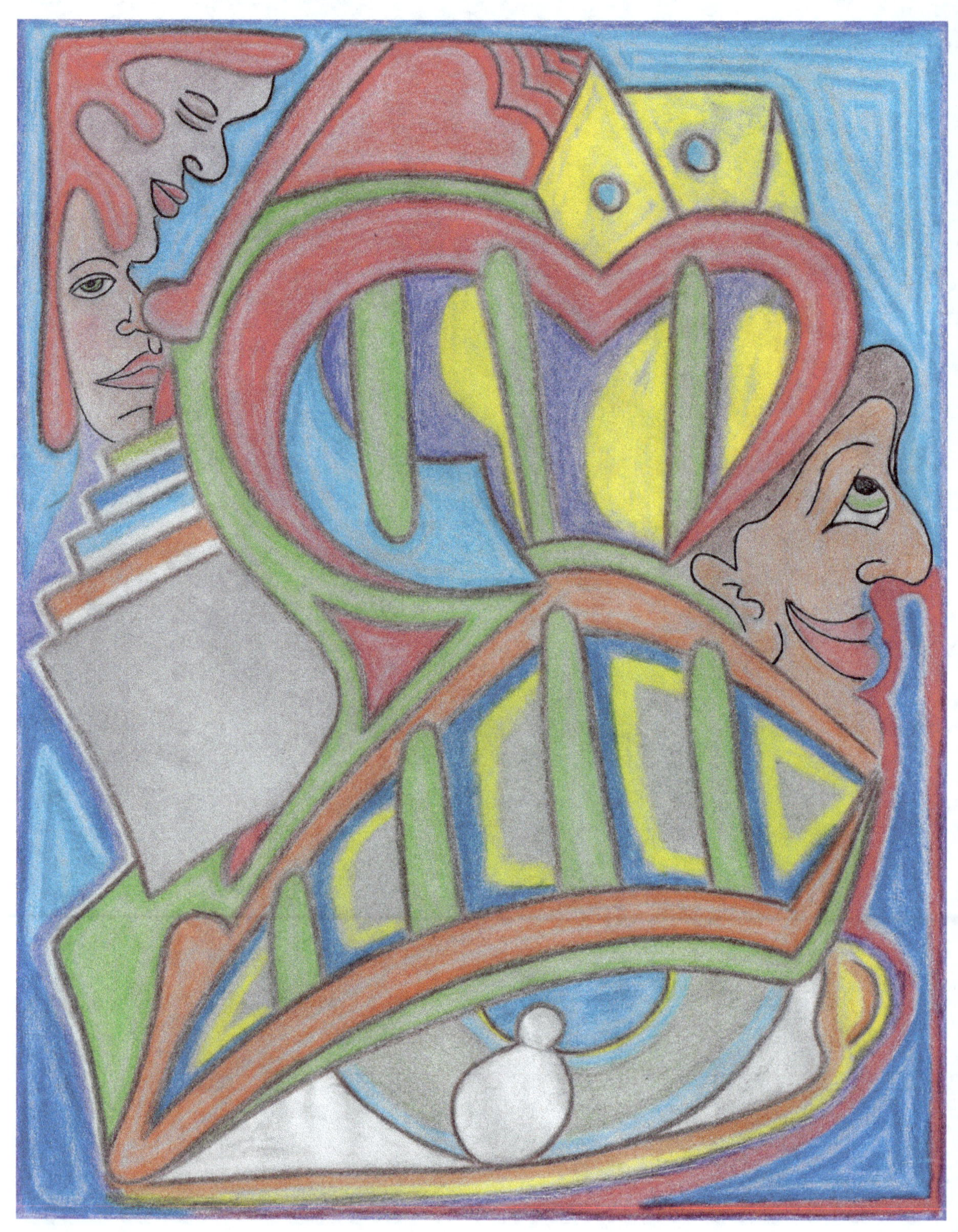

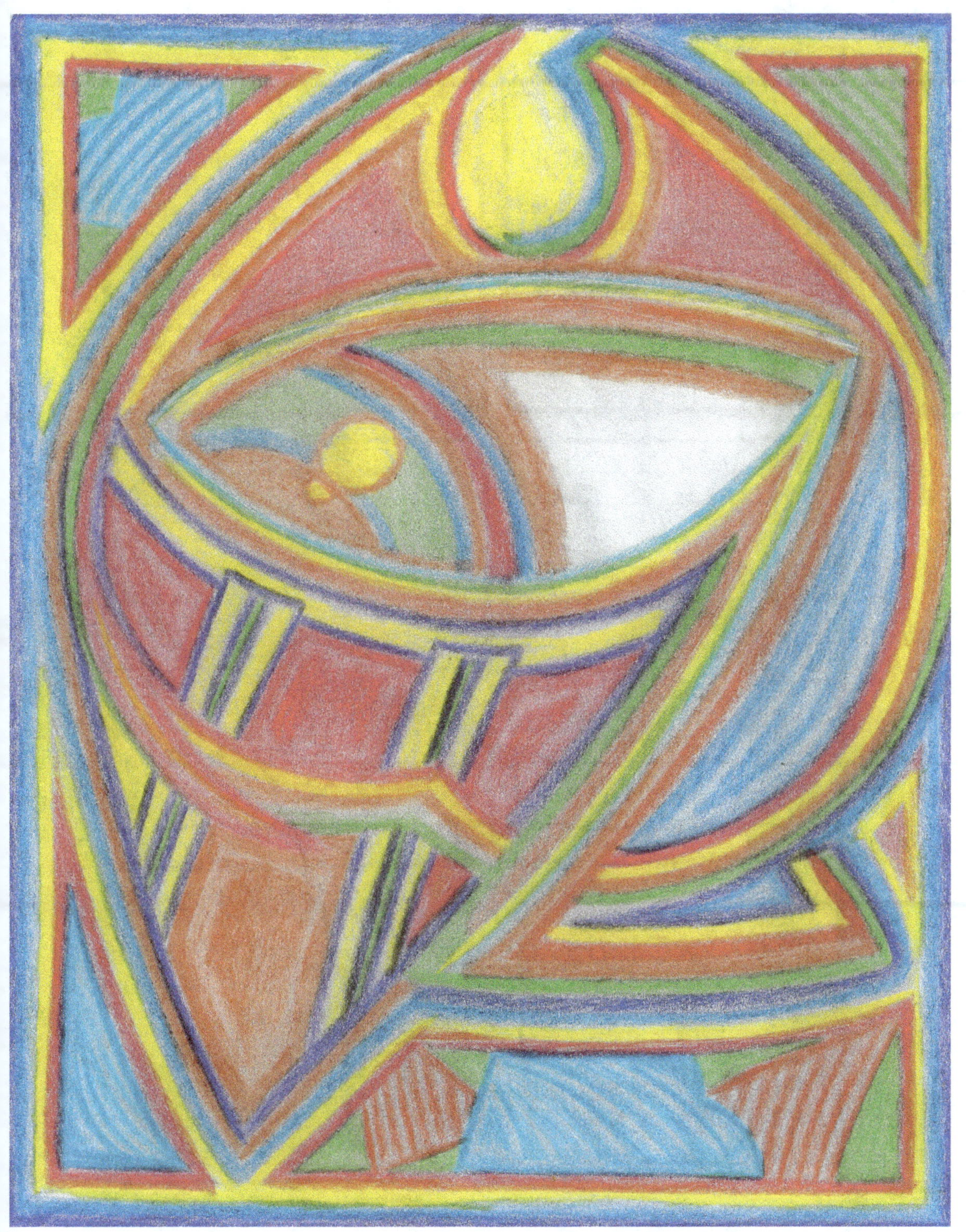

over,
Comeing
The
Heaters

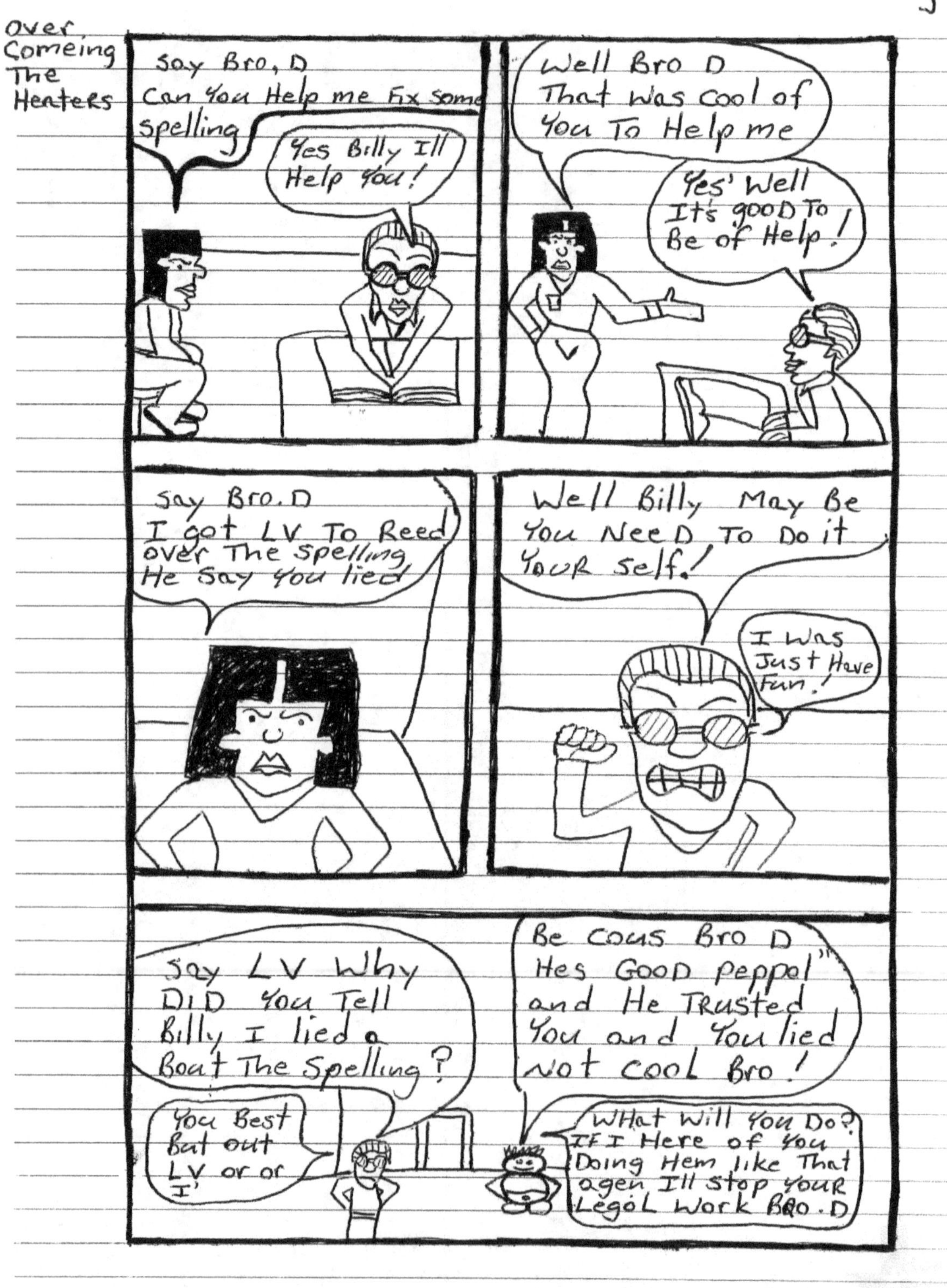

Billy . T

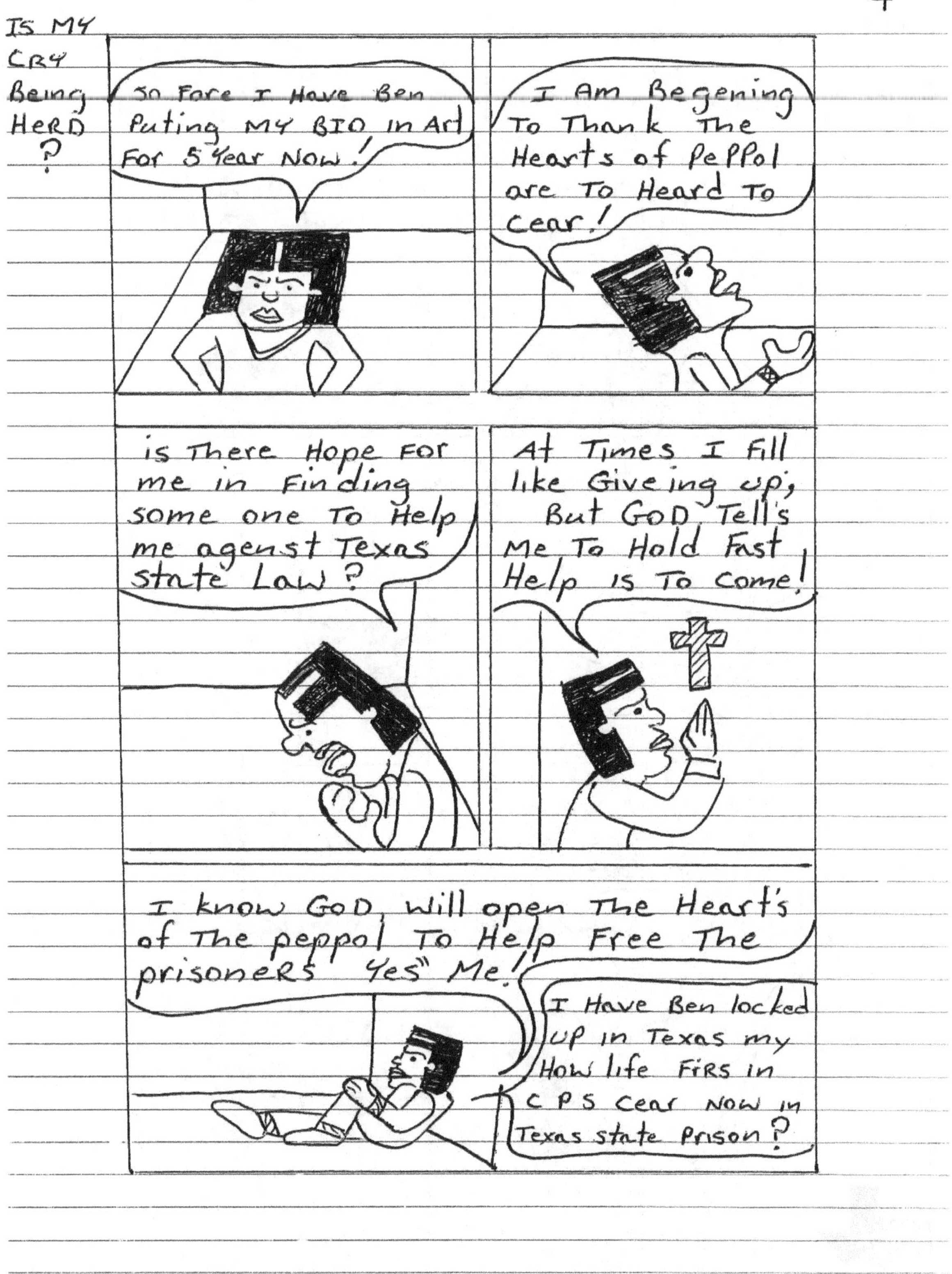
IS MY CRY Being HERD ?

So Fore I Have Ben Puting MY BIO in Art For 5 Year Now!

I AM Begening To Thank The Hearts of PePPol are To Heard To cear!

is There Hope For me in Finding some one To Help me agenst Texas state Law?

At Times I Fill like Giveing up, But GOD Tell's Me To Hold Fast Help is To Come!

I know GOD, will open The Heart's of The peppol To Help Free The prisoneRs "Yes" Me!

I Have Ben locked up in Texas my How life FiRS in C P S cear Now in Texas state Prison?

Faith

over
Comeing
Man's
Un Just
Law ?

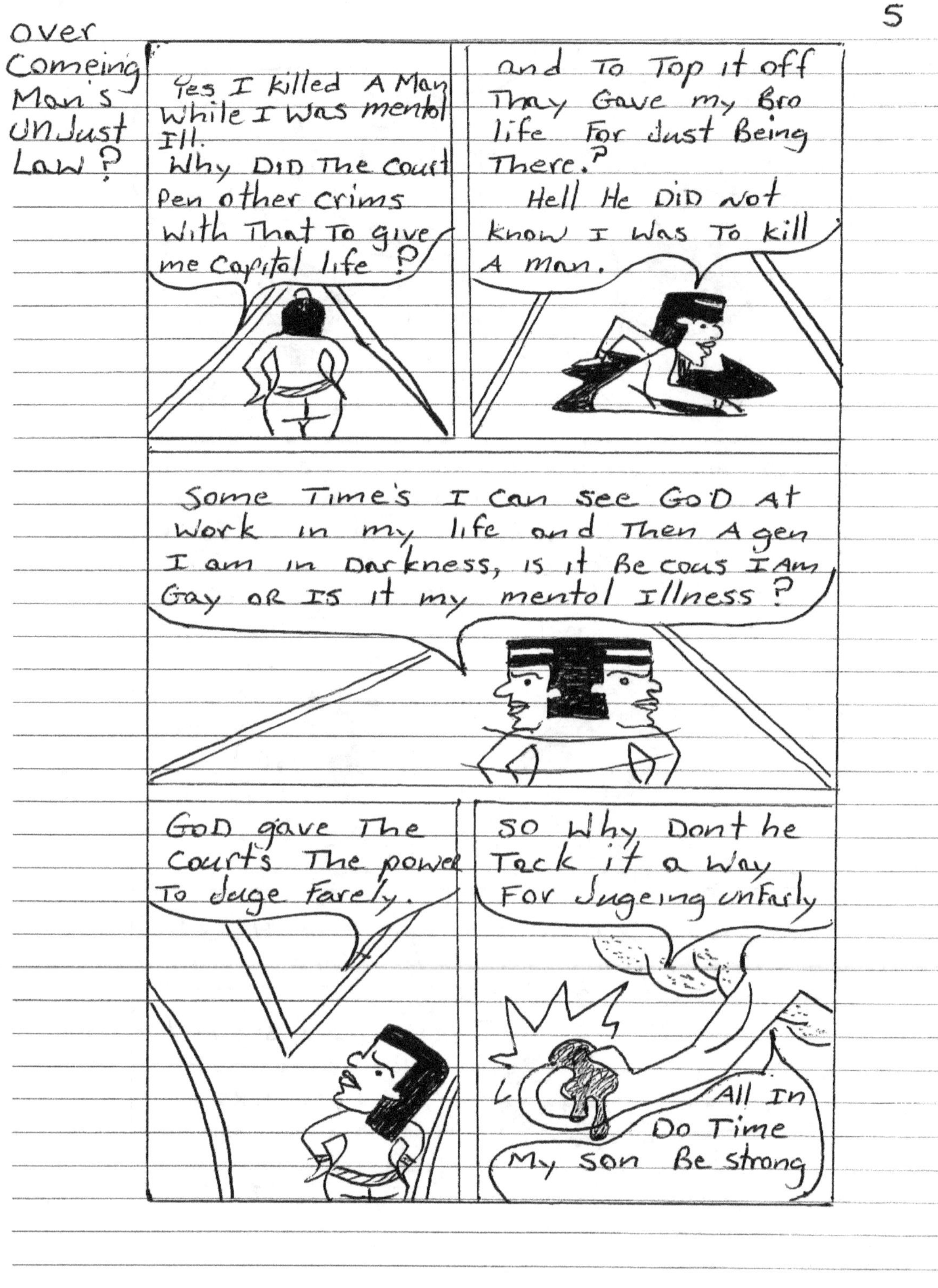

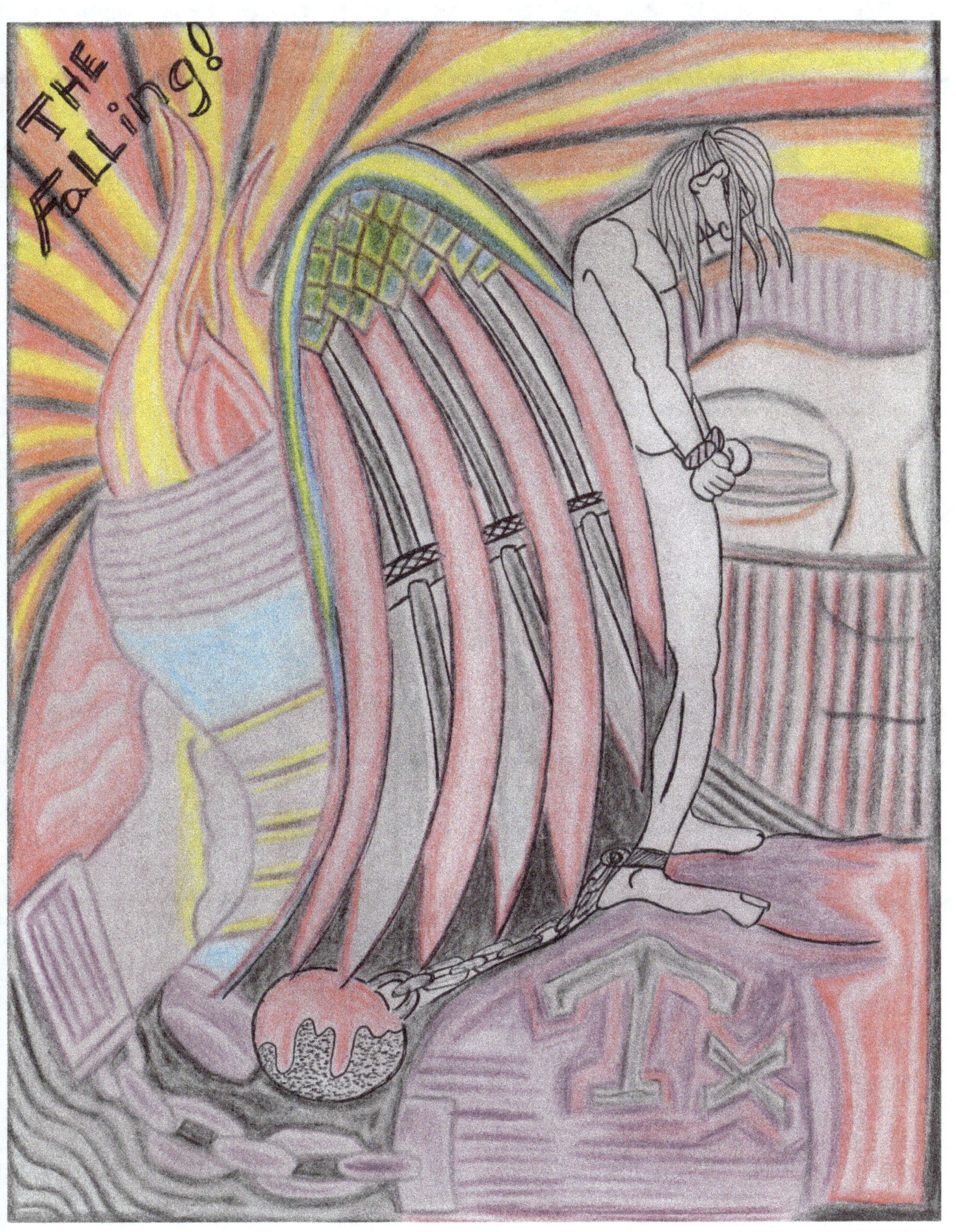
THE FALLing!

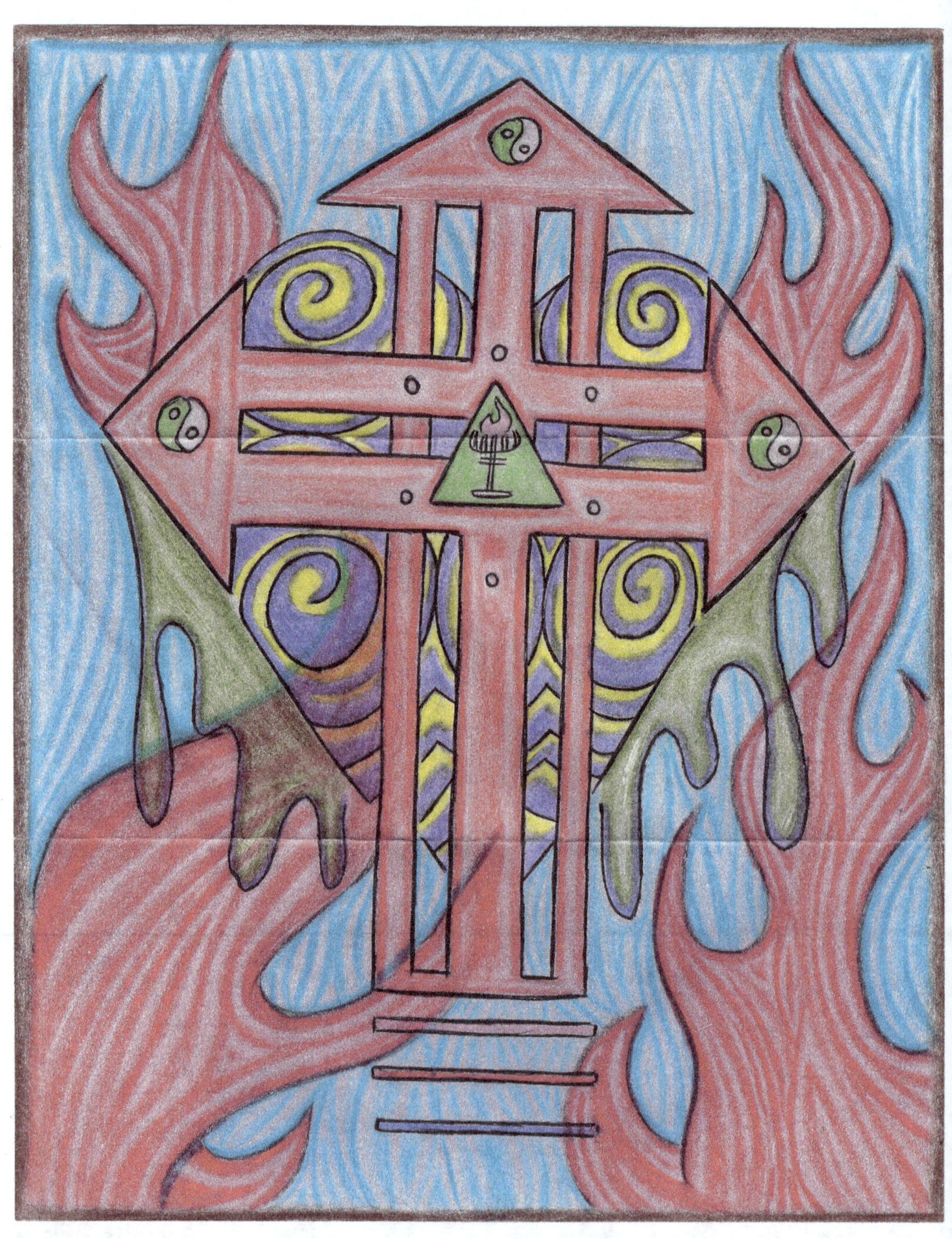

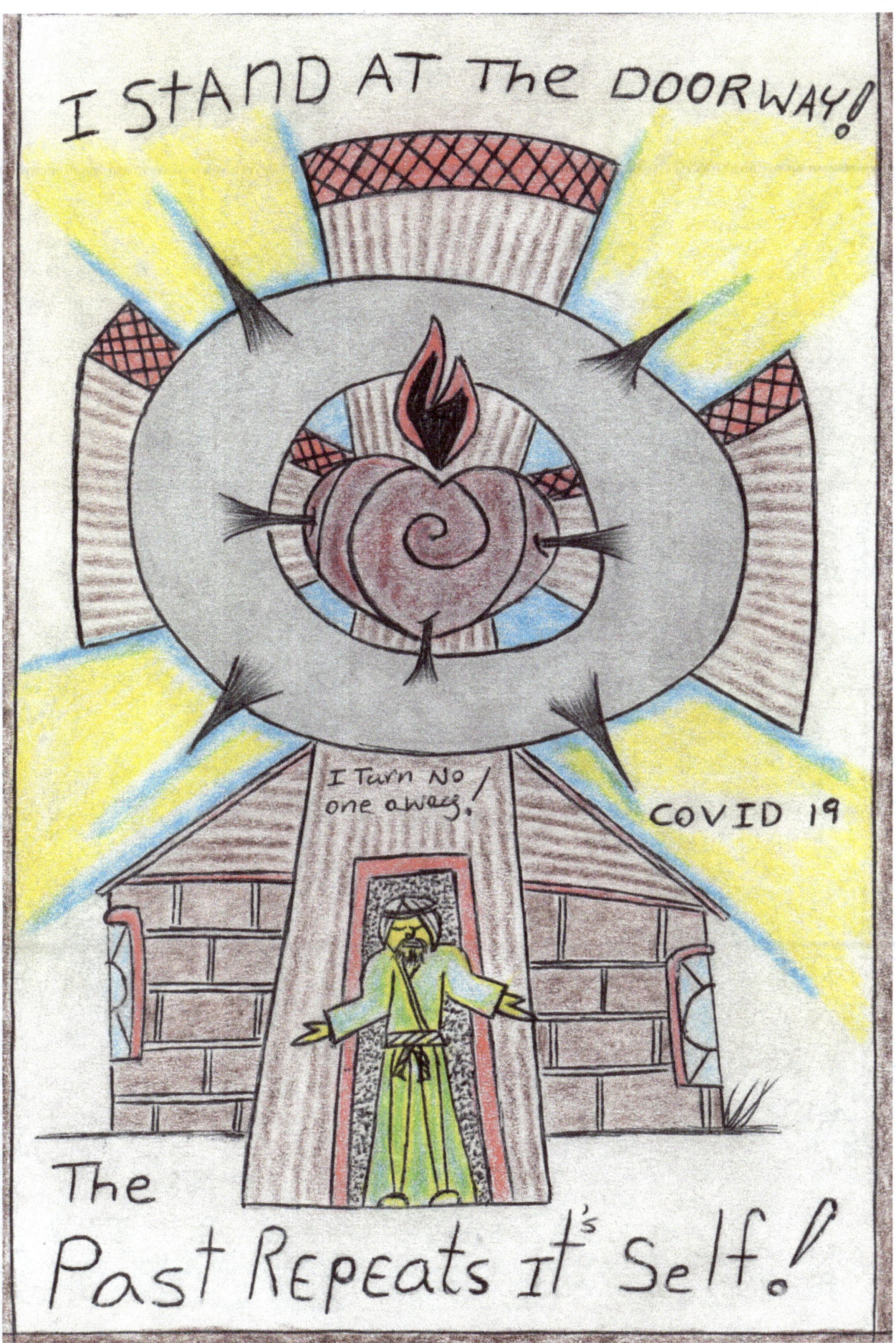

I STAND AT THE DOORWAY!
I Turn No one away!
COVID 19
The Past Repeats It's Self!

Faith

DePRIVED MY Fath
BY: Billy D. Thomas
#1275621
TDCJ
TDCJ
PRISON PALICY'S
NO FEAST
NO PASS OVER
USA Texas State Prison

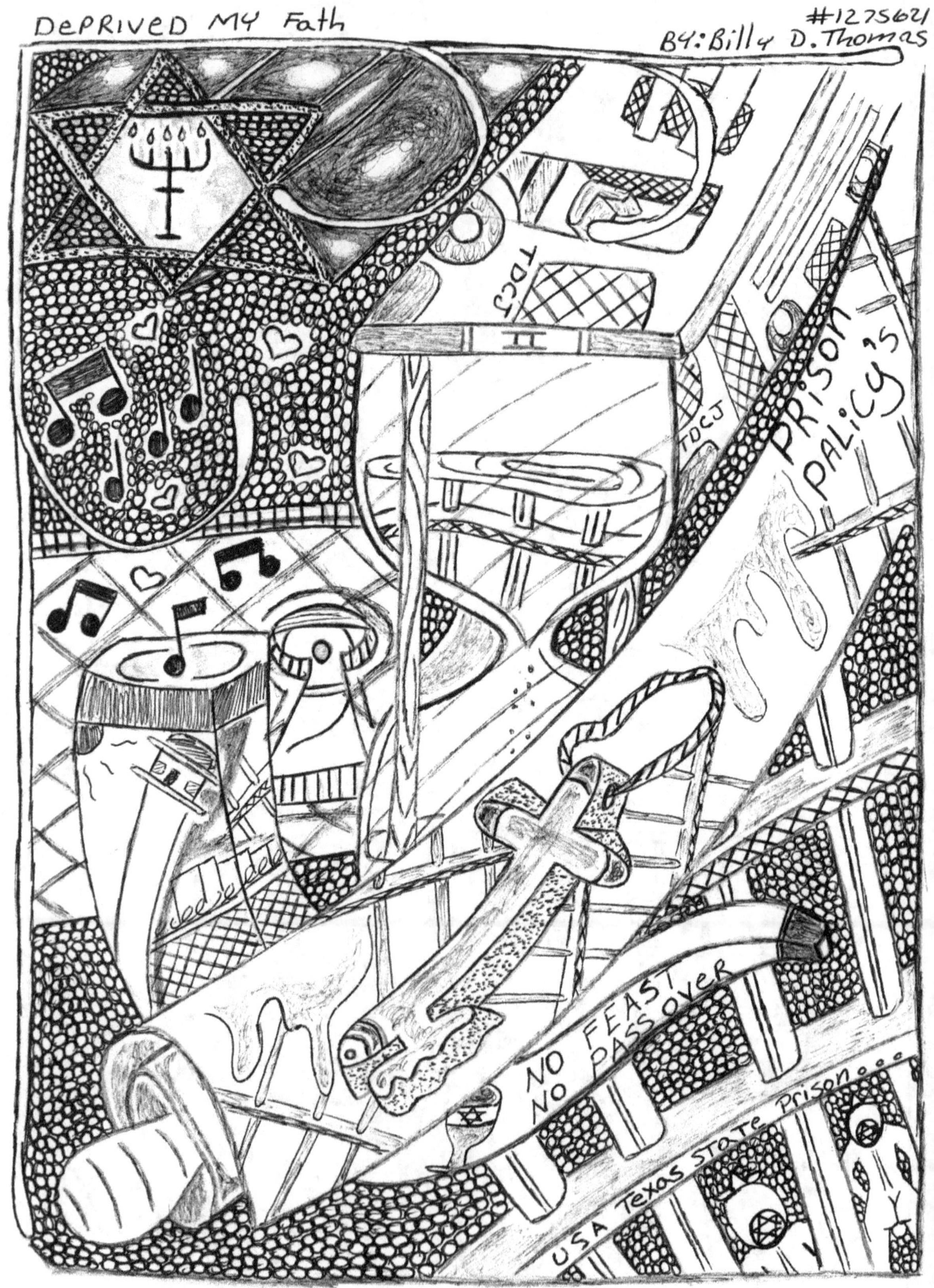

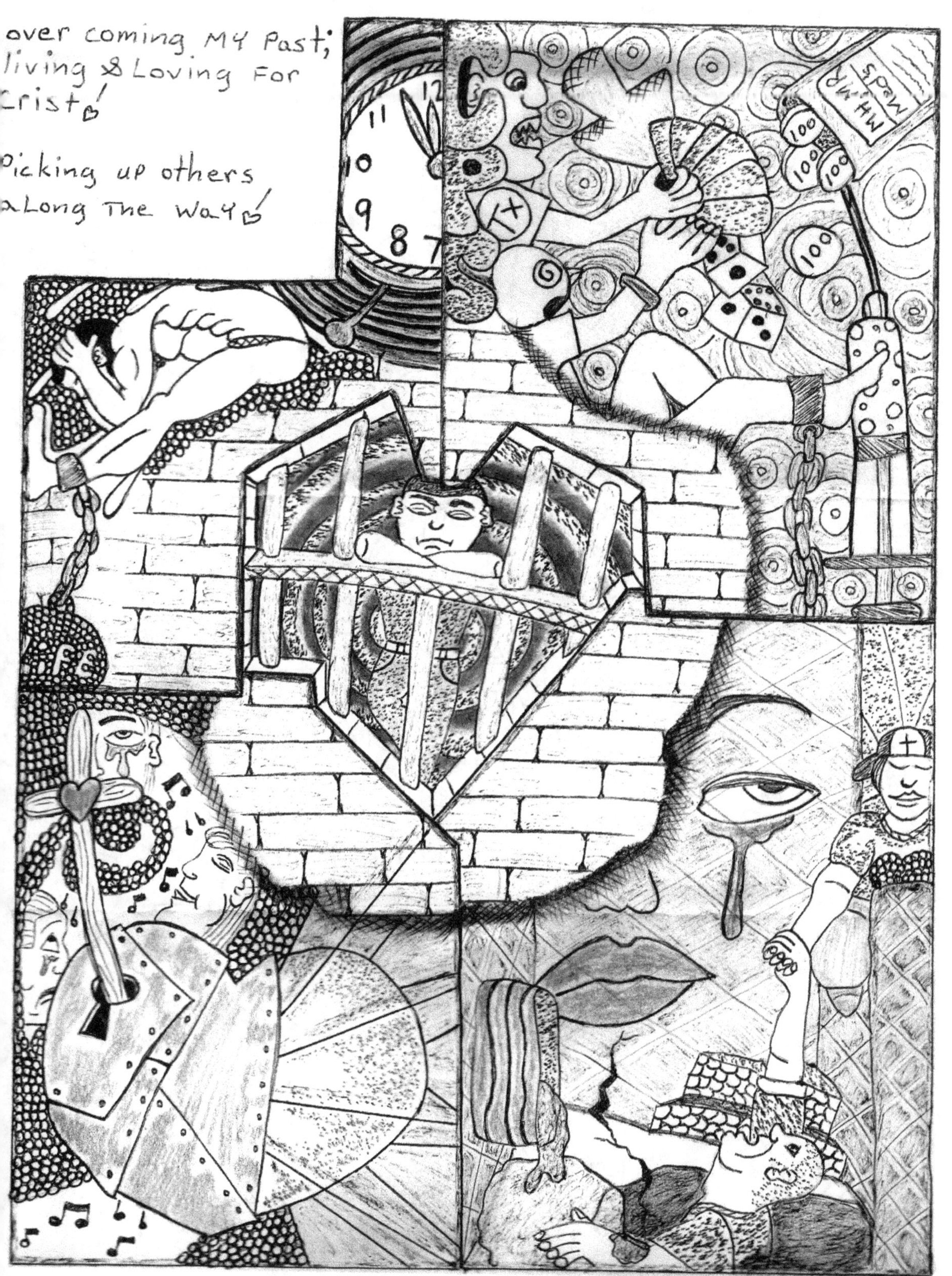
over coming MY Past;
living & Loving For
crist!

Picking up others
along The Way!

Faith

A World without Bar's ?
2002 F,W,Tx.
BY: Billy D.Thomas
Free
100
1275621
A Place To Call Home!
A Trow Friend Hand
A.B.O. Comix

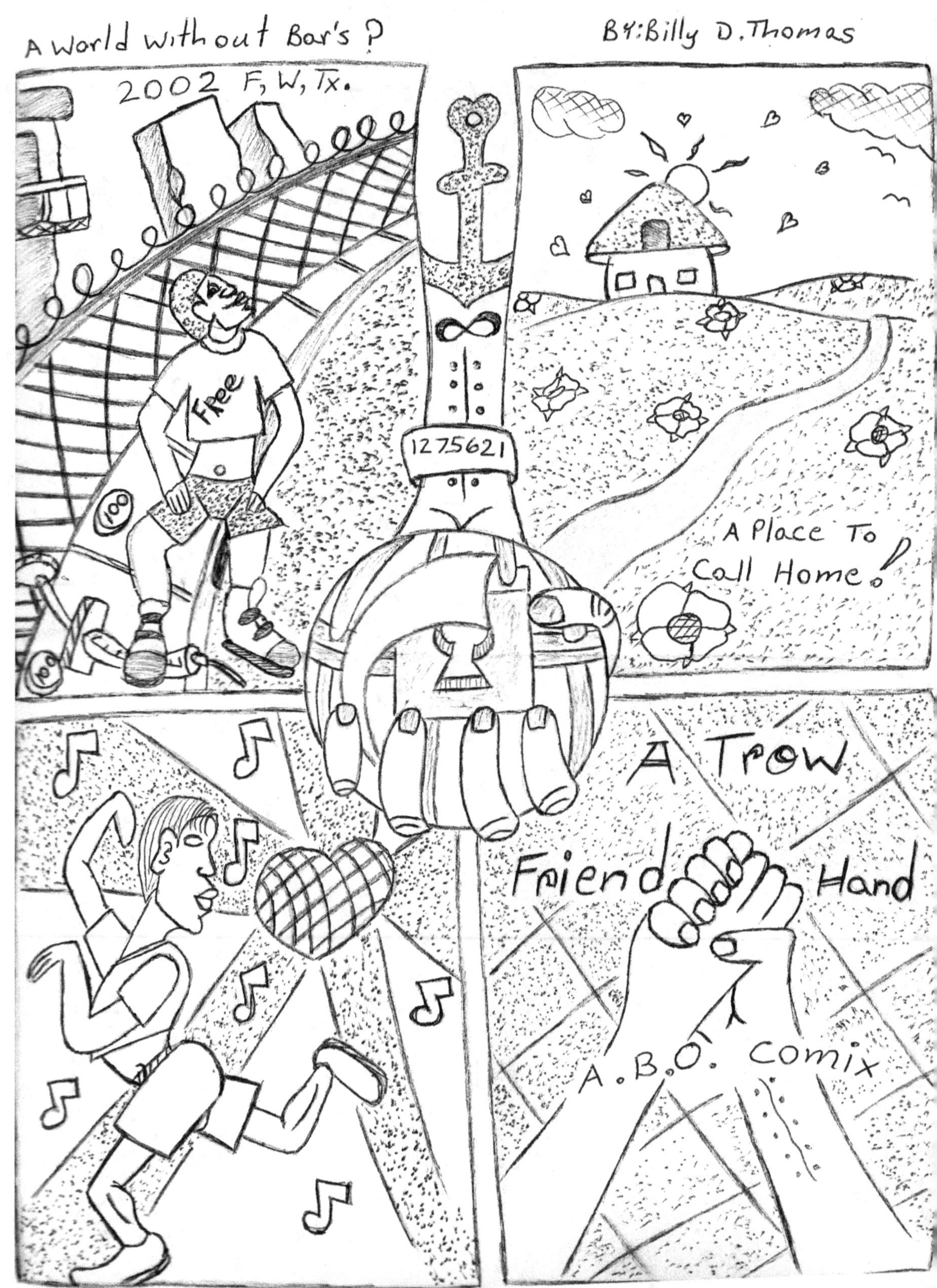

I in prison
You Came and
Show   me
The Love of
crist.......

You Being A
Trans Put Forth
crist like Frut.

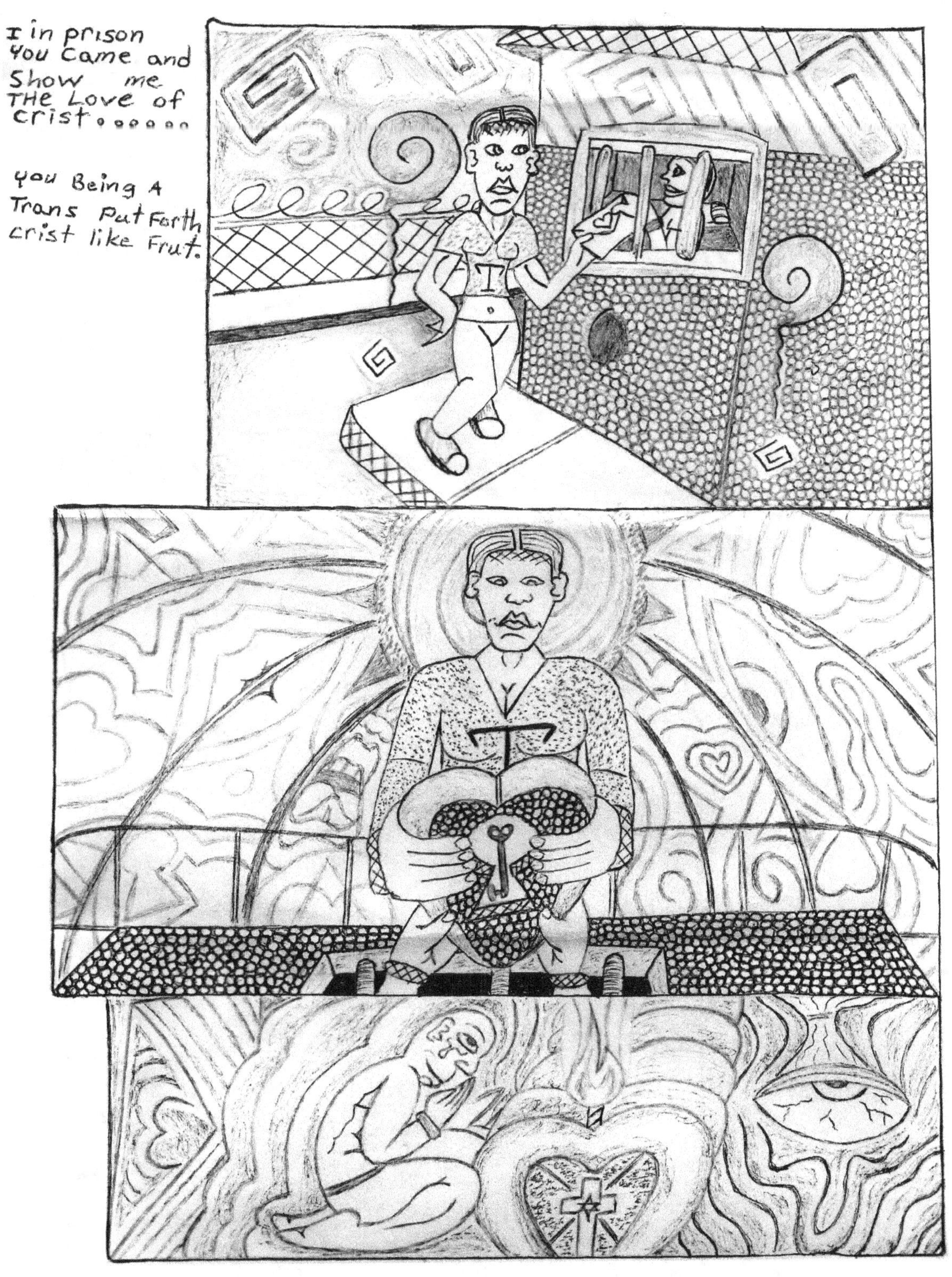

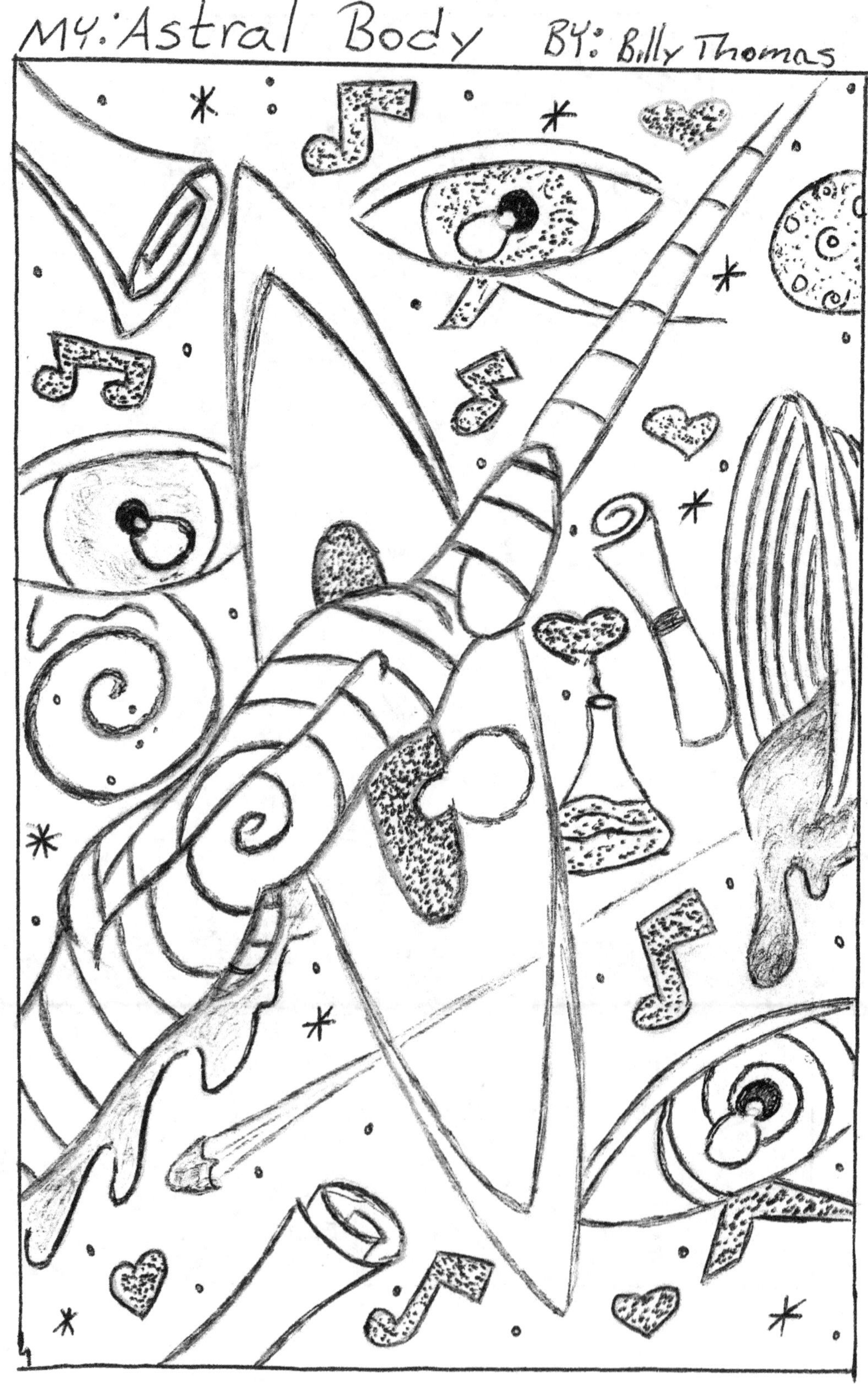
MY: Astral Body   BY: Billy Thomas

What I See With MY: BY: Billy Thomas
Therd EYE
LOVE
GTBQ
No Room For Heart
IF You Know

Faith

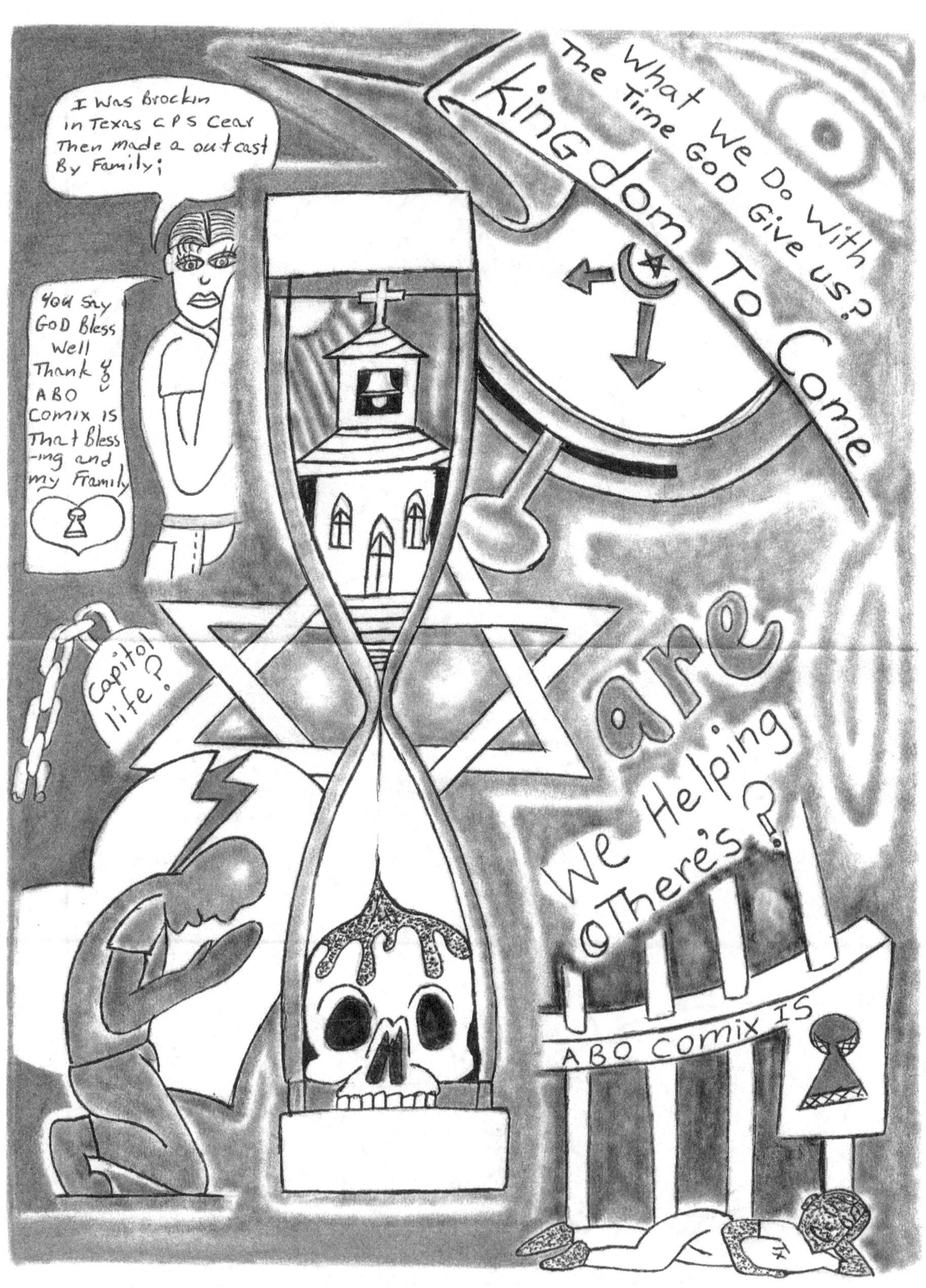

I Was Brockin in Texas C P S Cear Then made a out cast By Family;
You Say GoD Bless Well Thank y ABO Comix is That Bless -ing and my Framily
Capitol life?
What We Do With The Time GoD Give us?
King dom To Come
are
We Helping Others?
ABO Comix IS

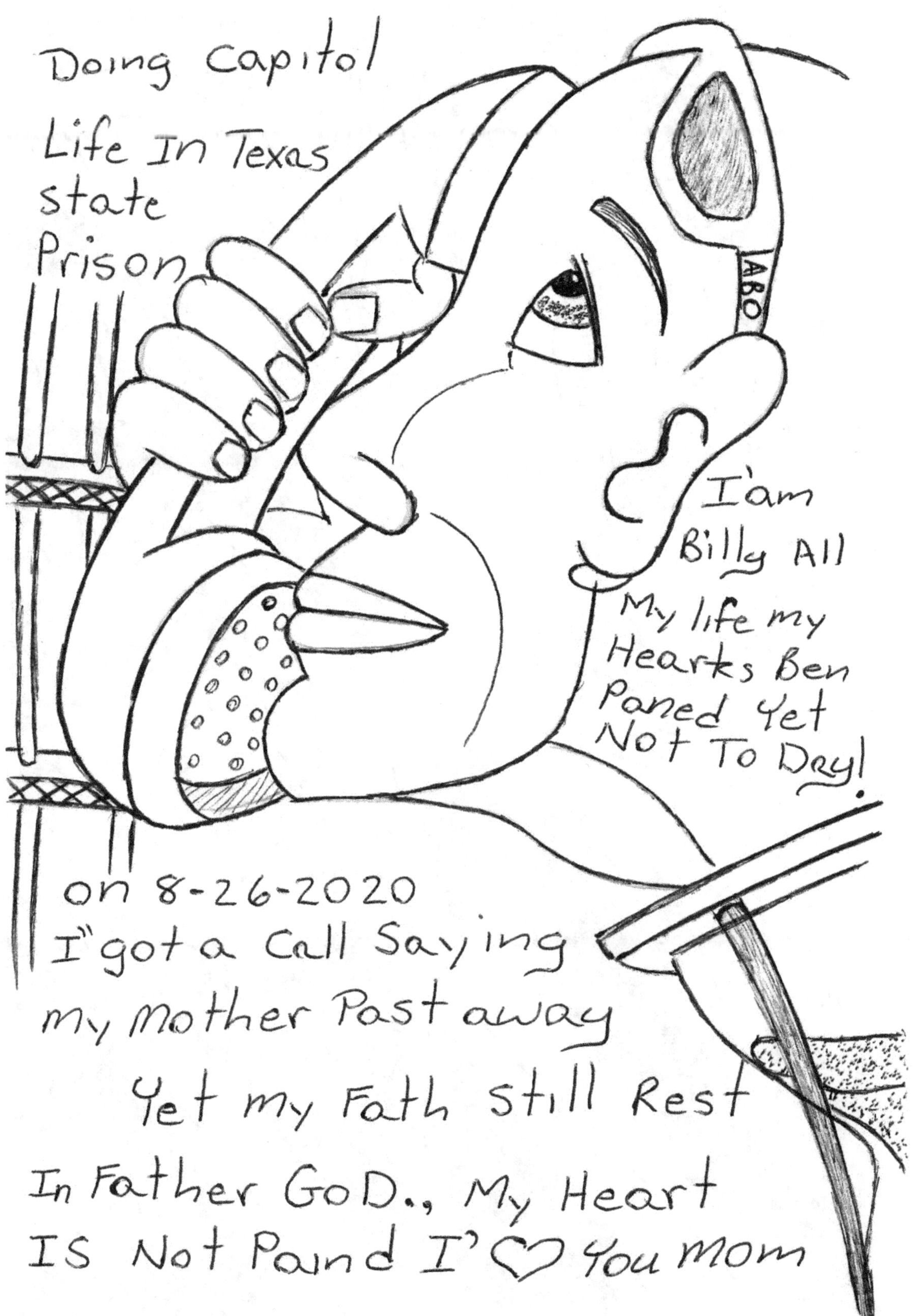

Doing Capitol
Life In Texas
state
Prison
I'am
Billy All
My life my
Hearks Ben
Paned Yet
Not To Dryl
on 8-26-2020
I"got a call Saying
my mother Past away
Yet my Fath still Rest
In Father GoD., My Heart
IS Not Paind I'♡ You mom
ABO

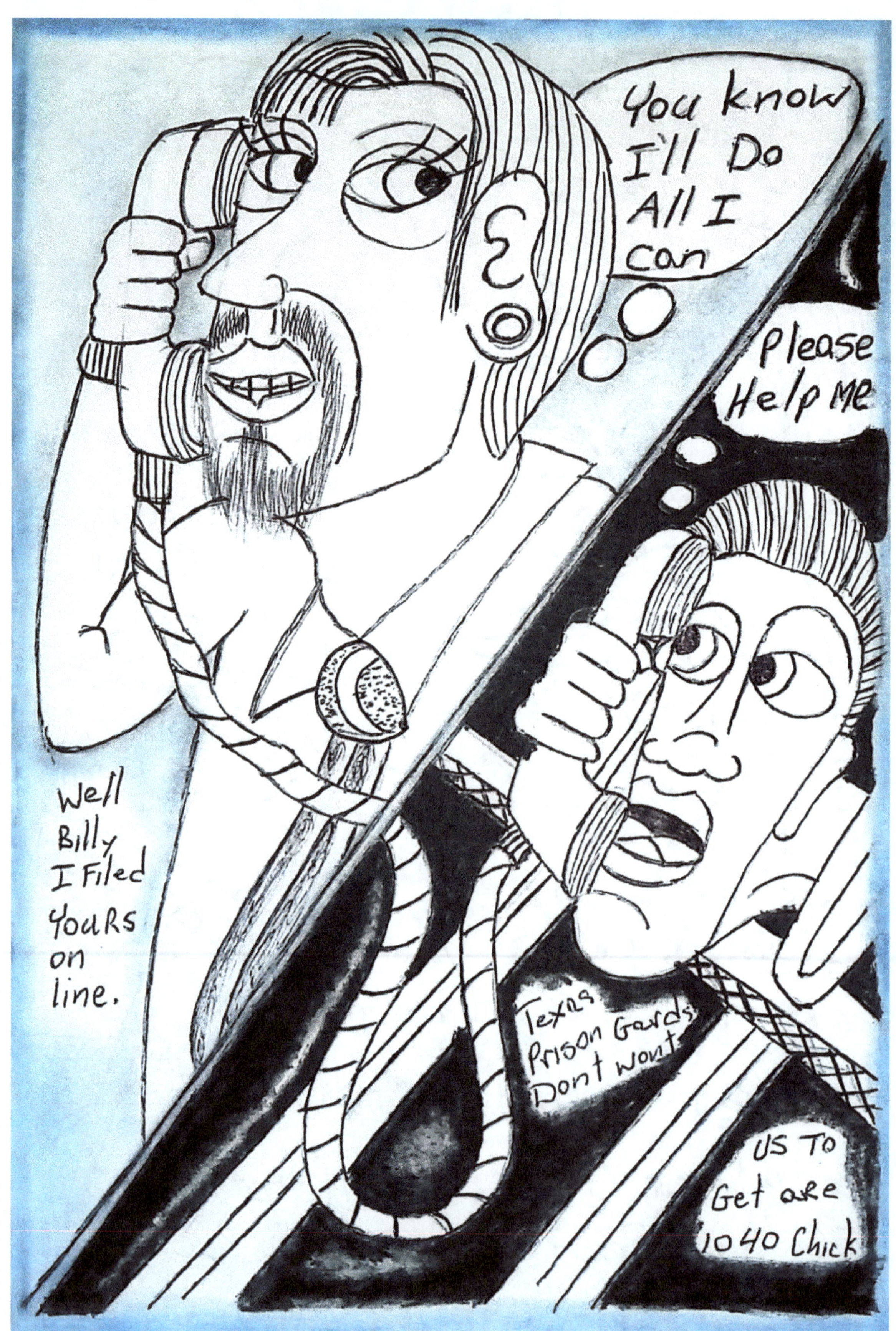
You know I'll Do All I Can
Please Help Me
Well Billy I Filed YouRs on line.
Texas Prison GaRds Dont wont
US TO Get aRe 1040 Chick

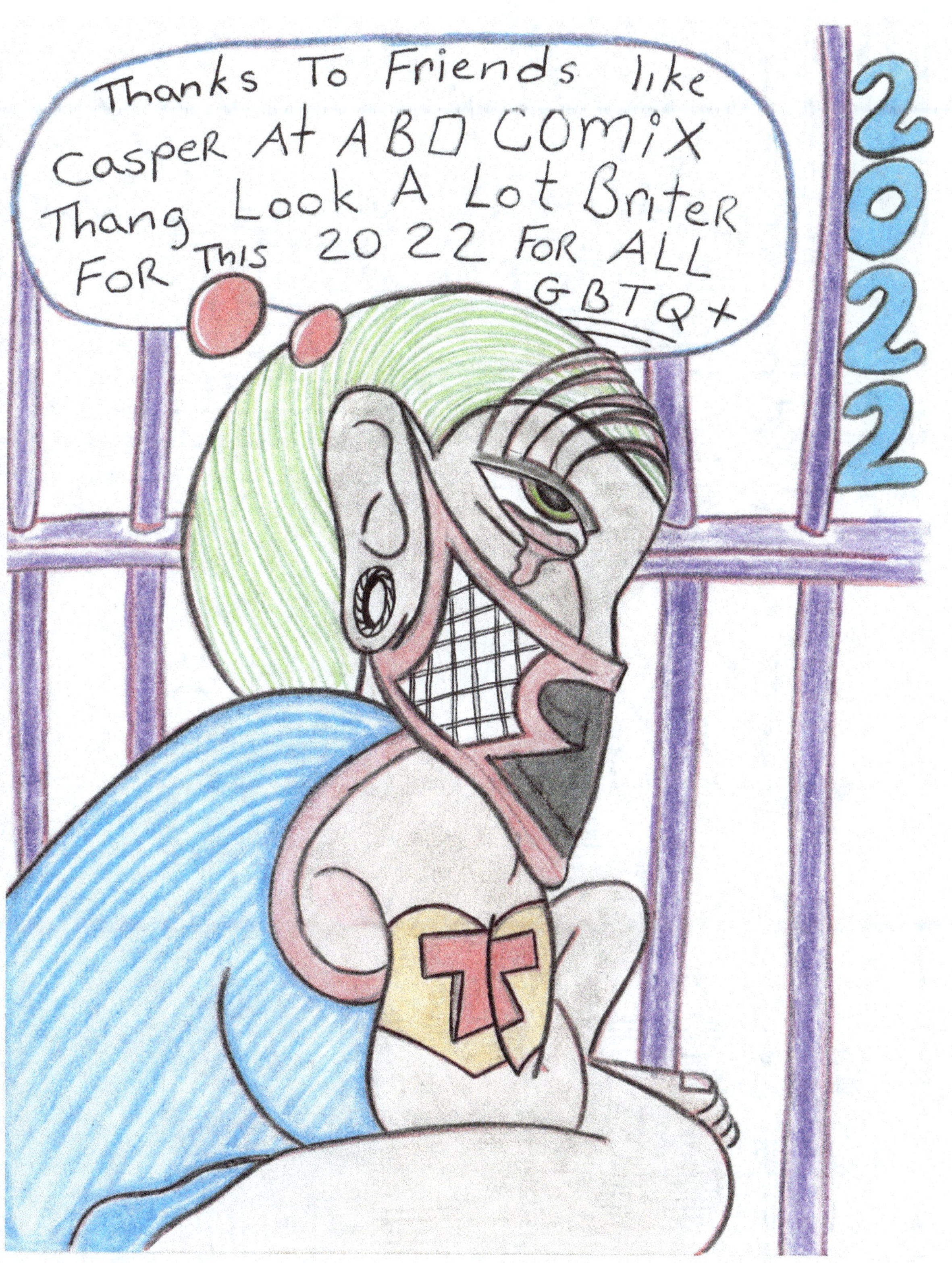
Thanks To Friends like
Casper At ABO Comix
Thang Look A Lot Briter
For This 2022 For ALL
GBTQ+
2022

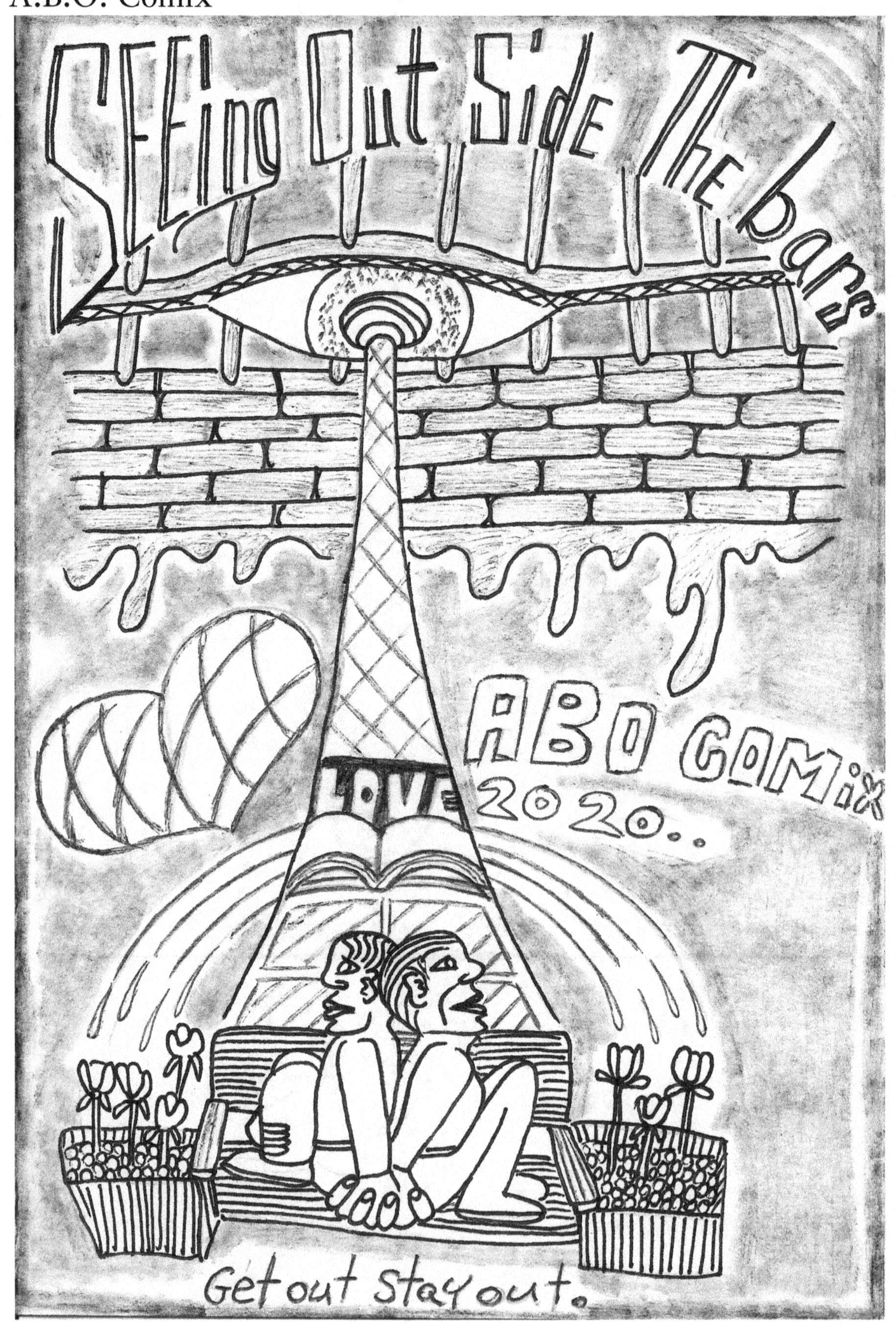

SEEing Out Side The bars
LOVE
ABO Comix
2020..
Get out stay out.

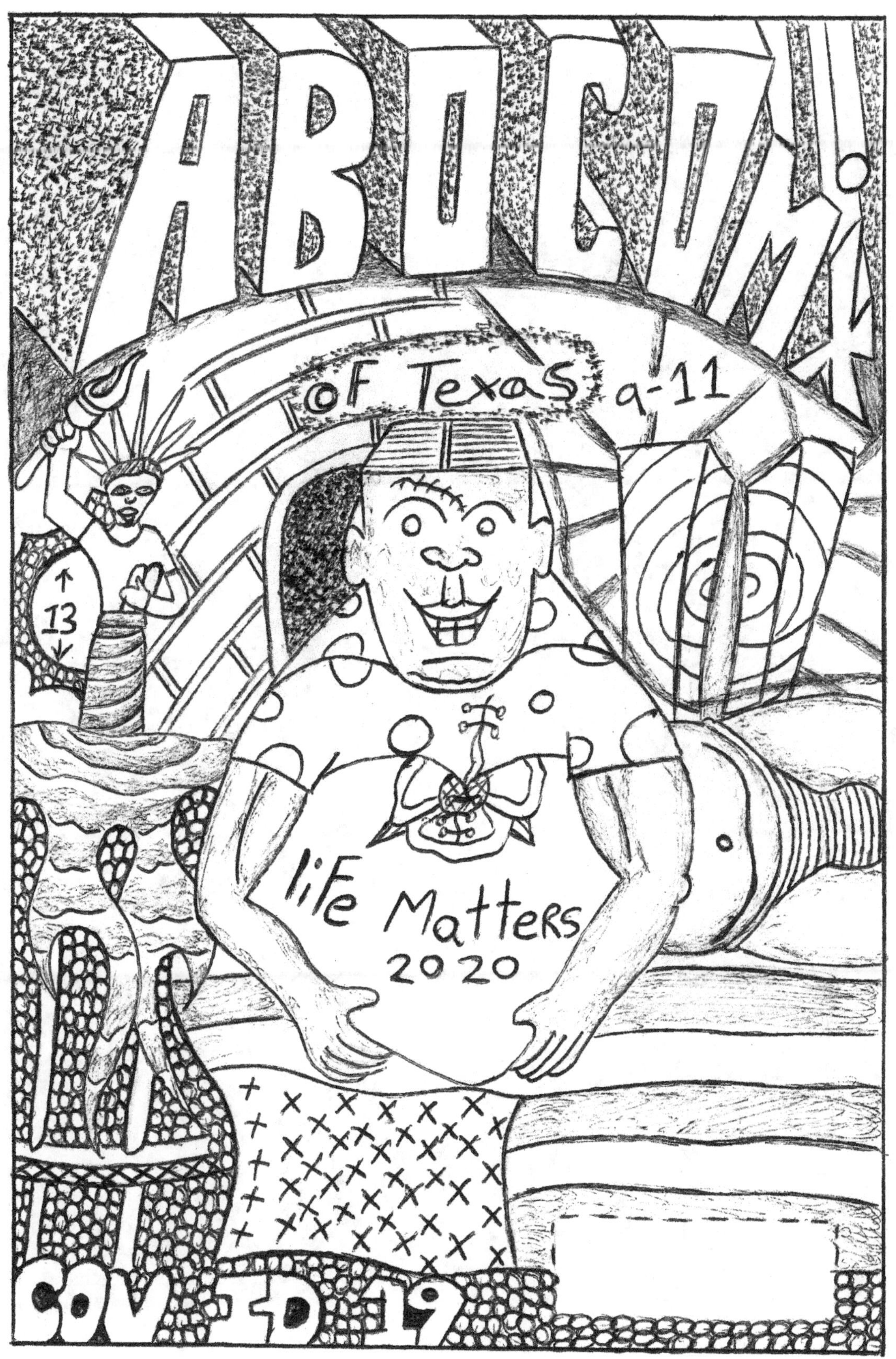
ABO COMX
oF Texas q-11
13
LiFe Matters
2020
COVID 19

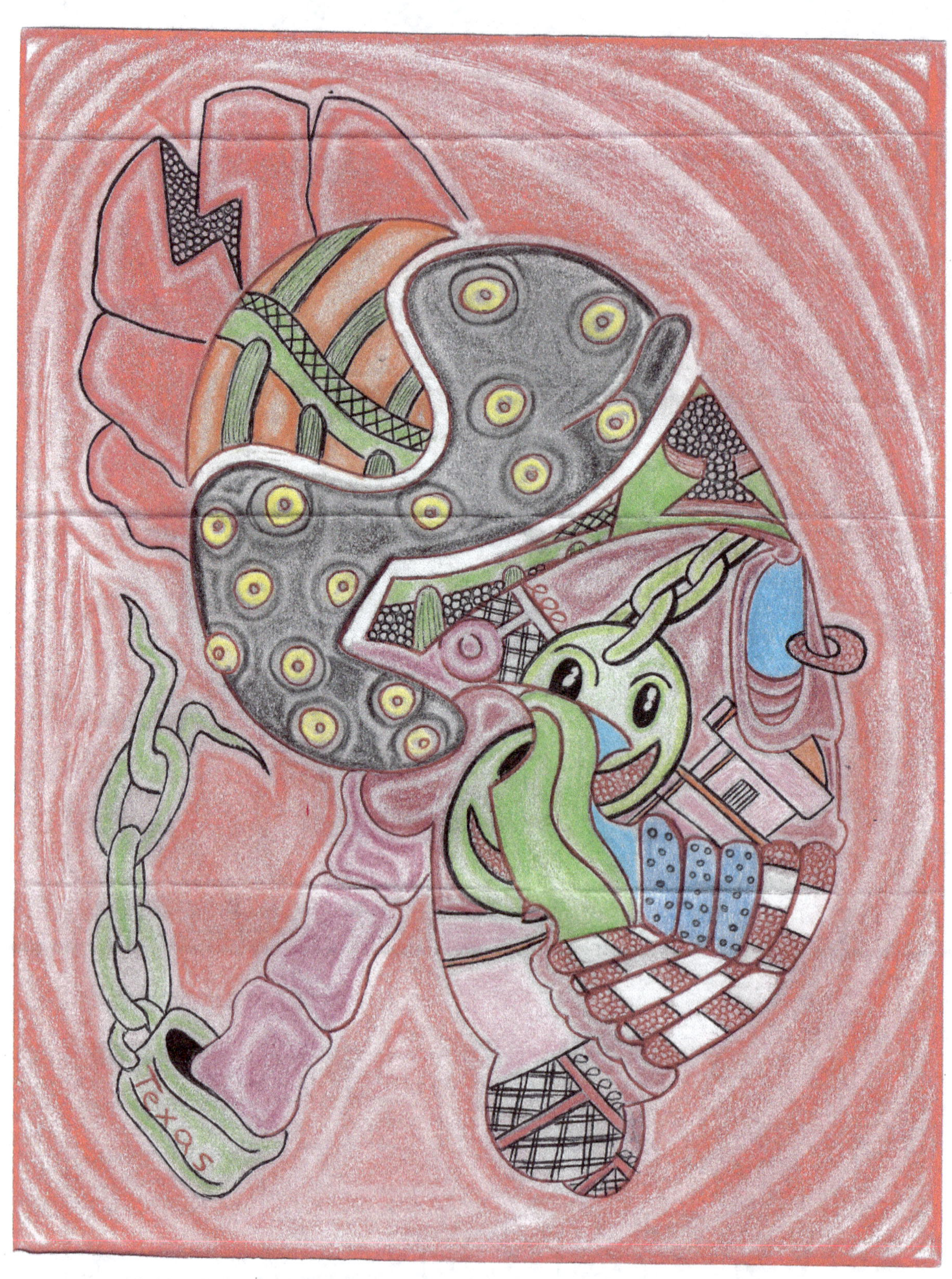
Texas

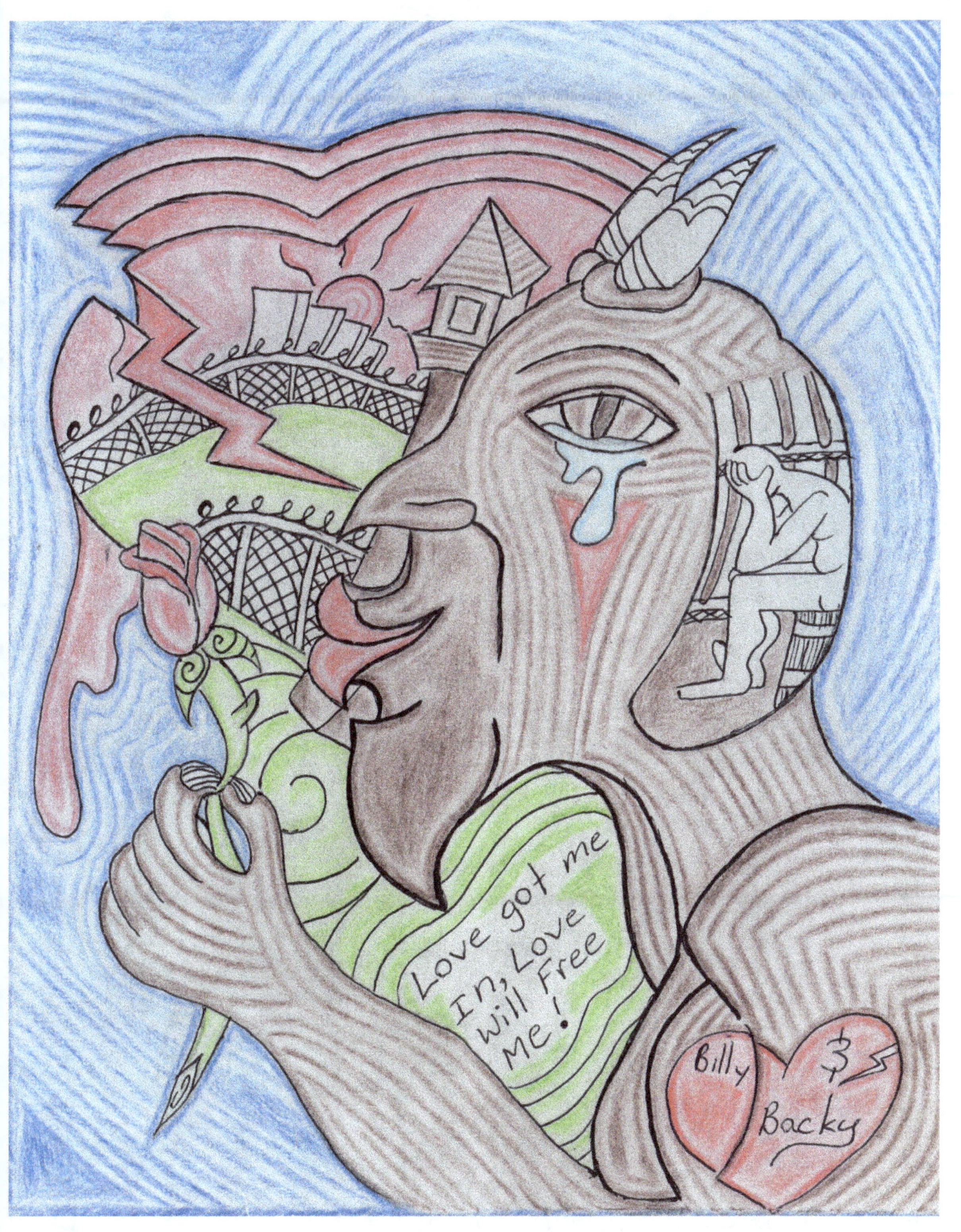

Love got me In, Love will Free Me!
Billy Backy

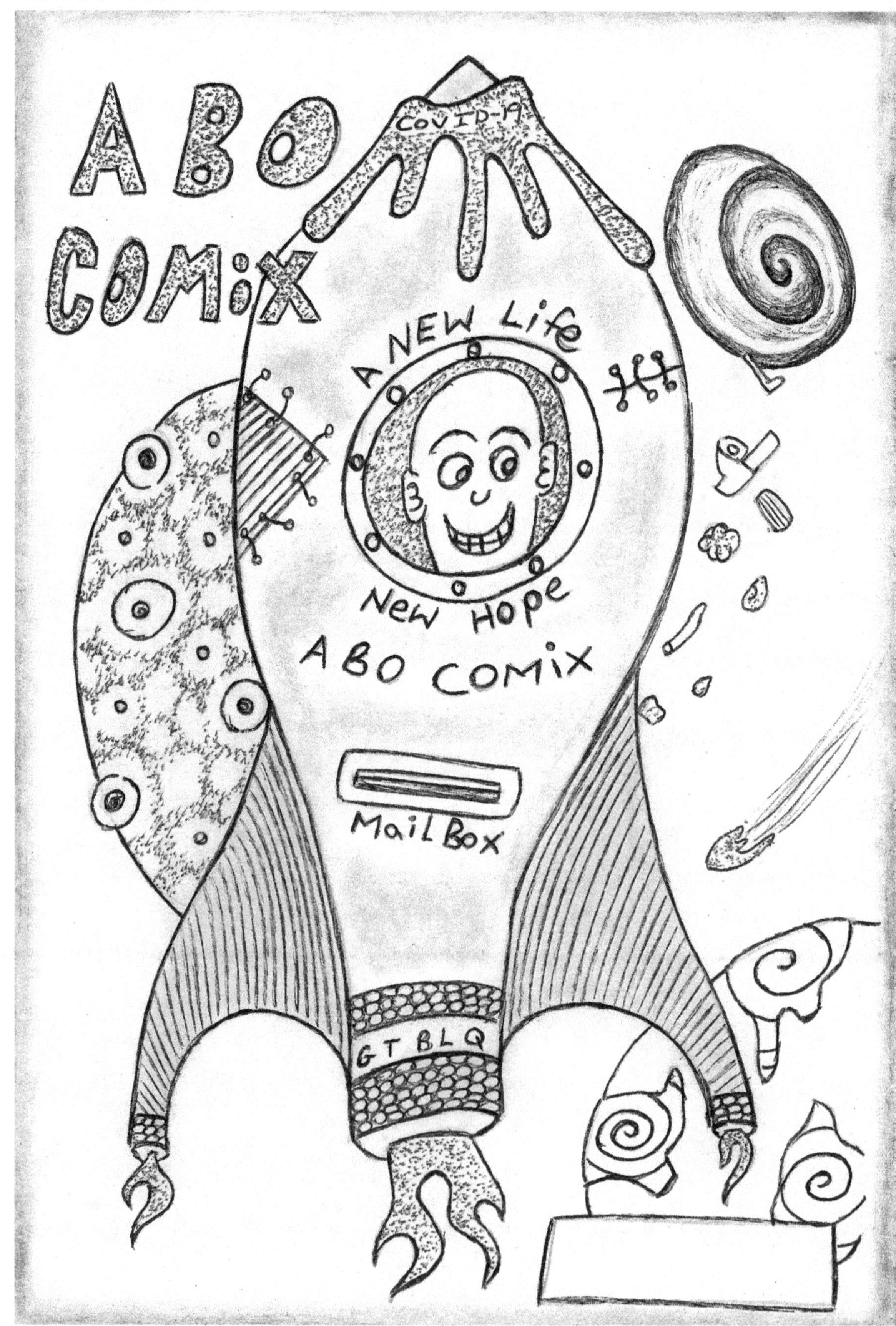
A B O
COMIX
COVID-19
A NEW LiFe
New HOPe
A BO COMiX
MailBox
GT BLQ

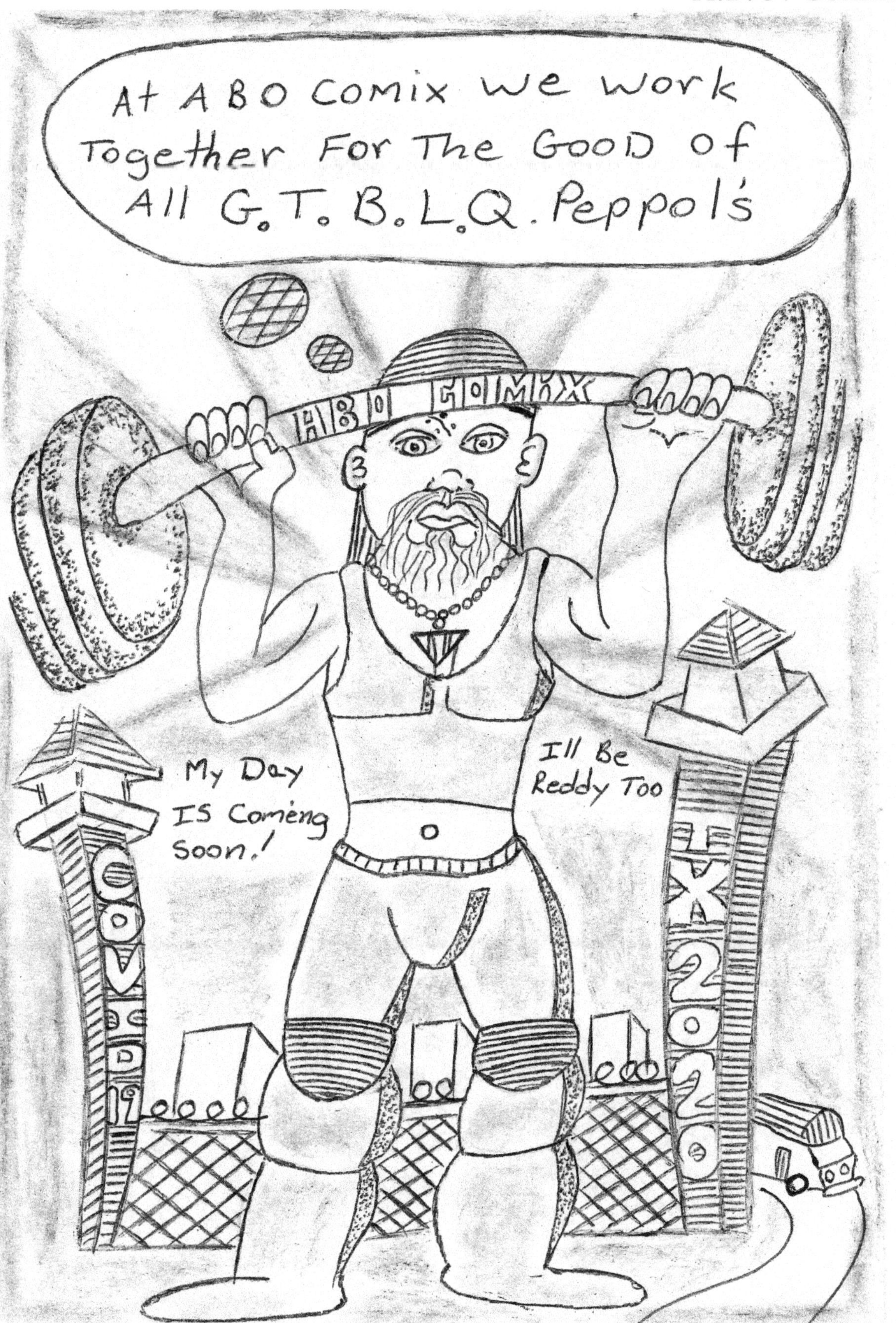

At ABO Comix we work Together For The Good of All G.T.B.L.Q. Peppol's
ABO COMIX
My Day IS Coming Soon!
I'll Be Reddy Too
COVID 19
FX 2020

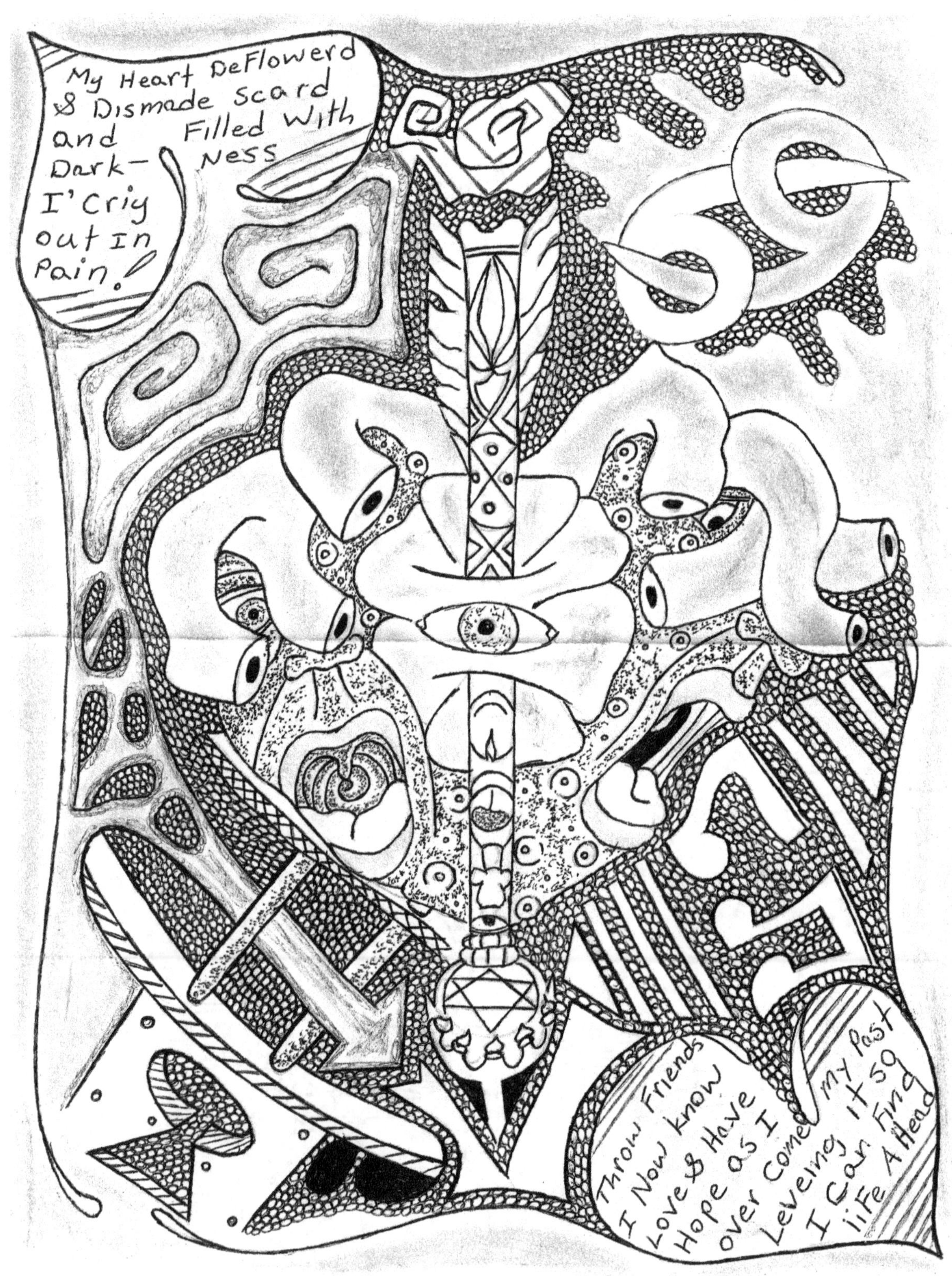
My Heart DeFlowerd
& Dismade Scard
and   Filled With
Dark—   Ness
I' Criy
out In
Pain!
Throu Friends
I Now know
Love & Have
Hope as I
over Come
Leveing it so
my Past
I Can Fing
liFe Afterd

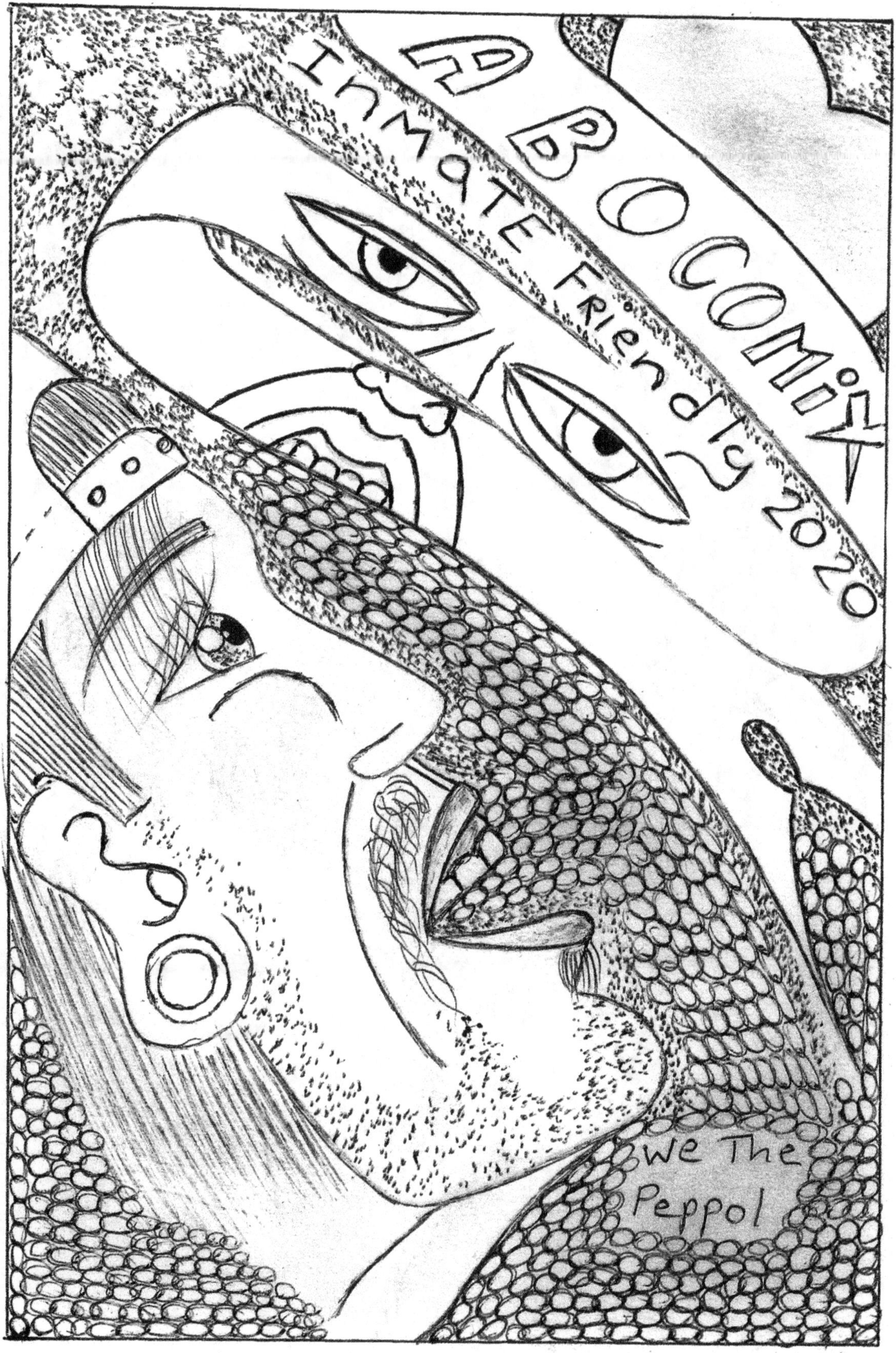
A B O Comix
Inmate Friendly 2020
We The Peppol

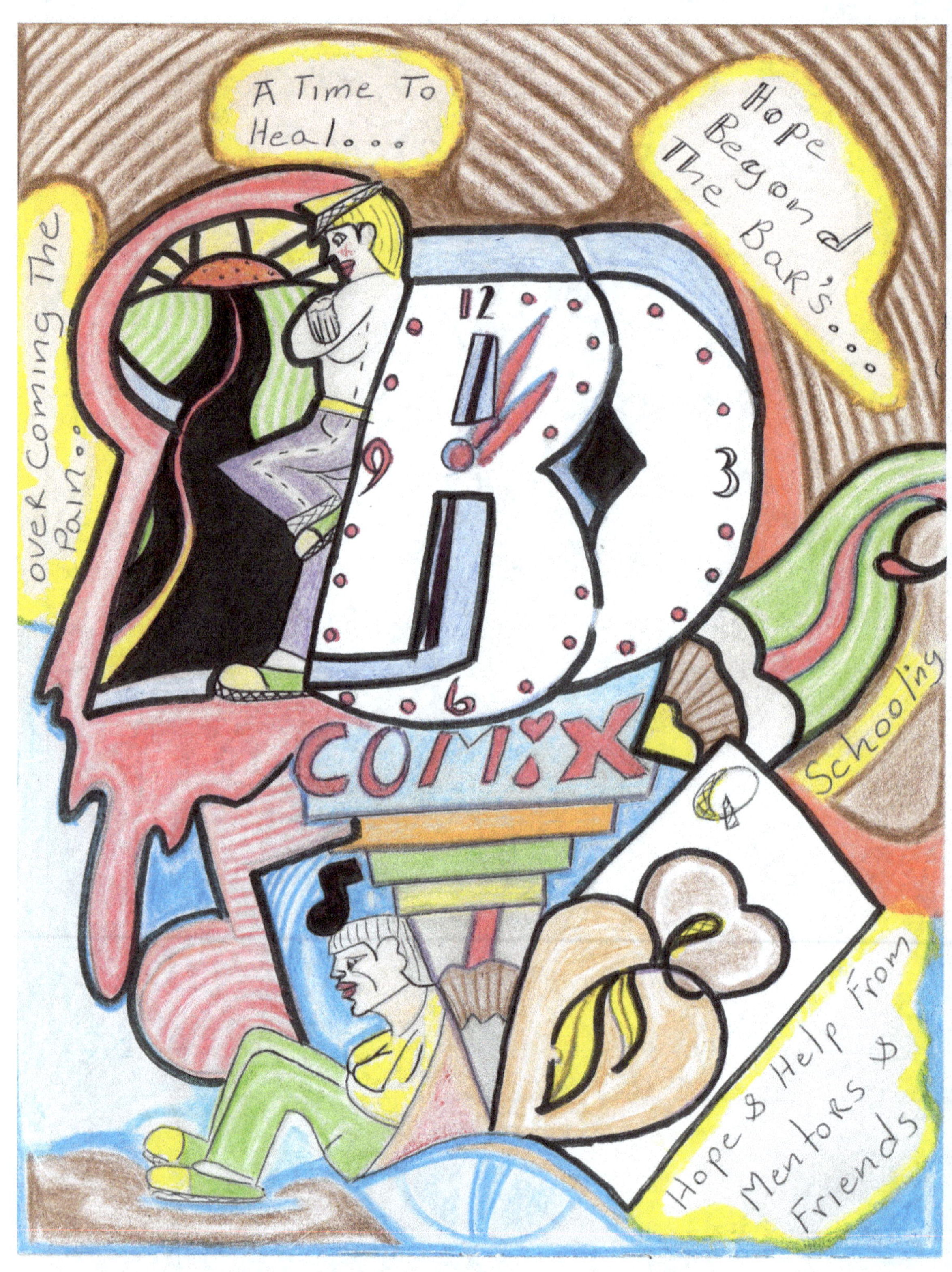
A Time To Heal...
Hope Beyond The Bar's...
over Coming The Pain...
Schooling
COMiX
Hope & Help From Mentors & Friends

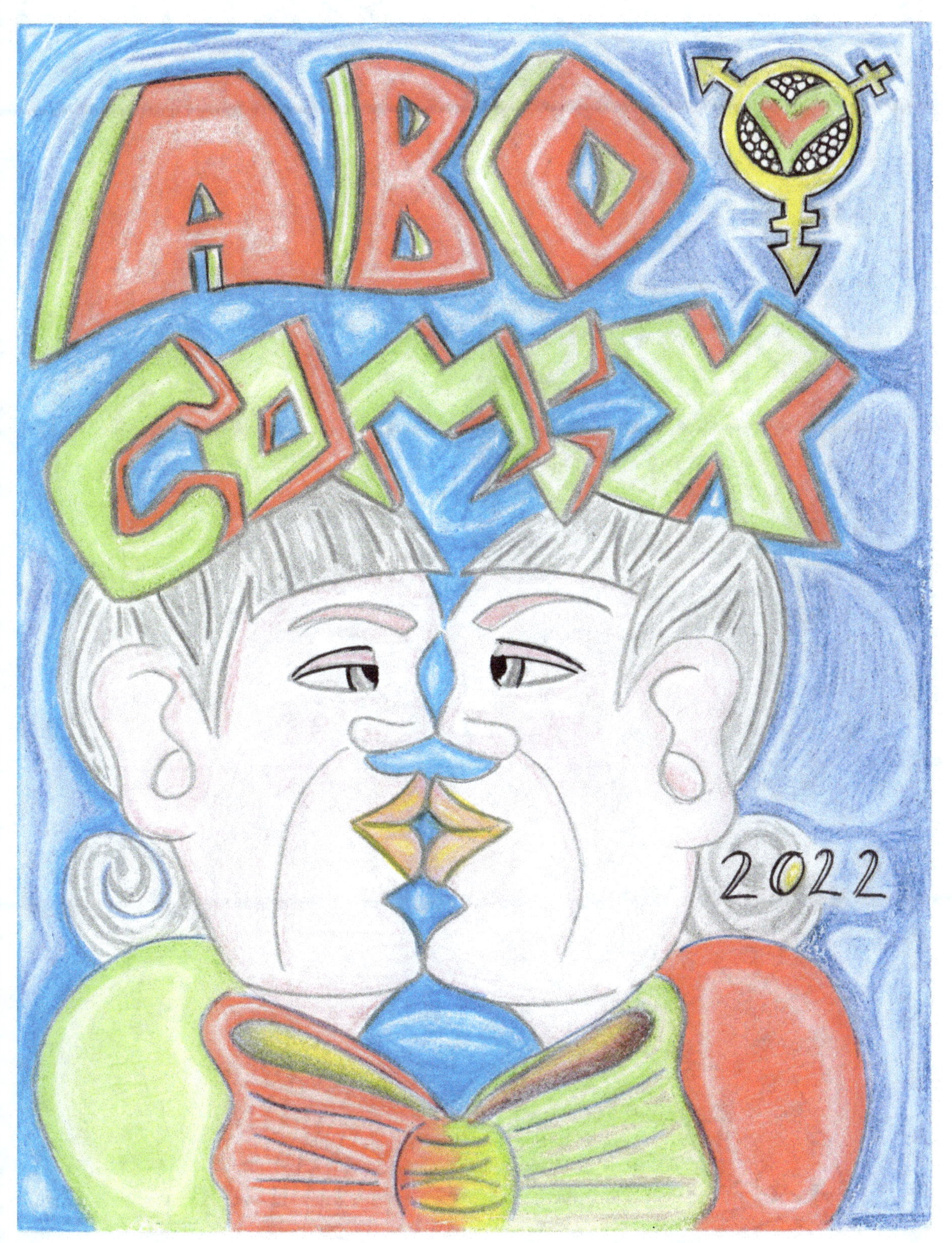

ABO
COMIX
2022

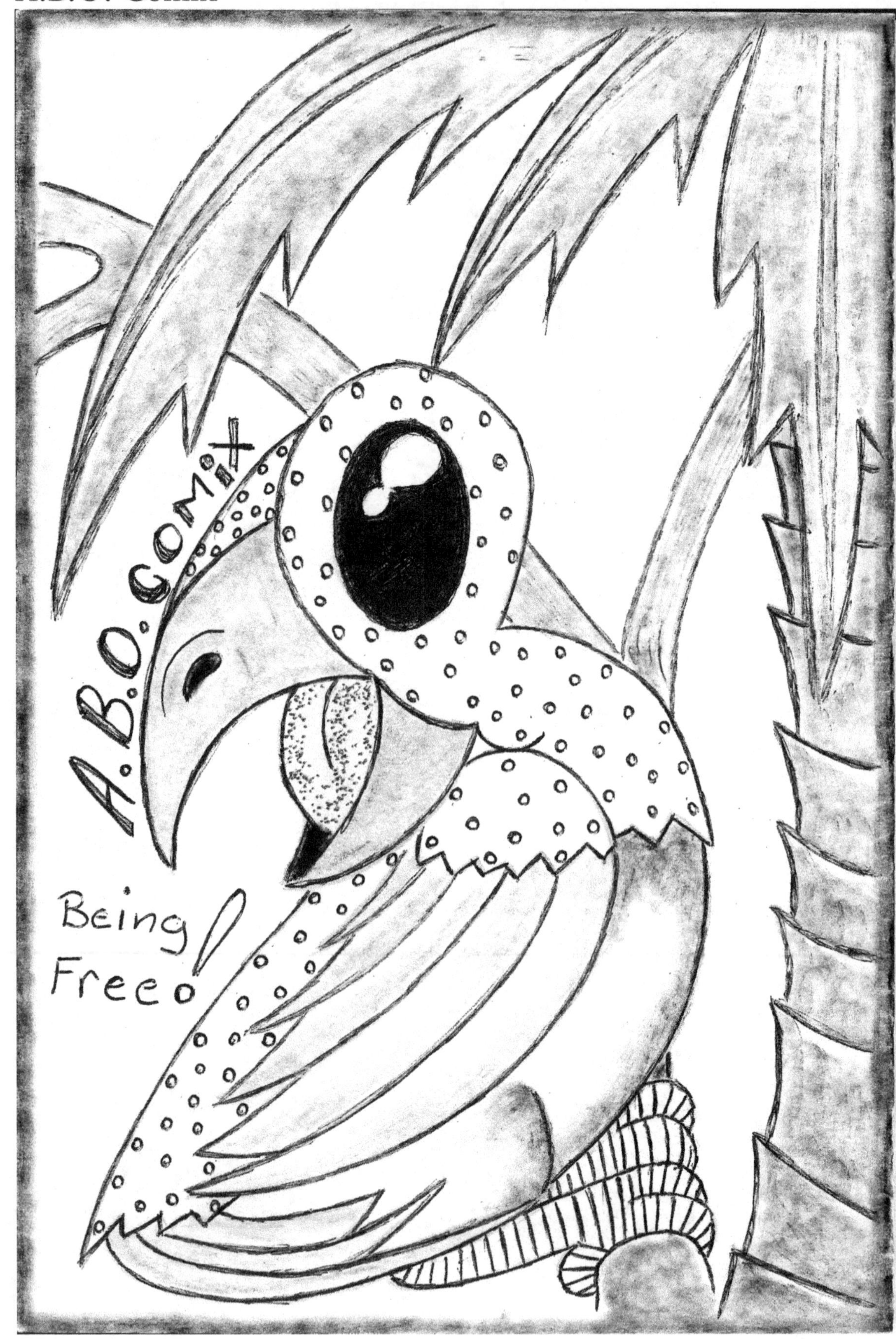
A.B.O. Comix
Being
Free!

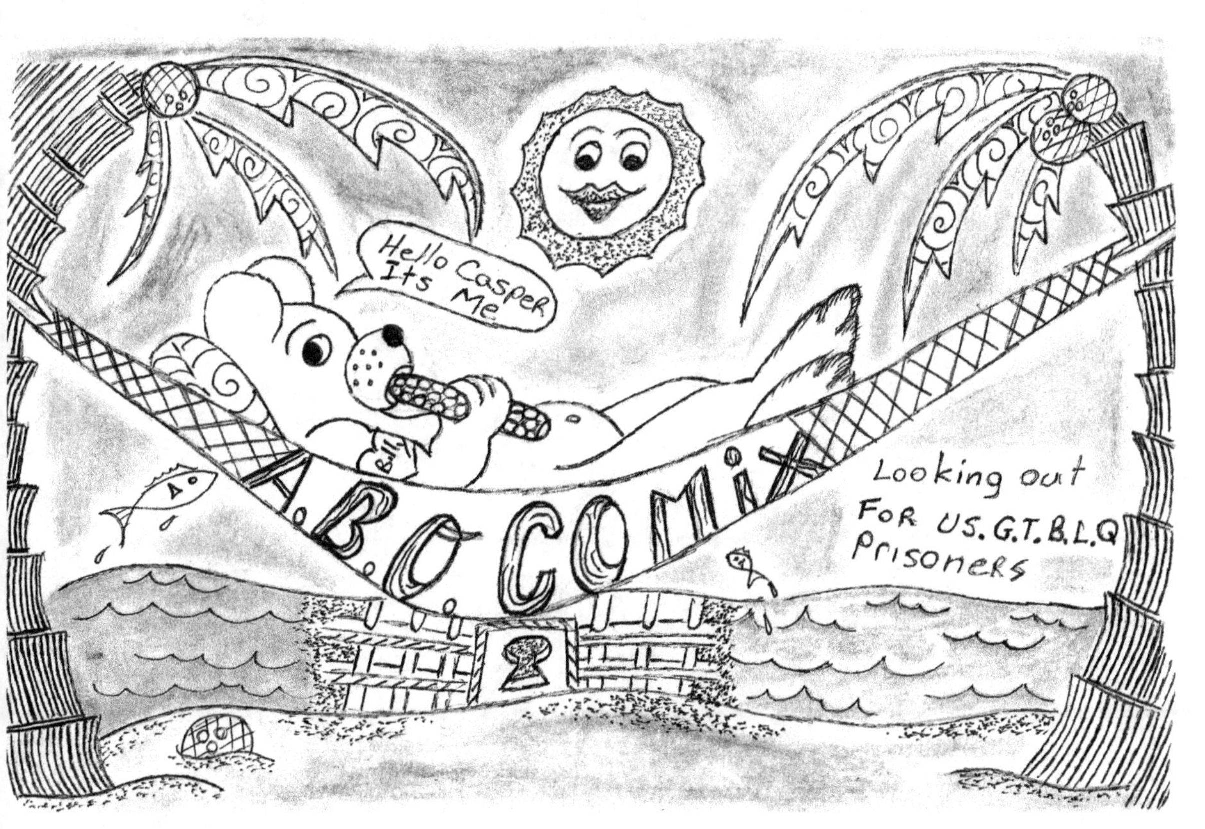

Hello Casper Its Me
A.B.O COMIX
Looking out FoR US.G.T.B.L.Q Prisoners
Billy

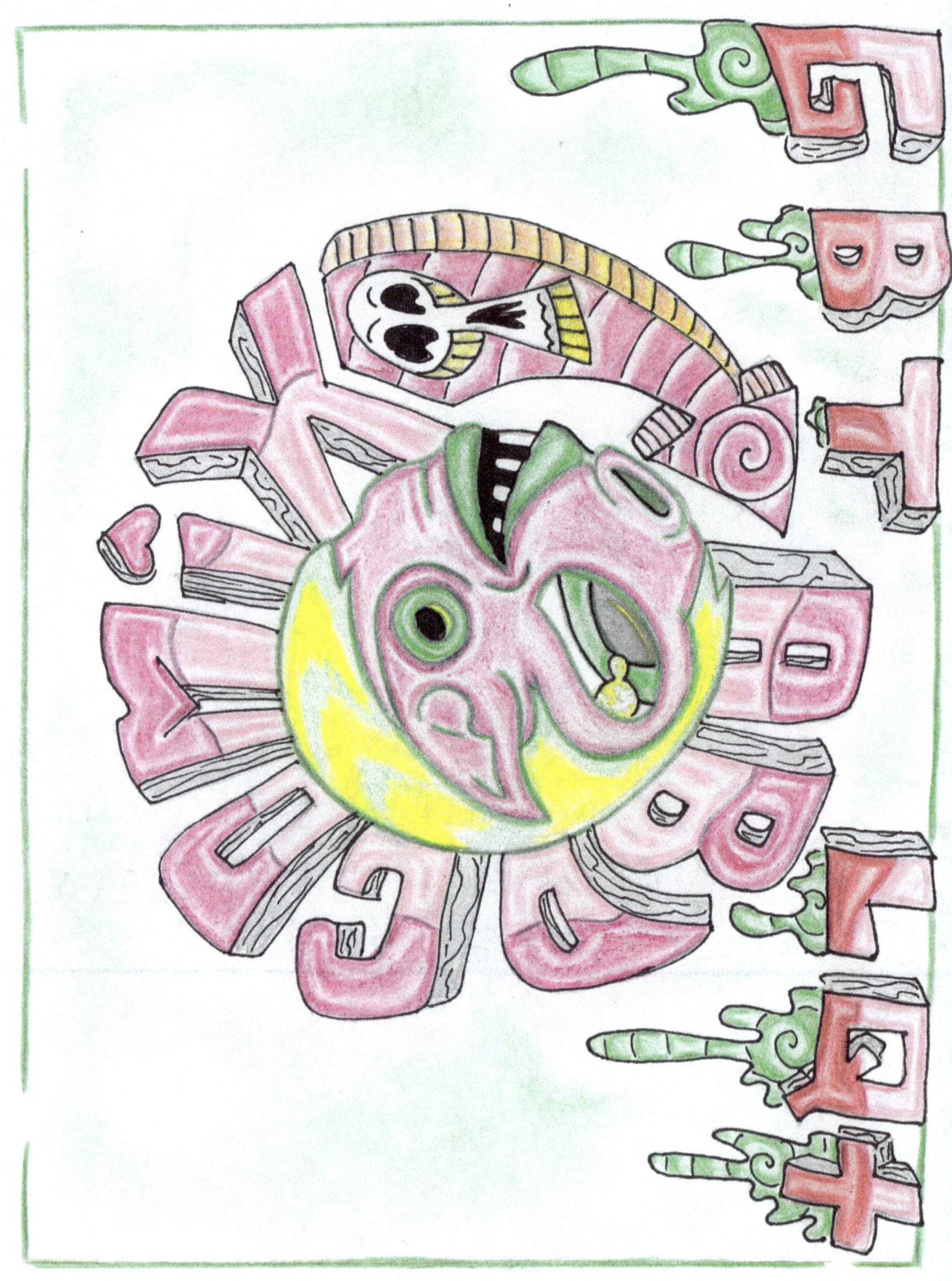

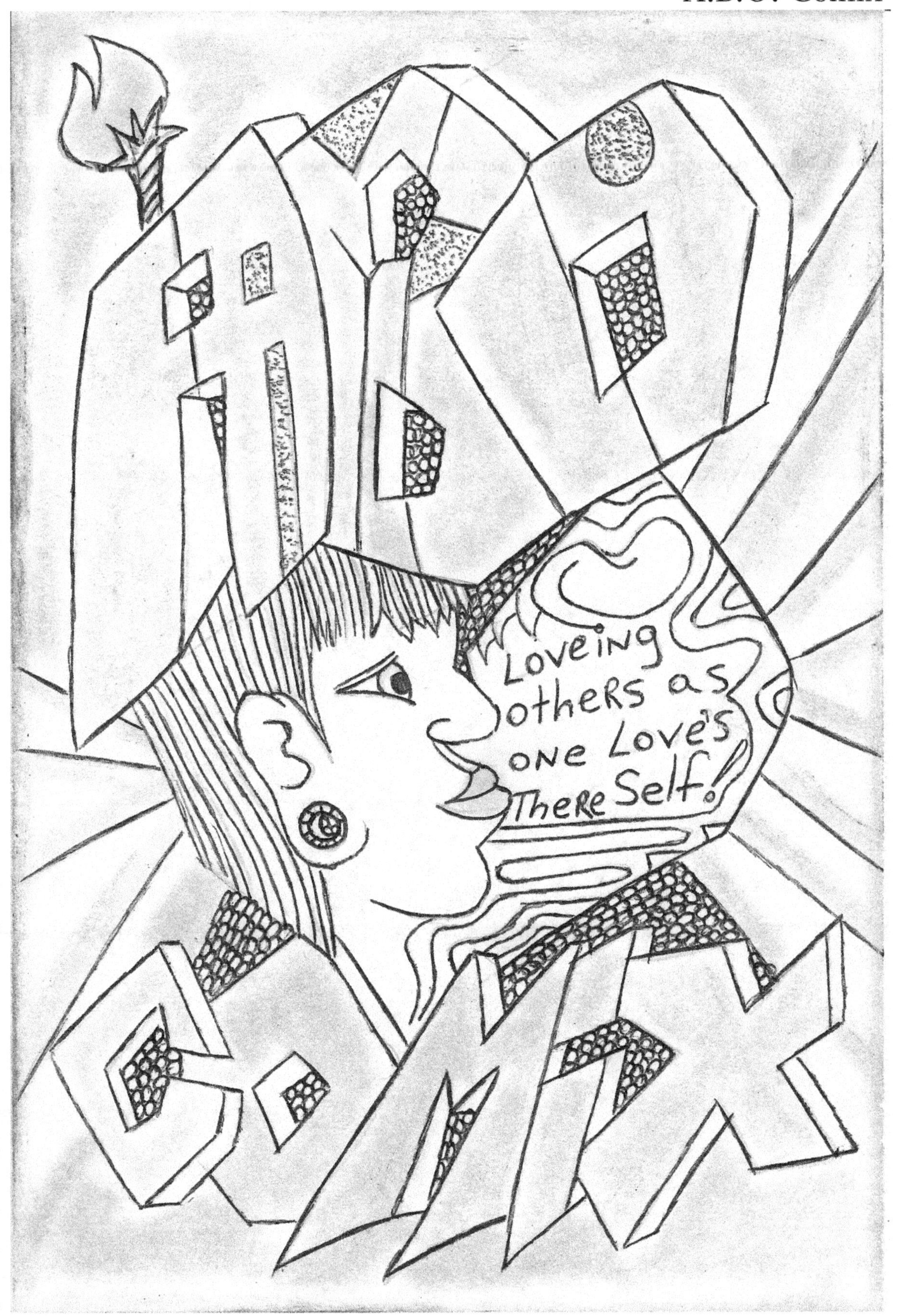
Loveing others as one Love's There Self!

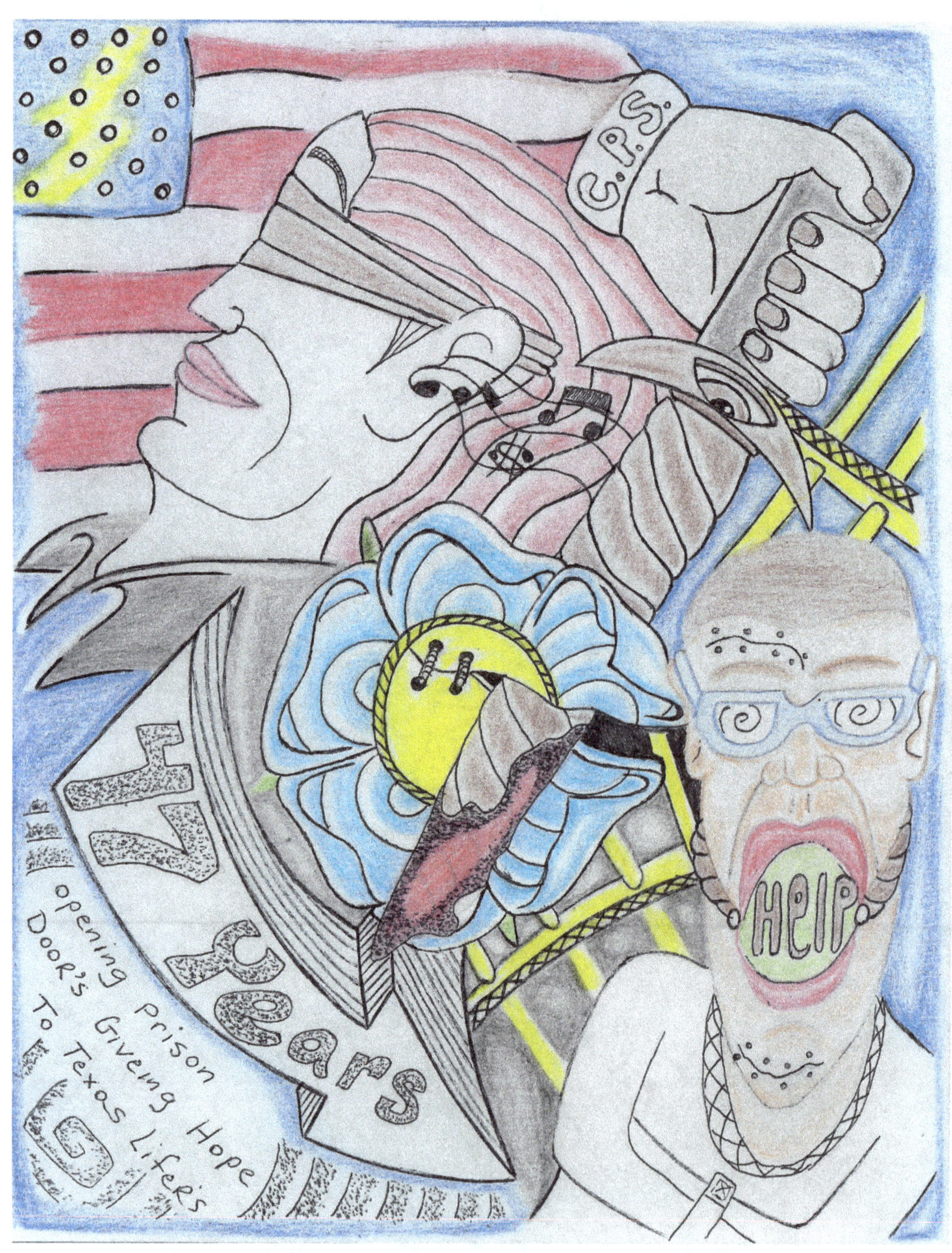

C.P.S.
HELP
17 Years
Opening Prison Door's Giveing Hope To Texas Lifer's

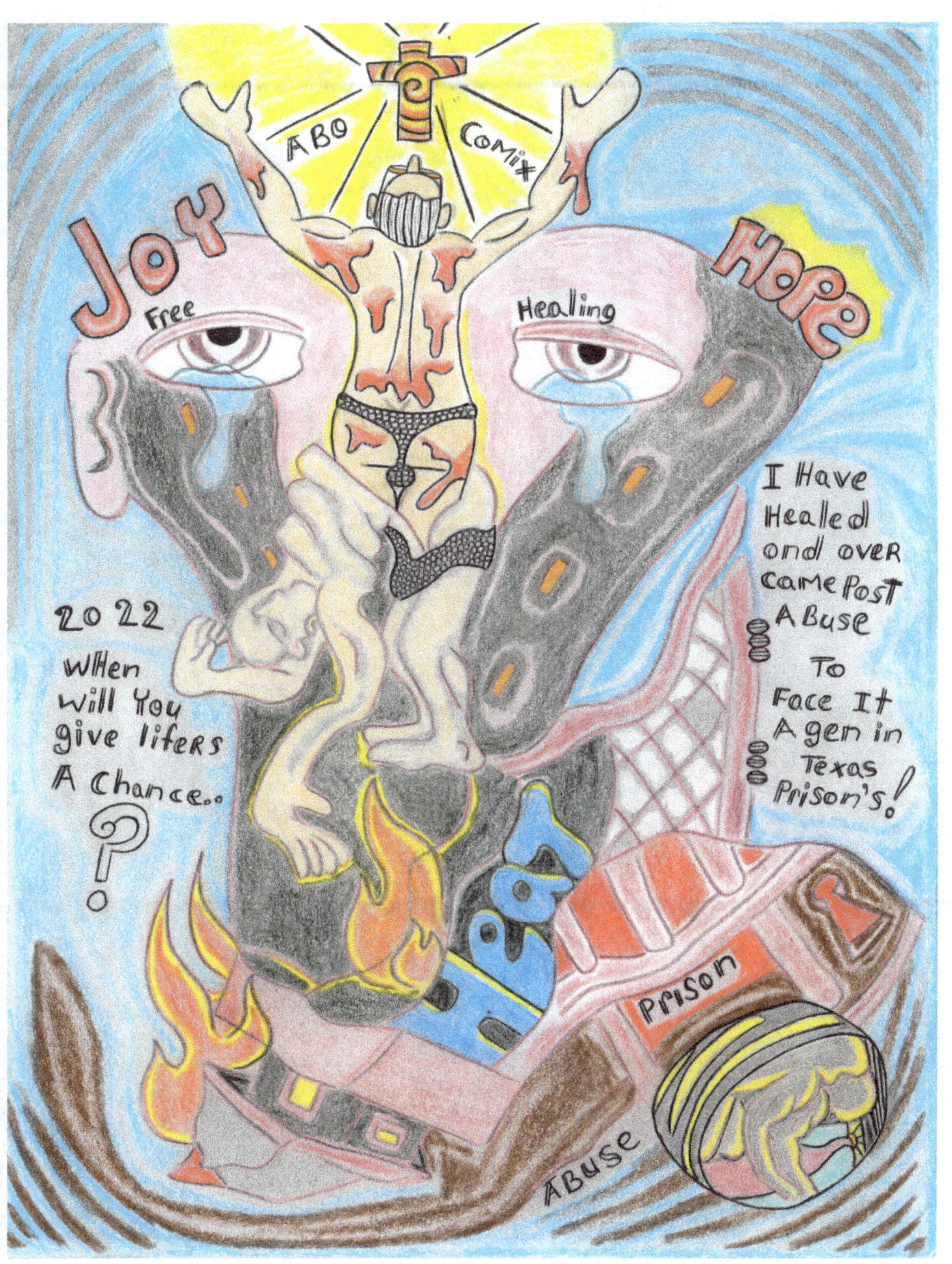

ABO Comix
JOY
Free
Healing
HOPE
I Have
Healed
and over
came Post
Abuse
To
Face It
Agen in
Texas
Prison's!
2022
WHen
will You
give lifeRs
A chance..
?
Heal
Prison
Abuse

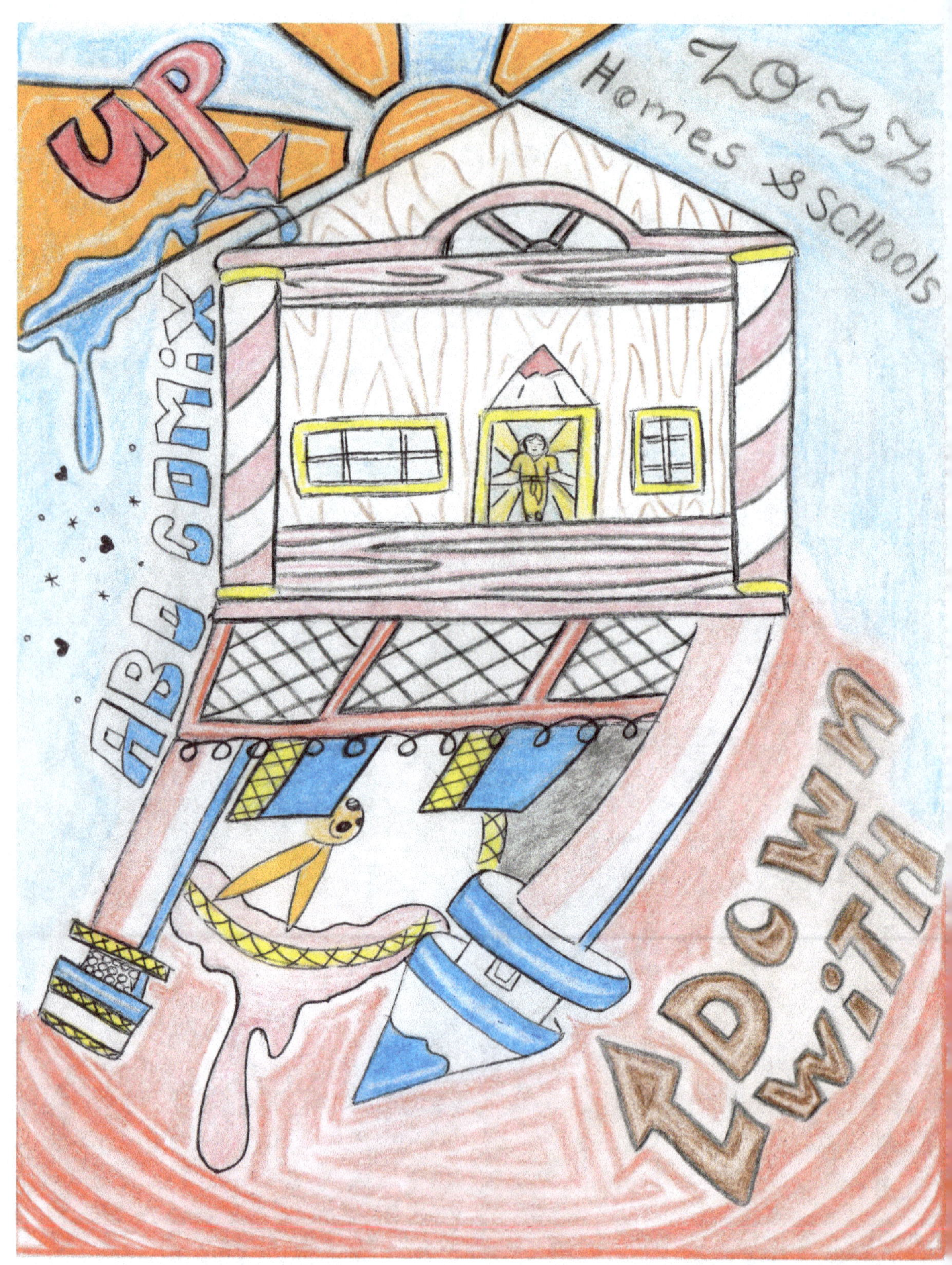
UP
2022
Homes & Schools
ABO COMIX
A.B.O COMIX
DOWN WITH

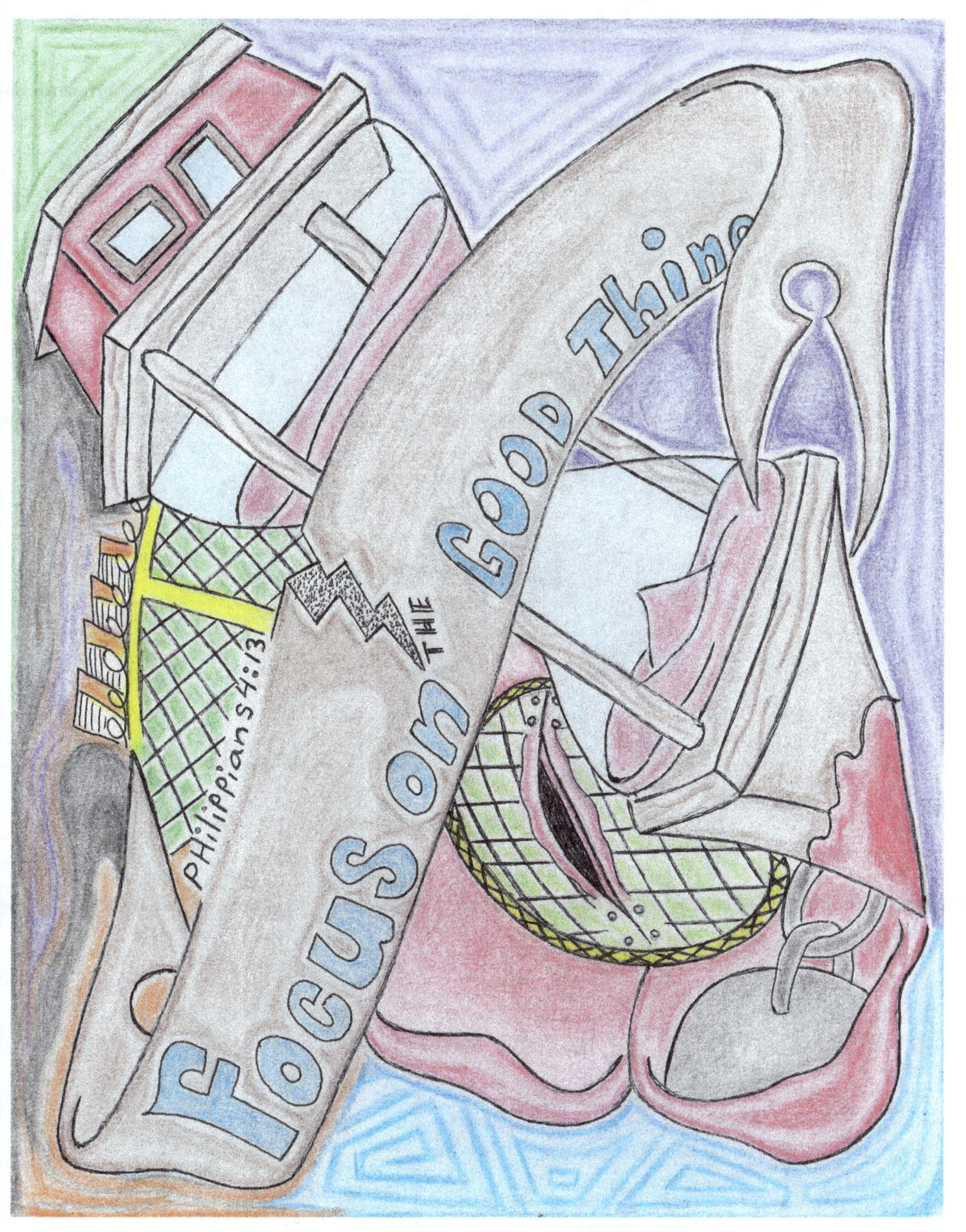
On
Focus on the Good Thing
Philippians 4:13

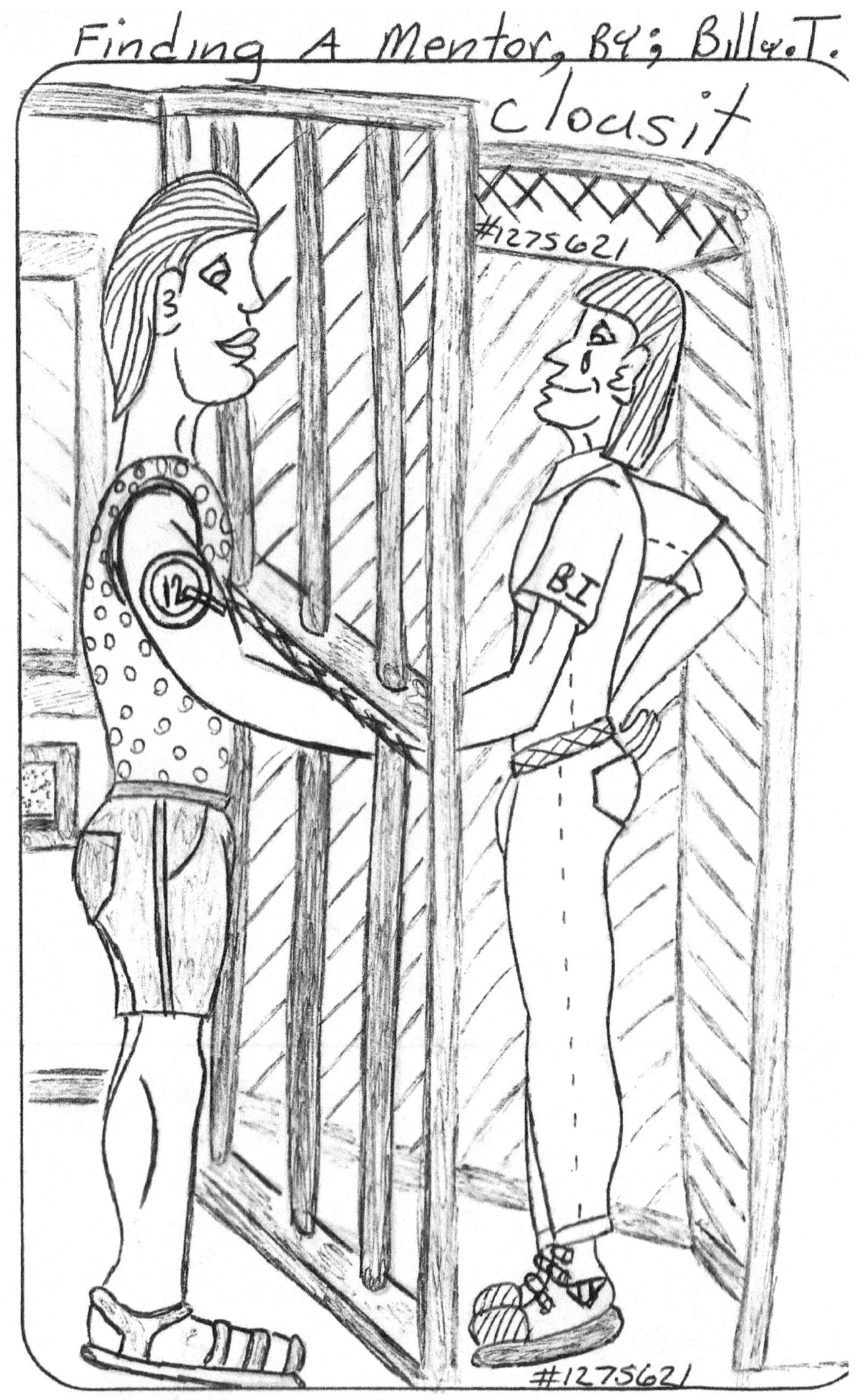
Finding A Mentor, BY; Billy.T.
clousit
#1275621
12
BI
#1275621

Friends Hart's   Billy Thomas

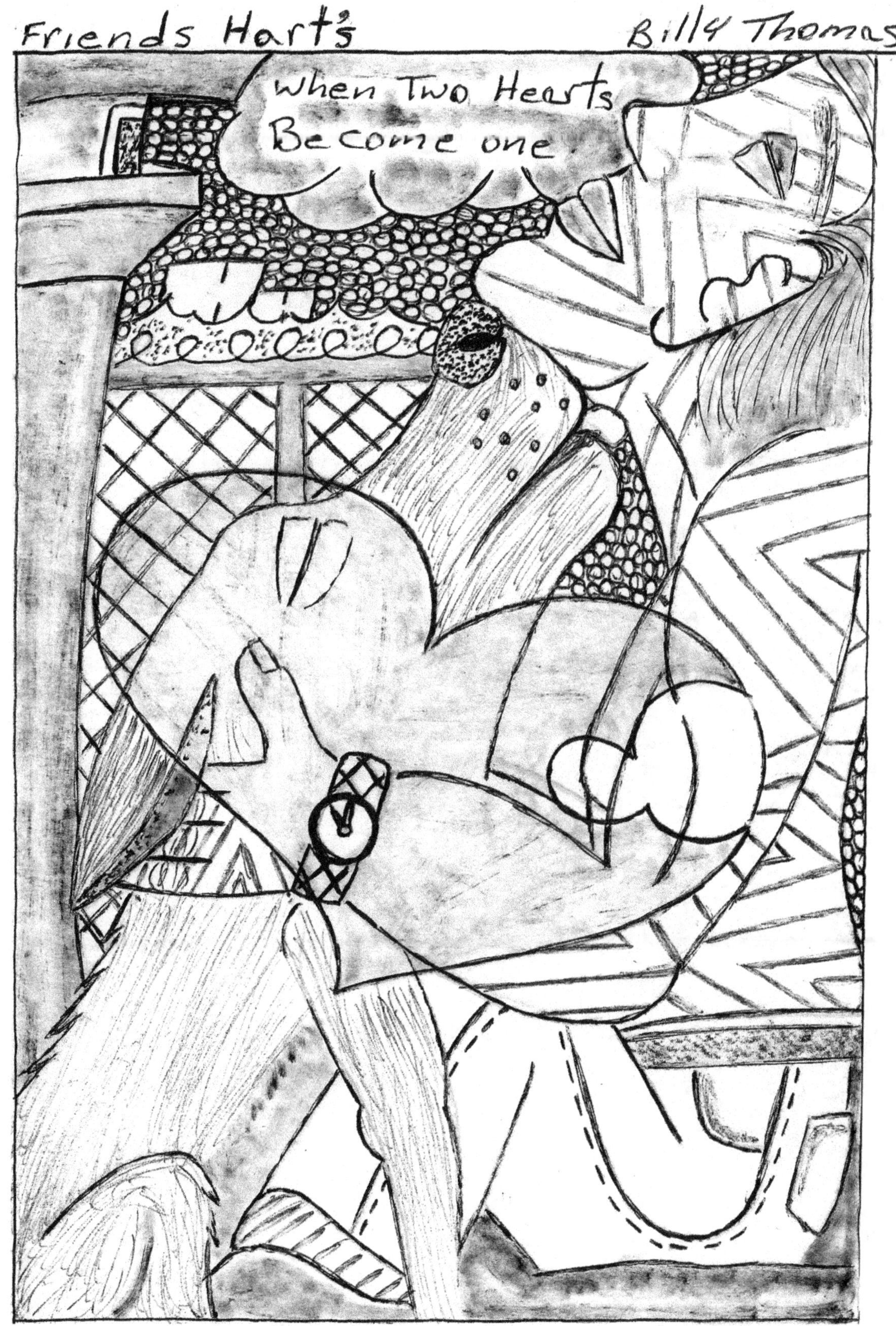

Finding The Time To Help OThers!

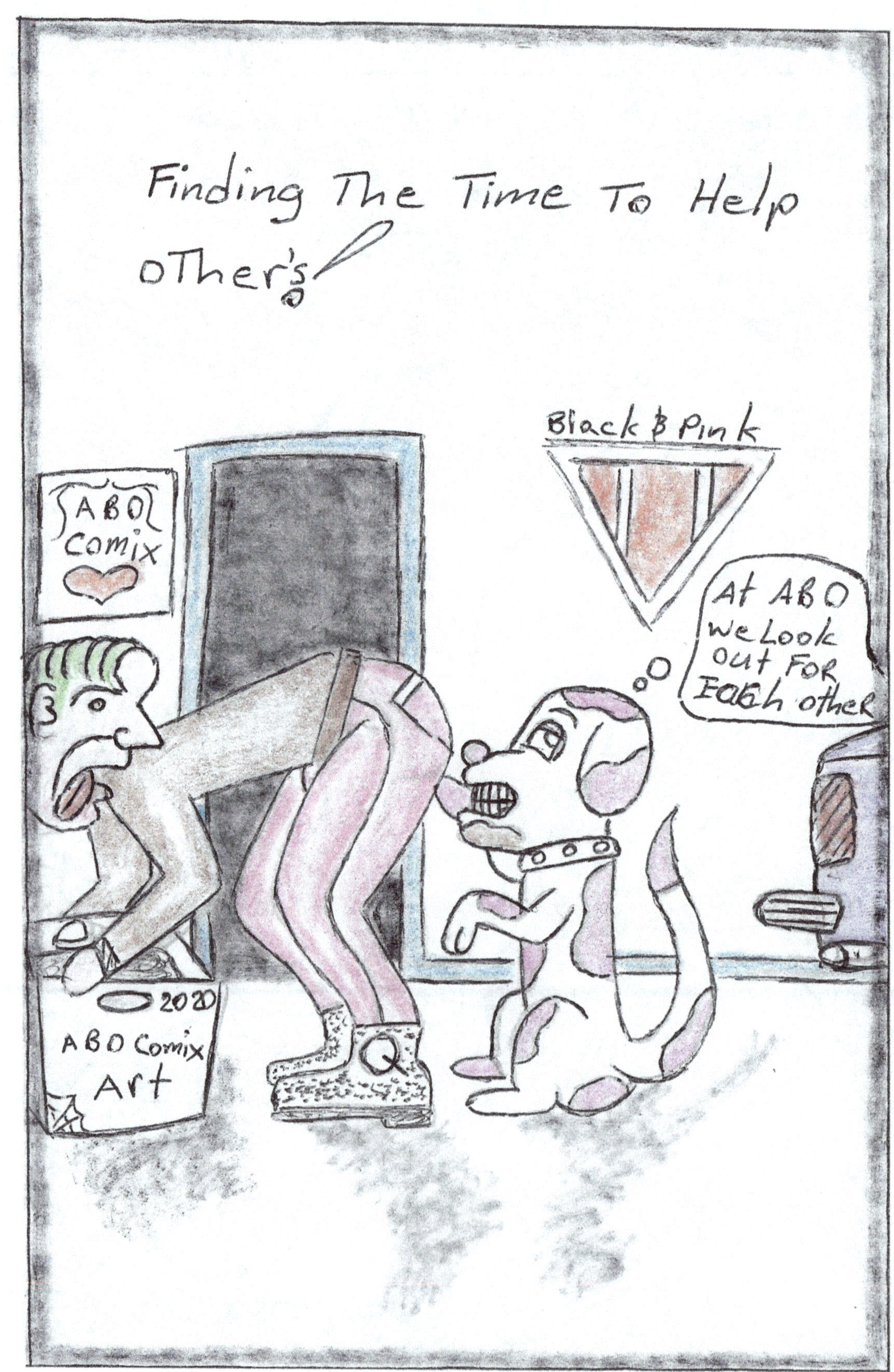

The Dree To Have.   BY: Billy Thomas

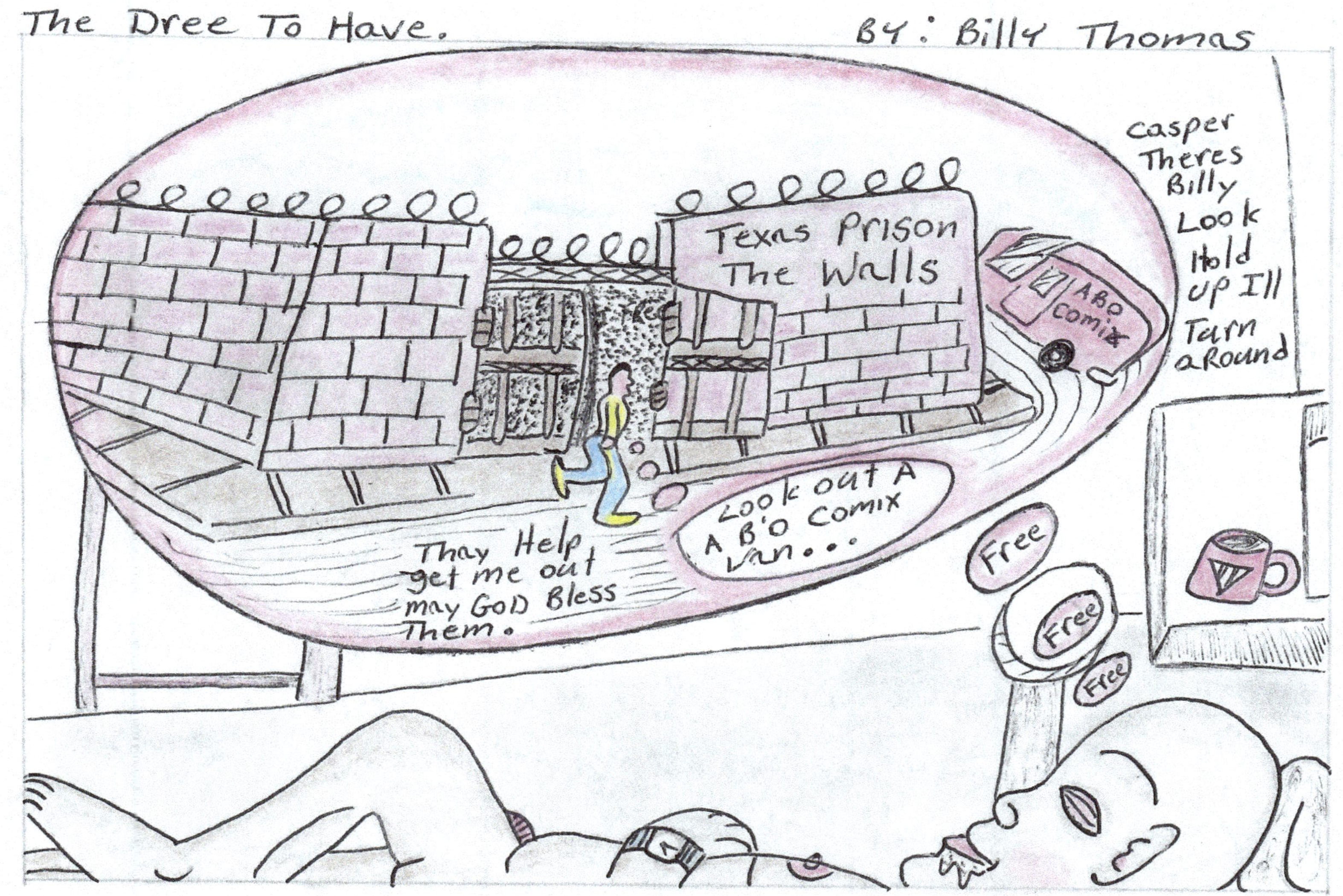

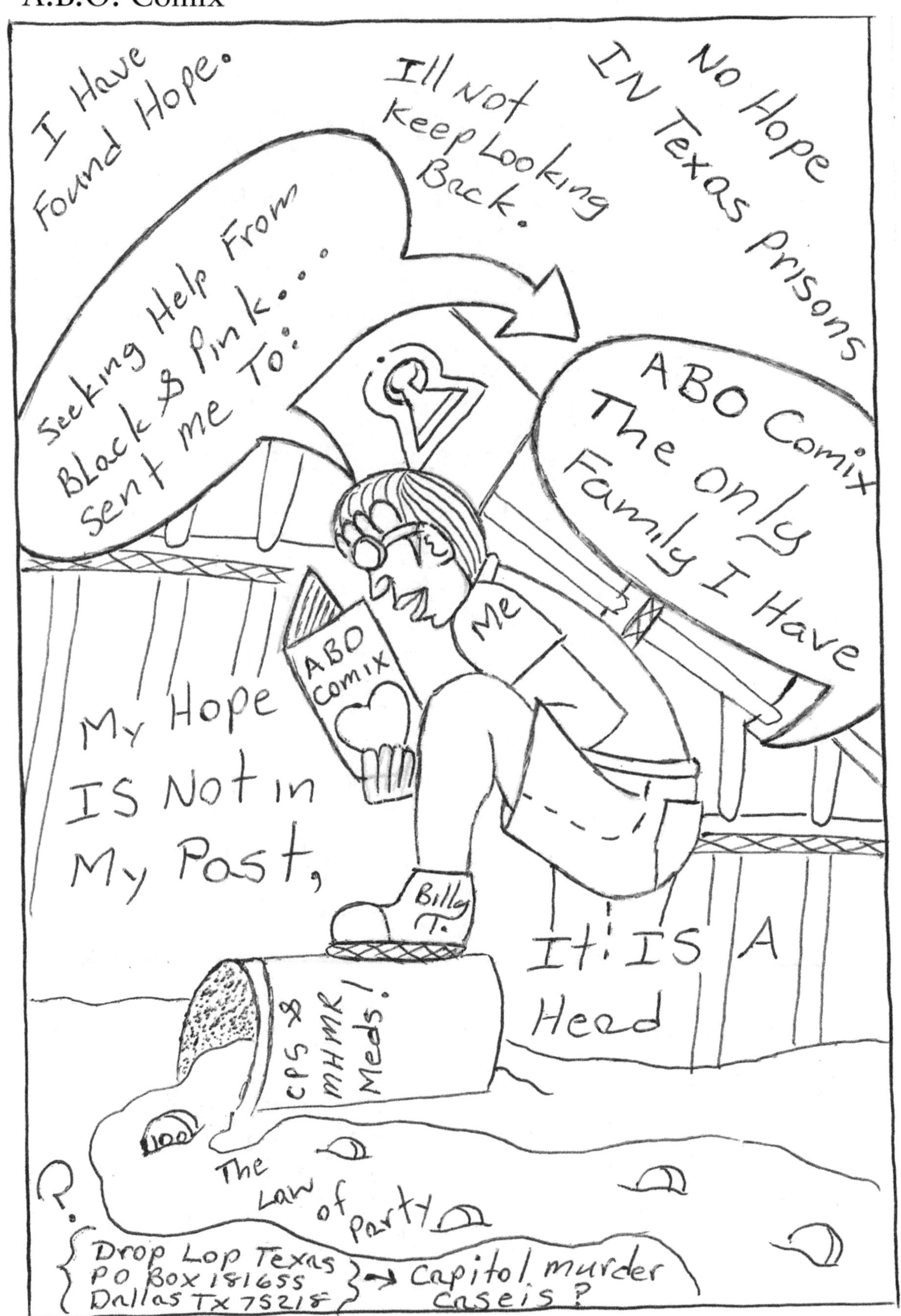

I Have Found Hope.
I'll Not Keep Looking Back.
No Hope IN Texas Prisons
Seeking Help From Black & Pink... Sent me To:
ABO Comix The only Family I Have
Me
ABO Comix
My Hope IS Not in My Post,
It IS A Head
Billy T.
CPS & MHMR Meds!
The Law of party
Drop Lop Texas
PO Box 181655
Dallas Tx 75218
Capitol murder case is ?

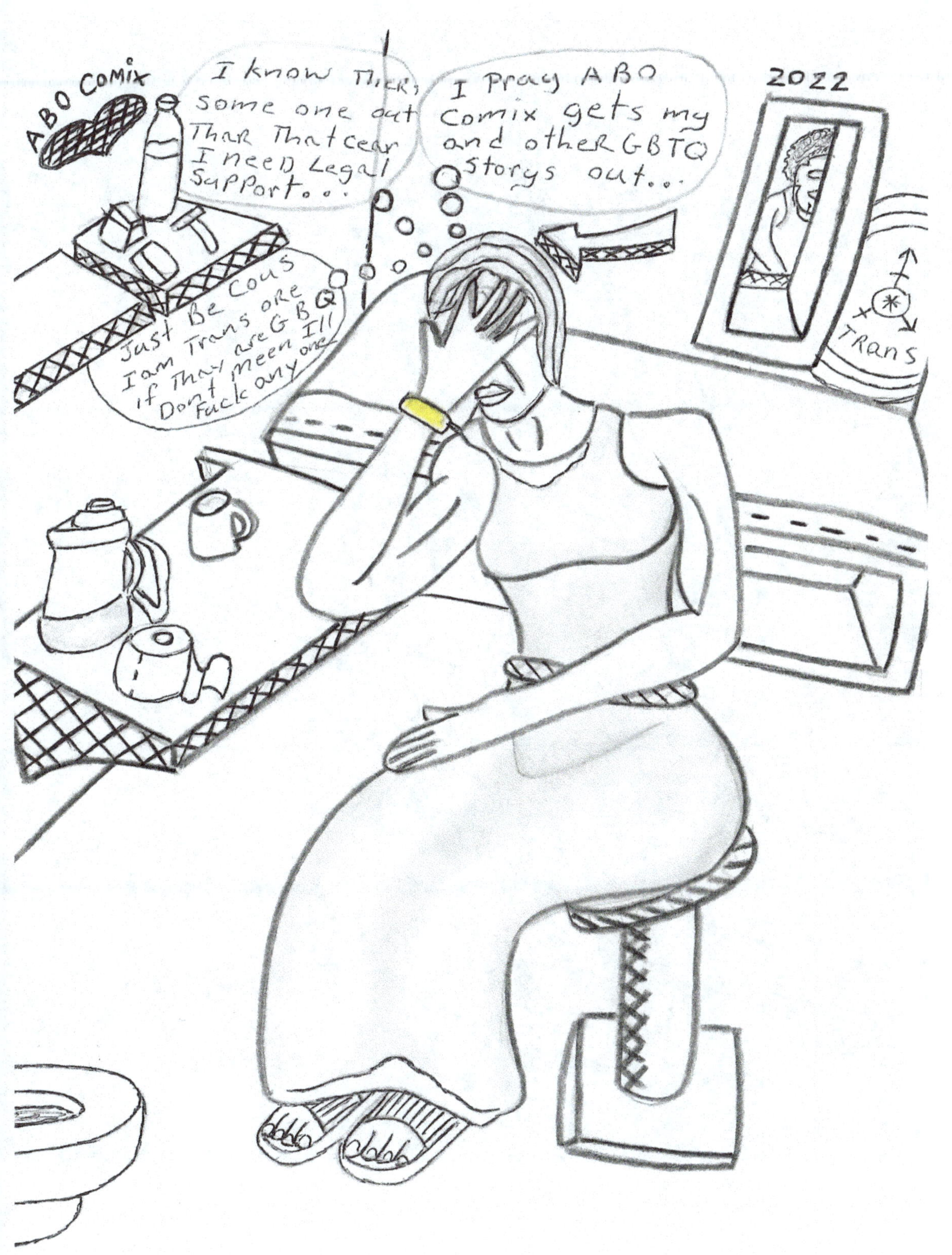
ABO COMIX
I know ther, some one out thar That cear I need Legal Support...
I Pray ABO Comix gets my and other GBTQ storys out...
Just Be Cous I am Trans ore if Thay are G B Q Dont meen Ill Fack any one
2022
TRANS

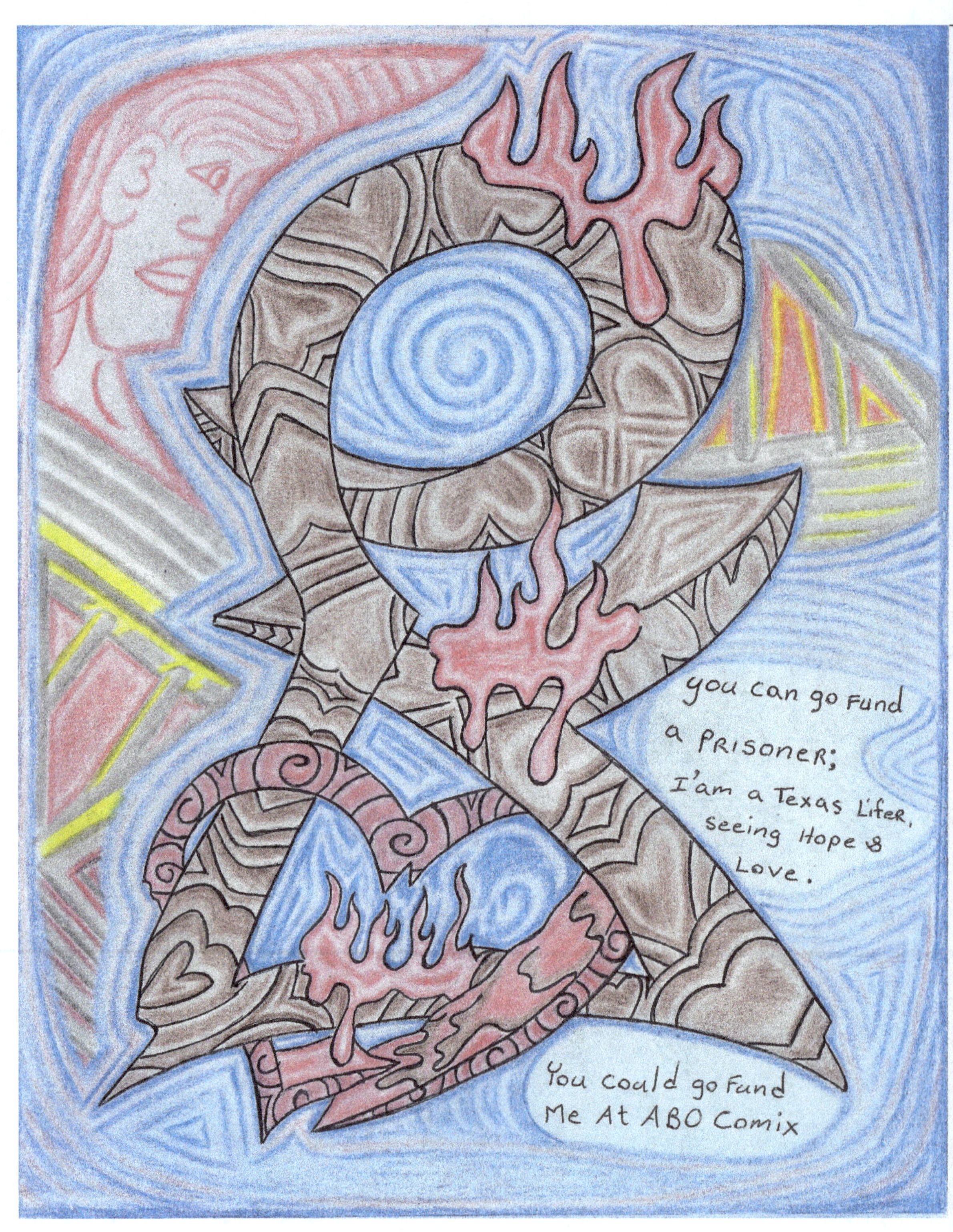
you can go Fund a PRISONER;
I'am a Texas Lifer,
seeing Hope &
Love.
You could go Fund
Me At ABO Comix

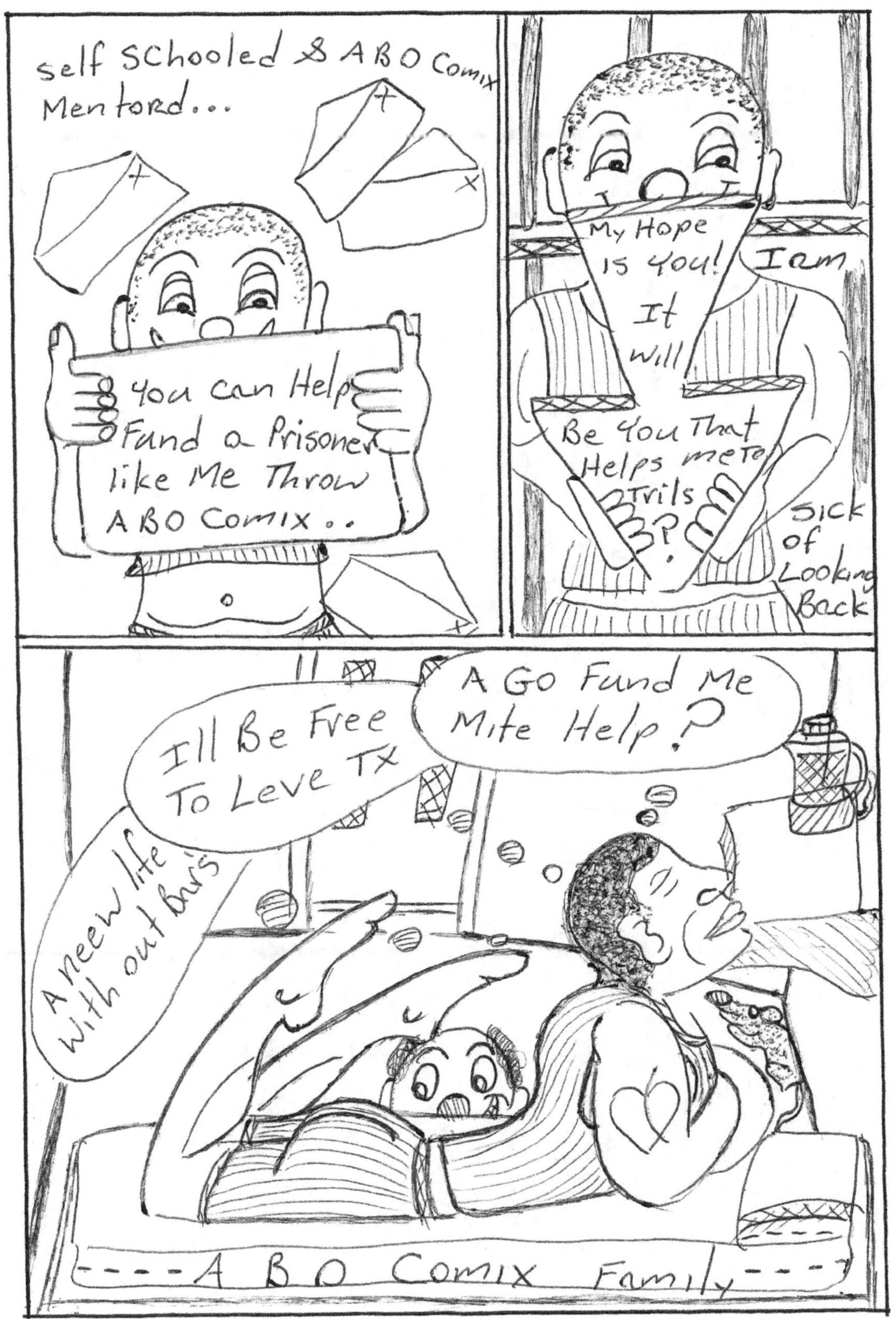
self Schooled & A B O Comix Mentord...
You can Help Fund a Prisoner like Me Throw A BO Comix..
My Hope is You! It will Be You That Helps me To Trils ?
I am Sick of Looking Back
I'll Be Free To Leve TX
A Go Fund Me Mite Help ?
A neew life with out bars
----- A B O Comix Family -----

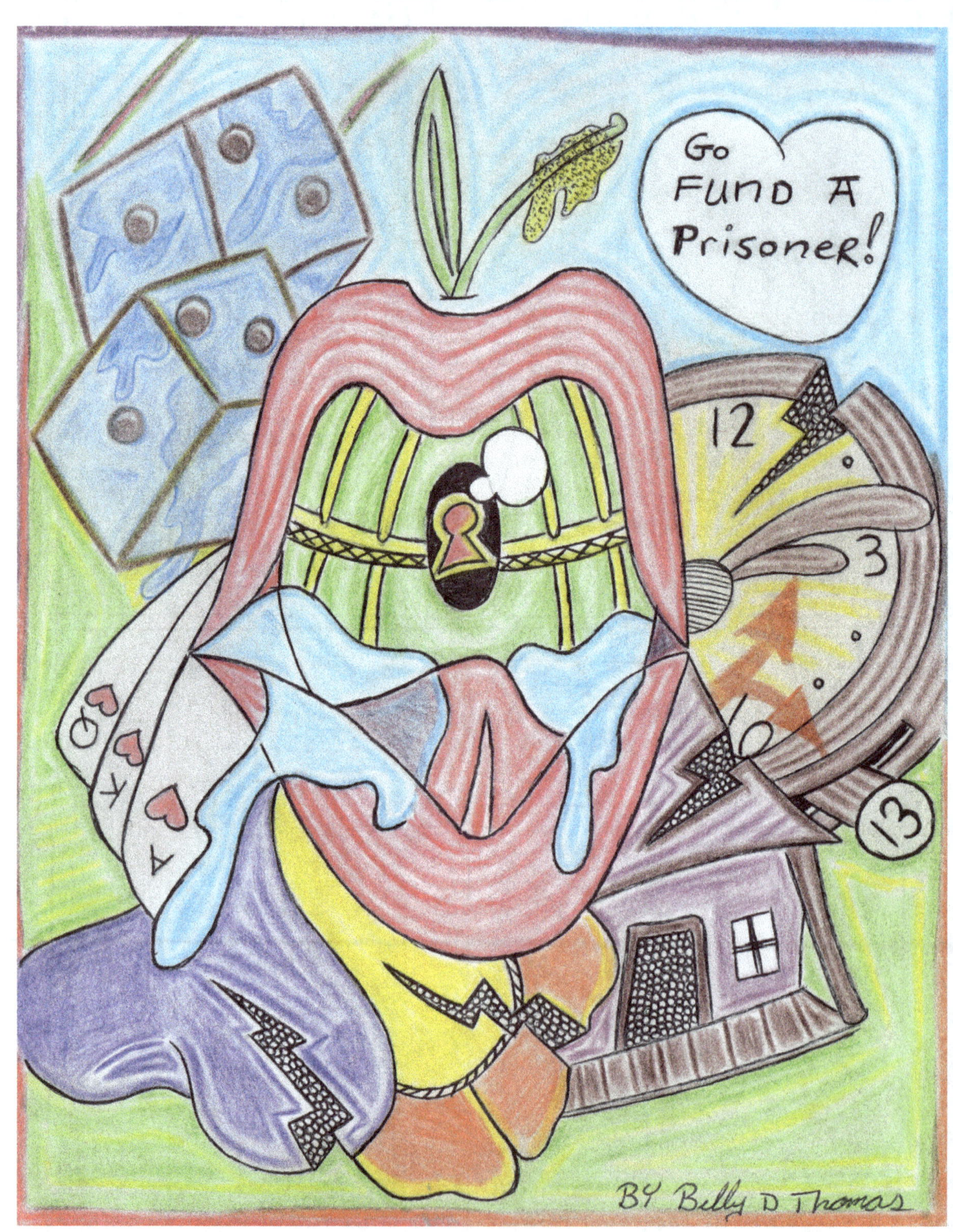
Go FUND A Prisoner!
12
3
13
BY Billy D Thomas

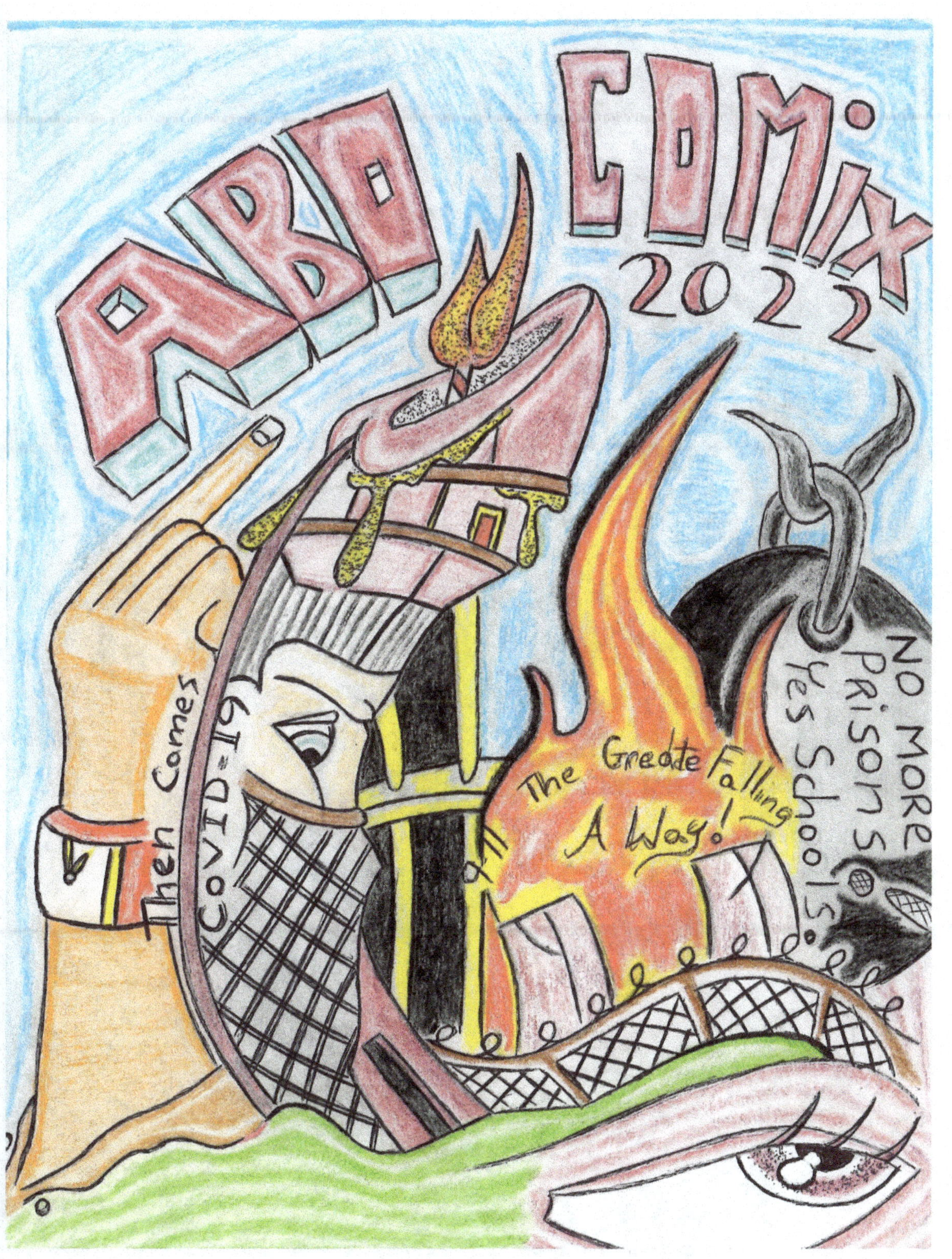
ABO Comix
2022
Then Comes
COVID-19
The Greate Falling
A Way!
NO MORE
Prisons
Yes Schools

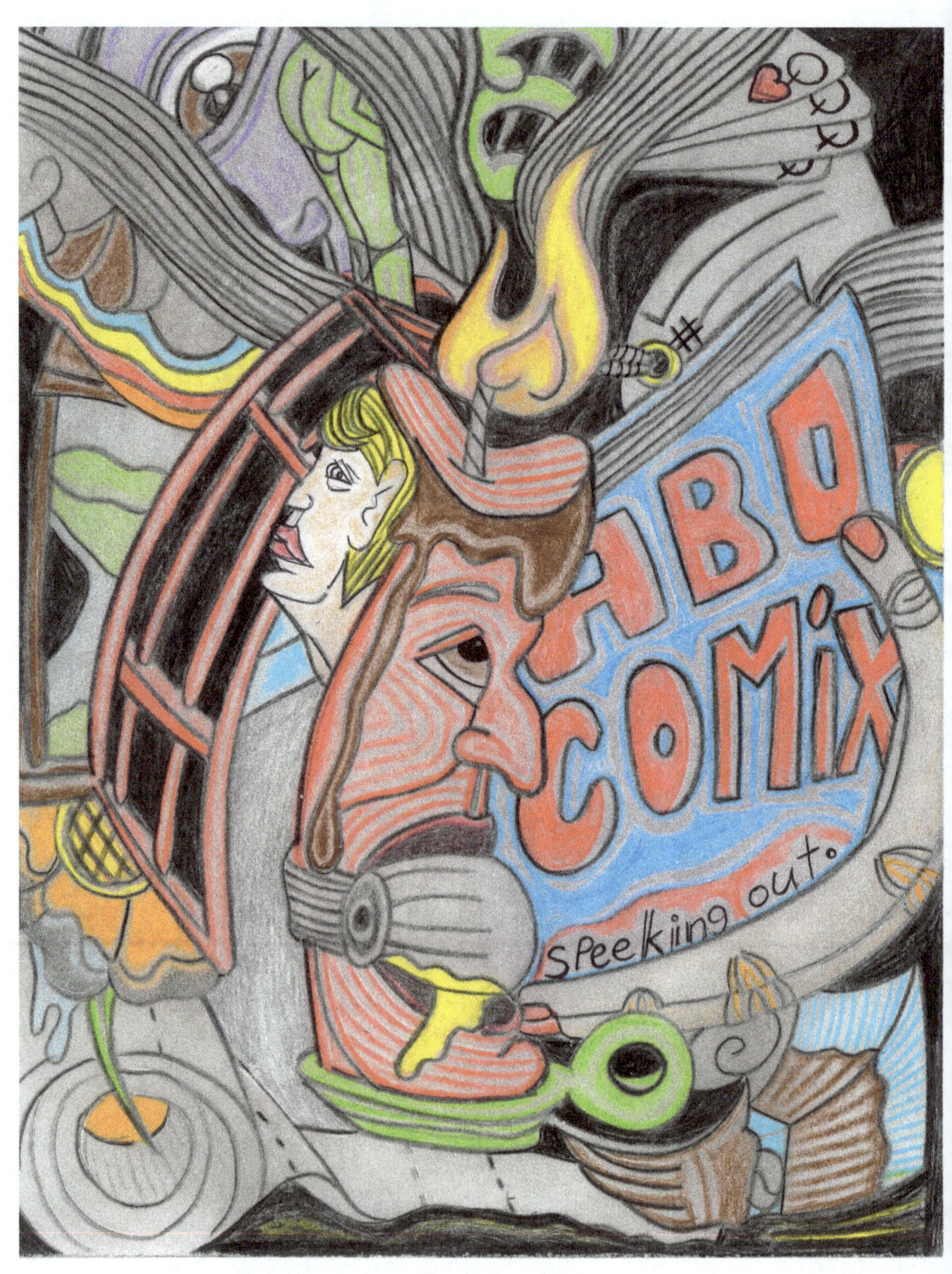
A.B.O.
COMiX
speekiing out.

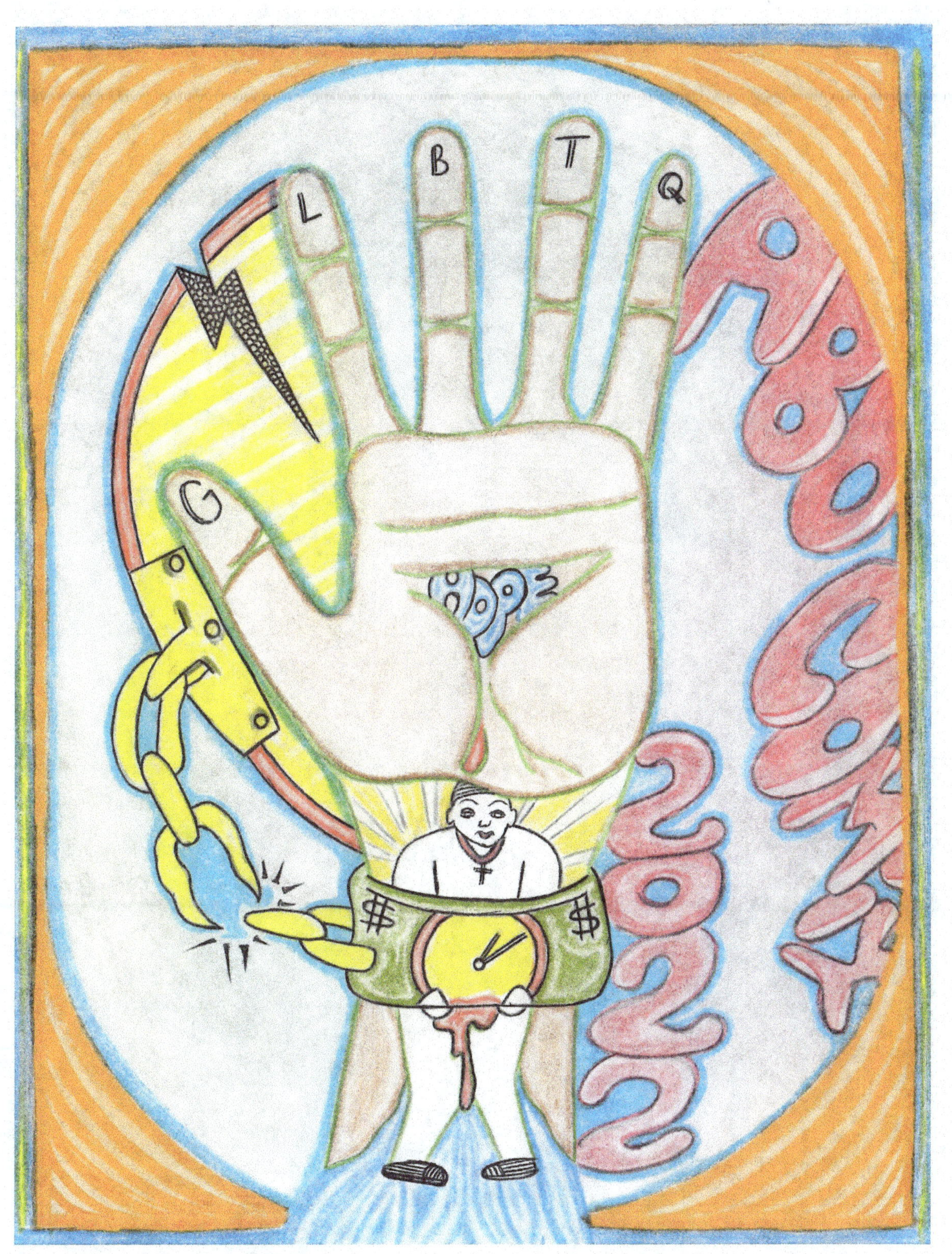
L
B
T
Q
G
HOPE
$
$
2022

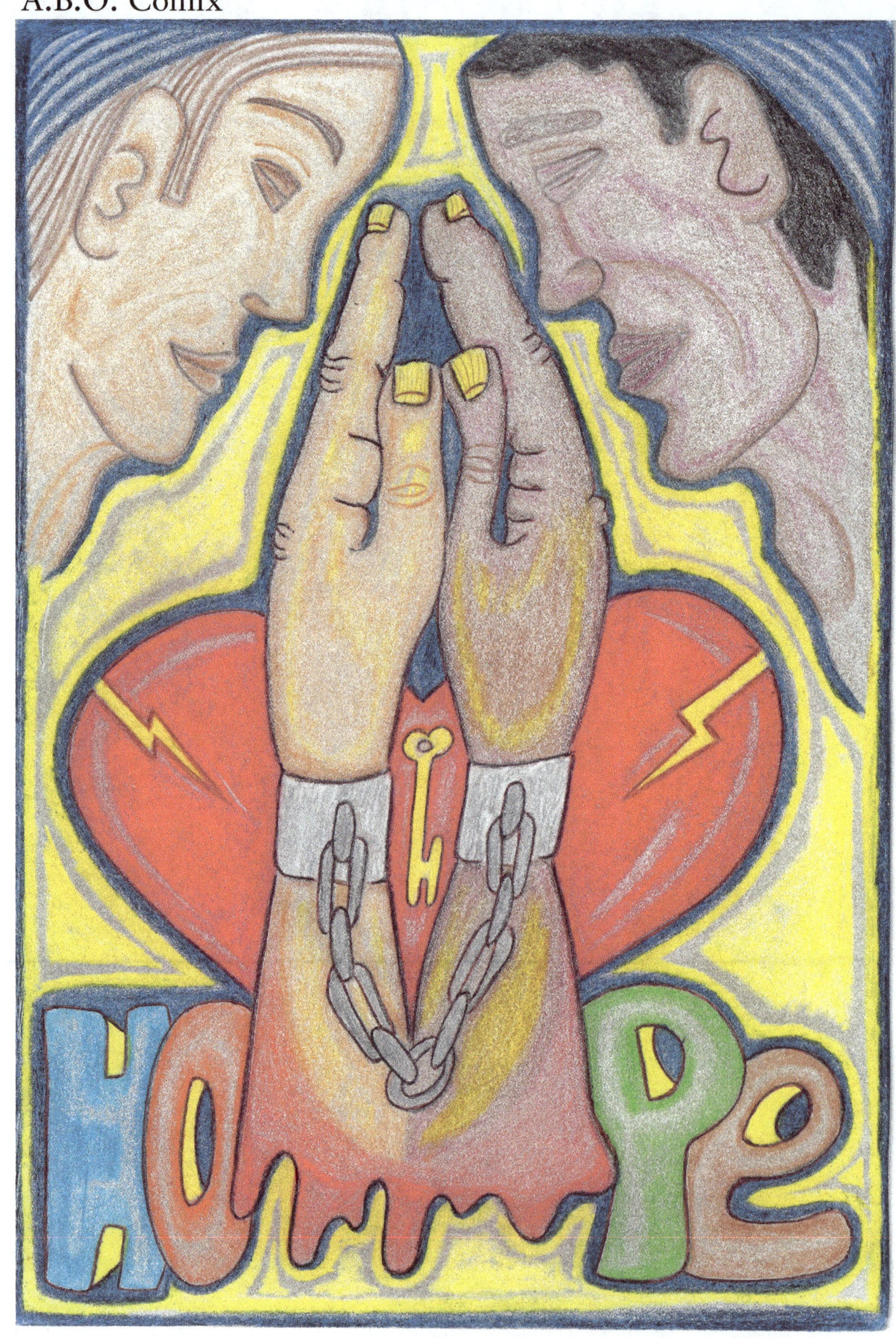
HOPE

Author Bio

Billy Thomas is an artist and friend of A.B.O. Comix whose art has been featured in all of A.B.O's annual anthologies since 2018. Billy has a wide variety of interests, including swimming, hiking, cooking, Dungeons and Dragons, sex, and watching movies. Billy has found hope in prison through God and his Jewish faith. His art is masterful and beautiful, and creating it has become his life's joy.

We are hoping the Texas Governor will look at the details of Billy's circumstances, pardon him, grant him early parole, or move him back to Vernon State Mental Hospital for treatment, not ongoing punishment. He is seeking legal support and a new trial.

How To Support Billy

If you are looking to support Billy, one of the best ways is to help is with our program to write letters to the Governor of Texas. We are looking to send letters with Billy's artwork to the Governor every week in hopes that Billy will be pardoned, granted early parole or be moved back to Vernon State Mental Hospital.

For a form letter to send to the Texas governor, please email us at abocomix.com. We encourage you to scan and print a piece of Billy's art from this book and send it along with your message!

If you know of any legal resources that could support Billy, reaching out to them and asking them to assist Billy in his attempt to receive a new trial would be immensely helpful.

Other ways to assist Billy include monetary donations or writing letters of support. For either of these options, reach out to abocomix@gmail.com for more information.

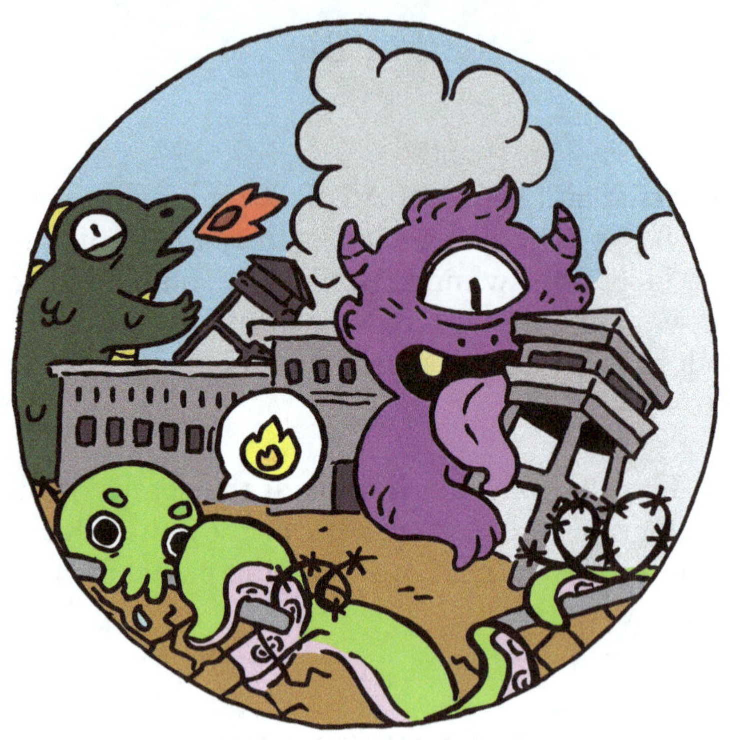

A.B.O. is a collective of creators and activists who work to amplify the voices of LGBTQ prisoners through art. By working closely with prison abolitionist and queer advocacy organizations, we aim to keep queer prisoners connected to outside community and help them in the fight toward liberation. The profits we generate go back to incarcerated artists, especially those with little to no resources. Using the DIY ideology of "punk-zine" culture, A.B.O. was formed with the philosophy of mutual support, community and friendship.

Our collective is working towards compassionate accountability without relying on the state or its sycophants. A.B.O. believes our interpersonal and societal issues can be solved without locking people in cages. Our mission is to combat the culture that treats humans as disposable and disproportionatly criminalizes the most marginalized amongst us. Through artistic activism, we hope to proliferate the idea that a better world means redefining our concepts of justice.